CONFESSIONS
OF A
CONGRESSMAN

by Jerry Voorhis

CONFESSIONS
OF A
CONGRESSMAN

GREENWOOD PRESS, PUBLISHERS
WESTPORT, CONNECTICUT

Copyright 1947 by Jerry Voorhis

Originally published in 1947
by Doubleday & Company, Inc., Garden City, New York

Reprinted with the permission
of Doubleday & Company

First Greenwood Reprinting 1970

Library of Congress Catalogue Card Number 72-110936

SBN 8371-2383-6

Printed in the United States of America

Contents

1	A DAY IN A CAMPAIGN	1
2	"WHY DID YOU RUN FOR CONGRESS?"	10
3	"HOW DID YOU GET ELECTED?"	20
4	I LEARN ABOUT CONGRESS	24
5	I LEARN ABOUT THE AMERICAN PEOPLE	40
6	POLITICAL LABELS	55
	THE STATE OR THE NATION?	64
8	THE NEW DEAL	75
9	FAIR LABOR STANDARDS	86
10	LABOR AND MANAGEMENT	96
11	"A BOLD PEASANTRY, THEIR COUNTRY'S PRIDE"	115
12	FARM "SURPLUSES" AND HUMAN NEED	140
13	MY BIG "CRUSADE"	161
14	EQUAL OPPORTUNITY FOR ALL, SPECIAL PRIVILEGE TO NONE	183
15	INVESTIGATION OF "UN-AMERICAN ACTIVITIES" —THE DIES COMMITTEE	207
16	"WHEN IN DOUBT, DO RIGHT"	232
17	POSTWAR PLANNING	250
18	ATOMIC ENERGY—CURSE OR BLESSING?	263
19	THE "LITTLE" BILLS	278
20	THE CONGRESSMAN'S JOB AS IT IS	291
21	THE CONGRESSMAN'S JOB AS IT OUGHT TO BE	302
22	THE ROOTS OF DEMOCRACY	323
23	THE FALL OF 1946	330
24	A BETTER WAY	350
25	BLIND ALLEY OR THE ROAD AHEAD	361

CONFESSIONS
OF A
CONGRESSMAN

Chapter 1

A DAY IN A CAMPAIGN

The warm sunshine of a late California summer fills the room. We are home for the campaign. We have to be. Congressmen either campaign every two years or they don't remain congressmen. Sometimes they don't anyway.

"Daddy, which is stronger, a buffalo or a mountain lion?" I try to pry my eyes open. I shake my head. I manage to push my feet out of bed and somehow my legs follow them. I get myself tipped up to a sitting position. It seems only a moment ago that I crawled into bed.

Fumbling for the watch—twenty minutes after seven. Should have waked up sooner.

"But, Daddy, which is stronger, a buffalo or a mountain lion?" Our eight-year-old really wants to get some information.

I try, as I stagger into the bathroom, to defend the buffalo, but to no avail, because the picture in the book shows the mountain lion getting the best of it.

I should be downstairs already. But first comes the seemingly interminable job of shaving. Suppose the phone rings, or someone comes. Thursday, Friday, Saturday—then Sunday—maybe I can do something with the children that day. Have to speak at a breakfast that morning, then at a morning church service. But

I should get home by one o'clock. Maybe we can have the afternoon. Maybe. Anyway, hurry up now. Hope we get through with breakfast before something happens.

But we don't. The phone rings. A good friend is on the line to say: "They have a whispering campaign going on. They say you haven't done anything to help the district. No big government installations like they have in the Nineteenth District. They're comparing you with the congressman from over in that district. I understand they're fixing up an ad which will list all the government projects in the Nineteenth District and contrast it with a much shorter list of the ones here. How can we answer this?"

"We can't," I tell him, "because it's at least partly true. I never claimed to be much good at delivering projects unless there were good solid reasons why they should be located here. About all we can do is point out that the very same fellows complain because I don't induce the government to spend more money in the district and also because the budget isn't balanced."

My friend isn't very well satisfied.

We talk more about other subjects. Then we say good-by.

I go in and eat some breakfast. But the family is all through and it's no fun eating alone.

By now it is going on nine o'clock. In another hour and a half I should be clear at the other end of the district to attend a community meeting. But there is the mail to be answered before that and a great number of matters I have promised people I would attend to—soldier's dependents' allowances, housing priorities, rent adjustment problems, et cetera.

My secretary, Harold Herin, is in the office already. So we start. We get through part of the letters. While I'm dictating I make notes of other things that must be done. Who is going to speak for the state ticket at the South Pasadena meeting? I must phone about that. Does the AF of L primary endorsement carry over into the finals or does it have to be renewed? Can we publish it in our campaign leaflet? Better find out for certain. Will Mrs. Voorhis or our daughter, Alice, please type the news release we wrote last night? It ought to be in the mail today.

All of this interrupts the dictation. But it can't be helped. Phone calls keep coming in, and we try to do both jobs at once.

I look at my watch—almost ten. I ought to be on my way. I can barely make it to Monterey Park by ten-thirty. Just one more letter, then I'll go.

The phone rings again. This time it's about an allocation of scarce material for one of the district's small companies. Unless they get it, they're out of business. It takes several minutes to work out the facts, decide what steps to take with the Department of Agriculture. I look at the watch again—ten-fourteen!

I grab my brief case, climb in the car, and dash off. All the way to Monterey Park I wonder if I'll be in time. Traffic is bad and I seem to hit every single red light. As I drive along I have a pad on the seat beside me to jot down more things to remember.

At last, here's Monterey Park. I go to the place appointed for the morning ceremonies. I am too late. They began exactly on time and were very short. A friend tells me my not getting there wasn't "too serious."

There are forty minutes left before I have to speak to the Lions Club. So I call at the newspaper office and pay my respects to the editor and his staff. His main trouble, he says, is getting enough labor. And Congress didn't help any when it reduced the "on-the-job training" payments to veterans. In fact he has lost a very promising young man as a result of this action. The editor and I talk briefly about current problems and then I say good-by.

I call at a couple of other places.

By this time it is noon, and I am due at the Women's Club-house for the Lions Club meeting. I start to walk. As I pass the drugstore a young veteran who works there comes out and stops me. He is president of a new organization of veterans who are trying to find homes to live in. A certain very new construction and real estate company has taken deposits from them of a hundred dollars and more each. But no homes have been completed and there seems to be great doubt whether more than a handful will ever be built. Most of the boys, therefore, stand to lose their deposits unless something can be done to force the company to pay. Everybody is fearful the company won't have funds to do so, and now something new has come up. I was at their meeting the night before and made a few suggestions to them. One of the metropolitan Los Angeles papers has been carrying feature articles about their problems so they submitted a story about the meeting to one of its reporters. Just an hour ago the reporter called up to say the paper wouldn't run the story because Congressman Voorhis's name was mentioned in it. What do I think of that? Well, the first thing I think is that I have killed the veterans' story and my second reaction is that I am angry clear through over what the newspaper reporter has told them. I can't believe it is true—that the reporter has given the real reason. Anyway, I will call the paper just as soon as I can get to a phone.

I am worried over this as I enter the little building where the Lions are meeting. A lot of them are my good friends and it is good to see them. I try to put other things out of my mind. Pretty soon I'll have to start speaking. It is hard to eat. At last the program chairman takes over and introduces me. For thirty minutes I give a talk on the need for dynamic American leadership in the world and what will be required of each of us if our country is to give that leadership.

The talk is well received apparently. The meeting adjourns, and though I wish I could stay around for a few minutes and talk informally with some of the men, I have to break away almost at once because I am due at an old-age pension meeting in Whittier at two-thirty, and want to see a veterans' housing project on the way. So off I dash to see the housing project. It is really all right—neatly painted, and clean, and not too crowded, though the buildings are obviously temporary. At least families can be together—and alone! The trouble is, it's such a drop in the bucket, compared to the need.

On the way to Whittier I take the road through the hills. They are brown, of course, since it is summer. Here and there are some live oaks and occasionally a little house under them. A few patches of land where water has been piped are cultivated and there are some small groves of citrus—not very good ones. This is old California. If only we could go back to those times. But then we'd have to do the past couple of decades all over again. No. It's no good thinking that way.

I get to thinking about the speech I've just made.

Did I give them enough that was substantial, immediate, practical for today? Or was it too much about the long-run future? Should I have discussed government controls and housing and things of that sort? Well, no. Those problems will be things of the past in a few months. The ones I talked about won't. They'll be with us for a long time. Maybe it was all right.

I arrive in Whittier and go to the park where about a hundred people, mostly old folk, are sitting on the benches listening to the speeches. I find the president of the local club and he takes me up on the platform and, as he has promised, lets me speak almost at once. I only talk a few minutes about how I believe a national old-age pension system would help keep the nation's buying power in balance with production, and about some of the principles to which I believe such a system should conform. It takes a half hour, however, to leave the park because a number of people want to talk about various problems and I'm no good at cutting short such conversations. At last, however, I do go.

I glance at the lists I've been making of things to do that afternoon. Most urgent are some phone calls. At least I must find out about that veteran story not being printed. So I go to our congressional field office in the federal building in Alhambra and start putting in calls. I get through to the secretary of the Central Labor Council of the AF of L to ask whether their primary endorsement is still valid for the finals or whether further action by the council is necessary. He tells me it is still valid and that I can state publicly that I have their endorsement. I try to reach the newspaper but the man I want to talk to is out. I call an old friend, an elderly gentleman, and congratulate him and his wife on the celebration of their golden wedding anniversary. Then I try the newspaper again and this time reach the vice-president. Did the paper kill the veterans' housing story because my name was mentioned? He says he's sure that can't be the case. Will he make certain their story is run? I ask. If it makes any difference please omit my name—but run the story. He promises to find out about the whole thing and let me know by letter. (Next day a story is printed, carrying forward the *News's* campaign for a square deal for the veterans. And it does mention my co-operation with them.)

Well, the rest of the calls will have to wait. It's after five and

I have a dinner meeting and later a mass meeting coming along in only an hour's time. A man with a problem drops into the office, but he has all the facts written out and is most kind when I explain that I have to make my notes for the evening speeches. I start to outline the talk for the dinner.

I work quietly for a while. Then I look at my watch. Barely time to get to the poultrymen's dinner, twenty minutes away—but I make it in fifteen. Mrs. Voorhis is there ahead of me and it is good to see her. She asks me how I feel and I tell her I don't know. We find our places and sit down. This is the sort of meeting I like best—a group of salt-of-the-earth American citizens who through good times and bad times have done their work, carried on their businesses, loved their families, their country and their church and, without quite realizing it, made up the backbone of America's democratic social structure.

During the meal I make some notes of what I want to speak about—the problems poultrymen have faced and how we tried to meet them, the dangers in our faulty monetary system that make both inflation and deflation profitable to the private financial interests which create the money our country uses, the outlook for American farmers generally, how co-operatives have helped and can play an even more important role in the future in helping farmers to be the masters of their own economic fate, and finally about the problems of peace among the nations. As people call one another by name I jot them down—so I won't forget next time.

They let me speak first so we can leave for our other meeting. I have trouble in cutting my speech as short as it ought to be, but finally I sit down. We shake hands with those at the head table, slip out, and get into the car.

Now comes the crucial meeting of the whole day—a joint meeting with my opponent. I can guess some of the questions that will be asked. But I don't mind them so much. The hard part will be to cut my main speech to the allotted time. Friends and advisors have told me I must be more aggressive, must not allow myself to be put on the defensive. I'll try, but the world is in a good deal of trouble and, of course, since I have been a congressman I am at least in a measure—however small—responsible.

Another trouble is, I'm tired. If only meetings like this could come at times when a fellow could quietly prepare for them. I get my notes out of my pocket and ask my wife to read them to me. They sound dull. I'm certainly not very good company for her.

Here we are. A little crowd is waiting outside the auditorium to give last-minute advice. But the meeting is about to start so I rush down to the platform. Almost before I know it I have been introduced and am facing the crowd. Each of the main speeches is only fifteen minutes long. I know to start with that I cannot begin to do justice to the program I want to present. I talk first about foreign policy, outline what I believe our nation's duty is, say I believe our policy generally is now a correct one. I see there are only five minutes left. I attempt to pack into those five minutes as much as possible of the domestic full production-full consumption program in which I so earnestly believe.

There is only time to touch on the national debt and the monetary system, old-age pensions and a broader social security program, the school lunch bill and the hope it offers of a better demand for farm crops on the one hand and a healthier nation on the other. I contrast such a program with its opposite—artificial reduction of production in the face of an inadequate demand and point out the economic effects of monopoly in bringing this about. Then my time is up.

My opponent is introduced. He speaks easily and I wonder whether the audience may not prefer his lighter touch to my rather ponderous manner of presenting one big problem after another. He makes the expected attacks on "bueaucracy," bewails the state of the nation, and sympathizes with the people about the shortages that still persist. He says nothing specific against my record or the votes I have cast.

Then comes the question period.

Was I once a registered Socialist?

Yes, I was during the late twenties and the worst part of the depression when it seemed neither major party had any effective answer to the people's problems.

Why did I permit the bill to pass the Congress which reduced on-the-job training payments to veterans?

It was only on the floor for a very few minutes; no real explanation was made of it; it was passed under suspension of the rules without any record vote.

Should not I have been present at the time and stopped it?

Of course I should have been, but so should I have been doing a dozen other tasks, to one of which I was attending. Members of the House rely on committees having bills in charge to see that controversial measures are not slipped through in the manner this one was. In this case the committee did not keep faith.

Do I believe in a managed currency?

Yes, basically I do. But we have a mismanaged one now, and I believe management in the public interest would be an improvement.

What are these peculiar ideas about money I am supposed to have?

I do my best to explain in three minutes the monetary reform program I have worked on for fifteen years.

Don't I believe the American people can manage their own affairs without so much government interference?

I answer that wartime controls are temporary and should be. They have been put into effect either to control inflation or to direct all our resources to the most essential uses. These controls can be done away with soon, we hope. But government has some jobs it cannot in justice to the people fail to do. For example, if we mean what we say about believing in economic freedom, then the hand of government must be raised against monopoly wherever it exists.

And so on until at last about eleven o'clock the meeting is brought to an end. There is handshaking and talking afterward in the hall—and then some more outside. It is part of the job—meeting people, the American people, who were interested enough in their government to come.

We drive home.

As always at the end of a day in a campaign I am so exhausted I wonder if I can make it until Election Day. But it has been done before. It can be done again.

We are at home now. I go into my office at the rear of the house and sit down at the old roll-top desk. There is mail to be read. I am too tired to do more than skim through it to see if it contains anything urgent. Then I open one of the drawers of the desk. There are half a dozen notebooks in it. They are full of the talks I used to give to the boys when I was a schoolmaster. I read a couple of them. How clear most things seemed then—how clear and simple. Wish we could all be back at the school together again. But we can't. There's a different job to do now.

After a while I go to bed.

Chapter 2

"WHY DID YOU RUN FOR CONGRESS?"

Ever since I can remember I have been interested in politics. I recall asking my mother when I was a small boy why some people were so rich and others so poor and why something wasn't done to help the poor people have a more equal chance in life. She told me there were some men and women—not very many, she said—who were trying to bring this about. Ever since then I have been "for" those men and women. I guess that has been my main political motivation.

In college I experienced a very profound religious awakening, for which I shall be humbly thankful as long as I live. Out of this there developed the very disturbing and impelling idea that the Christian Gospel is to be taken seriously and that needless poverty and suffering on the one hand and special privilege and inordinate power on the other are entirely contrary to its precepts.

All during my years at college the barriers between "town and gown" as they existed in New Haven were a terrible thing to me. I know now, though I lacked the confidence in my own judgment to know it then, that I should have left school at some point along the way, gone out and found a worthwhile job, and gained a little of the knowledge that does not come from books, and then returned to finish my course. As it was, I felt it my duty to con-

tinue through the four years in the traditional manner and I
did so, at the expense of great emotional strain. I felt all the time
that I was not so much living as only "preparing for life" and
that the real world lay among the people beyond the college walls.
Consequently, once the diplomas had been distributed to our
class, I did the thing I had wanted to do for so many years. I
found a boardinghouse room and a factory job at thirty-nine
cents an hour. After a period of months during which we worked
a great deal of overtime (and were paid straight-time wages for
it), I reported for work one morning only to find that I was one
of the 2000 employees of the company who had been "laid off"
indefinitely. I got another job, this time handling freight in the
railroad yards. I caught the work train at six o'clock those winter
mornings and almost became accustomed to the unlighted cars
and to the ride to work in complete darkness. It was hard, hazard-
ous work. I shall never forget having seen two of my fellow
workers killed one day when a huge cogwheel, which they were
attempting to move from one car to another, slipped and pinned
them under it. I wondered what would happen to their families.

I left the freight handler's job to make a trip to Europe. It was
planned as a sort of good-will mission for the Student Friendship
Fund of the YMCA. I went to England first, then to Germany.
It was at the height of the postwar inflation. Postage stamps were
selling for billions of marks and people could be seen on the streets
clutching great bundles of bills which they were desperate to
turn into goods before prices doubled again. There was very little
food in Germany then. Students were in almost universal distress.
In each city I stayed in the home of someone to whom I had a
letter of introduction. In Dortmund it was with an unemployed
miner, father of ten children. There was no food except a little
cabbage soup and some sort of substitute for coffee. In Hamburg
I spent three days and nights in the home of a schoolteacher who
could afford neither light nor heat in his rooms.

Everywhere people were having meetings and talking about
"hunger" and "no more war."

Finally I contracted pneumonia, managed somehow to get
back to England, and spent six weeks in a nursing home. That
was all of the European trip.

Back in the United States I met a young lady doing social service work and promptly fell deeply in love with her. Then I went off to work for six months on a Western ranch, partly, at least, for the purpose of rebuilding the physical strength I had lost during my illness. I learned to plant and harvest grain, to "put up" hay, to handle a team, and to build fences (not the political kind). I found out how ranchers in that section drove their cattle and sheep to the railroad in the fall of the year, figuratively kissed them good-by, and then waited for a check from an Omaha commission house for whatever "the market" had allowed on the particular day when the stock was sold. That check represented in most cases almost the entire cash income of the rancher for a year's labor.

Louise Livingston and I were married that fall and we went to North Carolina where I hoped to secure work in a textile mill. But that proved impossible. Strangers were simply not hired by the Southern mills in those days. I discovered also that I could not have supported the two of us on what I would have earned at such a job. So I tried elsewhere, and one day was lucky enough to be picked out of a milling crowd outside the Ford assembly plant and given a job on one of the "lines."

I started at five dollars a day, which seemed like big money at that particular point. After two months I made six dollars a day and we had saved enough to buy a secondhand Ford by the time spring came. The assembly-line job was the hardest one that I have ever held. The monotony was almost unbearable. I solved the problem tolerably by two devices. I memorized poetry and repeated it over and over during the long days—most of which consisted of twelve-hour shifts, with no overtime pay. Our line was adjacent to the freight siding and I could see the cars as they were backed in and pulled out. The names of the various railroads on the freight cars served to quicken my imagination and to conjure up thoughts about the parts of the country through which these railroads passed. This helped too.

When I left my job at the Ford factory I had not the least conscious idea of ever running for Congress or any other office. But I was quite sure I wanted to try to do something about the things I had seen and experienced, about low wages and long hours, arbitrary dismissals, inflation and deflation, the insecurity of farmers' incomes.

Our move from North Carolina was to a jack-of-all-trades job at Allendale Farm School in northern Illinois. This was both a home and a training school for boys, a sort of "boys' town." I taught the social science subjects in all grades, conducted chapel services, helped coach athletics, worked with the boys on the farm, and did anything else that needed doing. During this year our first baby was born. I was glad she was a girl.

The next year found us in Wyoming at the call of the Episcopal bishop of that state. The job was that of getting the first church home for orphan boys started. It was a tough assignment, principally because there was apparently almost no money to support such an institution in the state and I proved none too adept at raising even what there was. I traveled over the state for this purpose but everywhere I went I got boys to take care of and very little money to do it with.

Finally, the idea occurred to me of writing to people in all parts of the country asking them to sponsor—at three hundred dollars a year—one orphan boy in the projected home. This worked and our "family," some thirty-six boys, a big colored woman who was our cook and entire "staff," my wife, our baby girl, and I began living together in the fall of 1926. We had only one building and it was surrounded by red clay which in wet weather became red mud and was generously transferred to the interior of the building by everybody's shoes. The board of directors was principally concerned with good housekeeping, to the neglect, as it seemed to me, of the happy development of the boys. A variety of conflicts arose over this difference in point of view. Nevertheless, we lived a happy year with our boys in Laramie.

By this time my father was ready to retire from active business and anxious to make an investment in something far more worthwhile than stocks and bonds. He proposed that we found an institution which would be both a home and a school for boys who had lost their parents by death or separation. He preferred to do this in California and so, in the fall of 1927, with a dozen of the Wyoming boys for whom there seemed no other satisfactory solution, we moved to Claremont, California, and started constructing the Voorhis School for Boys at San Dimas, a few miles distant.

We rented from Pomona College a big old house that shook vigorously every time a Santa Fe train roared by a block away. The boys attended school in Claremont, little Alice passed her second birthday, and I took my master's degree in education at Claremont College.

By the next summer our school at San Dimas was ready and the first thirty boys had been selected to form our nucleus. By the end of our first year sixty-five boys were living there—our capacity. The "school" was, first of all, a home. All our boys were orphans, boys with but one living parent, or lads from broken homes. They lived the year around at our school and usually remained with us until they had been graduated from high school. Our chapel was the center from which a truly religious spirit pervaded our community. We taught the sixth, seventh, eighth, and ninth grades at the Voorhis School, and the older boys went to the regular public high school in San Dimas. We worked together in our fruit groves and our vegetable garden, in the chicken houses and rabbitry, the auto shop, the print shop, and the kitchen. These were happy years. The day began very early and didn't end till I had told the younger boys good night after they had gone to bed. But we compassed the whole gamut of life and made it something altogether worth while. Moreover, to bring an even greater fullness to our family life, our first son was born in the summer of 1931.

Not only did I teach the social sciences to our boys at the school, but for several years I gave a special lecture course at Pomona College. I was always telling the boys that we should put into practice the principles in which we believed. As time went on, therefore, the feeling grew that the time might sometime come for me to attempt some practical contribution toward carrying out the principles of government I had been teaching.

Just how it would ever be possible for me to do this through active politics was a question I did not then attempt to face, much less to answer. Certainly I would have at least two strikes on me if I tried, for I had been a political maverick ever since I was old enough to vote.

I cast my first vote for President in 1924. But I did not vote for John W. Davis, or for Calvin Coolidge. I voted for "Old Bob" La Follette. To make matters worse, in 1928 I voted for Norman Thomas and was, in fact, at that time a registered Socialist, since I could find no evidence that either of the old parties was genuinely concerned with the problems of the people. With the coming of the 1929 depression those problems became nothing short of desperate and my own concern markedly deepened.

It was virtually impossible for the graduates of our school to find worthwhile employment. Through intensive effort and the kindness of personal friends we managed to find some sort of employment for many of them. But seldom indeed was it the type of work for which the boys were so well qualified by their training and ability. On the wages and salaries which they were able to earn hardly any of them could look forward to the possibility of supporting a wife and children. To them and to millions of other young men and women America was saying, "We have no need for your talents and abilities. There are too many workers already. If you were put to work you would produce too much and it could not be sold, since the people, including yourselves, have so little money." To tell a young man you will not give him something he desires may make him angry; but to deny him the opportunity to make any worthwhile contribution to the society to which he belongs is a profound insult and a telling blow at his very hold on life. Not only did I believe this situation cruel to the individual young men, but I also suspected that it reflected some cockeyed economics and serious neglect on the part of those supposedly responsible for the health of the nation's economy.

Yet I found nothing on the political horizon which seemed to offer hope for a better future. President Hoover appealed to business to stop the disastrous downward spiral. But the effect of his appeal was to cause the very executives to whom he appealed to decide it was wise to lay off even more men and to curtail still further what little production was going on. The government's fiscal policies were exactly the opposite of those likely to lead to a checking of the depression. True, the RFC was established, and made a few loans to wealthy borrowers. But, in a feverish attempt to keep the budget balanced, government expenditures were severely curtailed, which circumstance undoubtedly contributed measurably to the fact that revenues fell off even faster. The Democrats, meanwhile, apparently sensing their first opportunity for political victory in many years, emphasized, as well they might, the mistakes and shortcomings of the Republican Administration but offered little which appeared particularly constructive in its place. From a purely political standpoint they were undoubtedly correct, but to a citizen as deeply distressed as I then was little cause for encouragement was given.

It came time for the campaign of 1932. I remember with great vividness coming out of a moving picture theater with Mrs. Voorhis and hearing the newsboys crying "Extra." We bought a paper and saw in the middle of the front page of the extra edition a large picture of the Democratic nominee for President. He was Franklin D. Roosevelt. I can still feel the poignant sense of being left out of the main stream of American political life which came over me at that moment. There was something in the expression around the eyes of the man whose picture appeared on those papers which made one sure that he would not be afraid to act in the crisis which the nation faced. His action might not be one hundred per cent correct in every instance but at least there would be movement.

The presidential campaign which followed was, however, a disappointment to me. Mr. Roosevelt gave us little inkling of his program for overcoming the depression and relieving the distress which stalked the country. But his victory in November 1932 was overwhelming and perhaps this proved the wisdom of his political tactics.

The new President was inaugurated on March 4, 1933, and within an hour the American nation knew that it was once more blessed with the vital type of leadership which, in time of trouble, has again and again brought new hope to our country. From the beginning there were features of his program which raised some serious questions for the future. But the President was telling us that mass unemployment must always be a matter of national concern and a cause for national action; and as his plans unfolded they evidently deserved the support of all Americans who, like myself, sought first and foremost an immediate answer to our nation's most critical problems.

For a variety of reasons California was ready to move somewhat faster than was the nation as a whole. Upton Sinclair, the author, became the symbol of this spirit.

In the fall of 1933, more than a year before the next California elections, he launched his campaign for the Democratic nomination for governor of California. His "EPIC plan" (End Poverty in California) was simple. It was this: that unemployed people be given an opportunity to produce for their own needs instead of being "cared for" by direct relief. The state was to buy or lease lands on which food products would be grown by some of the unemployed. Factories were to be erected where others among them would turn out such essential manufactured articles as clothing, furniture, and processed foods. The people were to be paid in scrip money, expendable only for goods produced within their co-operative "production-for-use" system.

Neither his nature nor his experience equipped Mr. Sinclair particularly well for the position of California's chief executive. But there were hundreds of thousands still unemployed in Los Angeles County alone; and national "recovery" appeared a long way off. Therefore to many Californians the hope in the EPIC proposal—hope of an end to destitution and the "relief" system, hope of a return to dignified self-support—seemed the one important consideration.

So it was that I decided to enter the Democratic primaries as a candidate for the nomination for state assemblyman from the Forty-ninth Assembly District. I was an avowed EPIC candidate and as such I shared in what was unquestionably one of the most bitterly fought campaigns in all the history of American politics.

On our side it was a crusade for what we believed was the best available solution for the profound problems of the great depression. Equally sincere, I now suspect, were our opponents who believed the EPIC plan would spell the end of the capitalistic system in America.

The primary results in August 1934 were, on the whole, a victory for the EPIC candidates. Mr. Sinclair was nominated for governor by a comfortable margin, and many of the candidates for the legislature, myself included, were likewise successful in winning their nominations. But thereafter it was a different story. Many Democrats joined forces with the Republicans to defeat the EPIC plan and candidates. Millions of dollars were spent against us and in the final event we lost. I was defeated by a margin that was not exactly overwhelming but was nonetheless decisive. I thought my political career was over.

But it wasn't.

The EPIC followers were terribly let down by Upton Sinclair's defeat. Tears were shed without shame or attempt at excuse in the post-mortem meetings held in the various communities. In many instances the people decided they would go ahead anyway and organize co-operative production ventures. We tried one in our town—a tomato cannery—which did give work to a number of people for a while but which eventually failed—primarily, as I now realize, for want of a skilled manager.

Time passed and the period approached for filing as candidates for office in the elections of 1936. I will say, as all politicians will, and generally with truth, that a good many people urged me to become a candidate for Congress. In the background, however, were the experiences in the factories and on the ranch, the problems the boys of our school had faced in the worst years of the depression, the failure of our co-operative and the reasons for it, the things I had seen in Europe—all the important events of my life. I believed there were answers to these problems. I saw that legislation passed by Congress was already getting the best of some of them. I believed the answers to more of them could be developed, in part at least, through wise action on the part of government.

It was essential that those basic American principles of opposition to concentrated economic power, equality of opportunity for the worker and the small farmer, and the preservation of the hopes of the common man should find practical political expression. I saw clearly then, as I have seen more and more clearly as the years passed, that the highest values in human life can be preserved only under a government which guarantees to its people a full measure of liberty—religious, personal, political, and economic. But the point was—and is—that the very existence of liberty depends directly on the maintenance of at least a reasonable degree of hope for economic betterment in the minds and hearts of the masses of people. Dictators have succeeded only in destroying free political institutions in nations riddled by economic chaos and despair. They have acquired power only through the willingness of a defeated people to sacrifice their liberty for the promise of employment and security. Ever since I was a boy I have had an abhorrence of the arrogance of power and every sort of totalitarianism—corporate, communist, fascist, or any other kind. Under dictatorship there can be no freedom of conscience. And without freedom of conscience true religious faith cannot flourish. And without such faith no people can be great, since the best single expression of human life is not present to drive them on.

For all these reasons I filed my name as a candidate for the Democratic nomination for Congress in the twelfth District of California in the spring of 1936.

When I did so I had little idea that I would be elected. Of course I knew that, should I be, I would have to be away from our school during a considerable part of each year. But I hoped and believed that the school would go on anyway and that during periods when Congress was not in session I could come back and take up my work with the boys where I had left it a few months before. Through the years the school had been not so much a job as an all-embracing life. It was a dynamic little community with its industry and agriculture, its education and its athletics, its newspaper and its library, its homes and its church. Had I known in 1936 that only two years later the Voorhis School for Boys was to become only a bright memory and its property a gift to the state of California, I am doubtful that I ever would have run for Congress.

Chapter 3

"HOW DID YOU
GET ELECTED?"

I have no very exact idea why I won the Democratic nomination or why I subsequently won my first election. In fact I have never been quite able to understand why I have been successful in any election. It has always seemed almost impossible that I could come out on top.

However, as I look back upon the events of the fall of 1936, I can see that there were a number of factors which gave me my first opportunity to serve in a public office in the United States.

In the first place the field was a very full one. The incumbent congressman was involved in some serious trouble over a West Point appointment and no less than eight candidates entered the race against him. In their philosophy they ranged from the very conservative to the very progressive. I suppose I fell roughly into the latter category. One of the men was the endorsed candidate of the Townsend organization, which was at one of the peaks of its influence. He "cross-filed" on both the Republican and Democratic tickets and ran second in each primary.

All the Democratic aspirants vied with one another in their expressions of support and admiration for President Roosevelt. In fact one of my problems arose when one of the candidates announced that he was not only "one hundred per cent for Roosevelt" but also one hundred per cent for any proposal, past, present, or future, which the President might make. He challenged me specifically to state whether I could match his one hundred per cent performance. I couldn't and said so. I declared myself in support of the broad principles which I believed President Roosevelt stood for but attempted, without too much political success, I believe, to explain that I could not conscientiously pledge myself in advance to be for any and all proposals which any human being, however wise and admirable, might advance.

I believe I won the nomination by my speeches. I know that most modern politicians minimize the effectiveness of public speeches as factors in winning elections. But in this case I feel fairly sure they were the deciding factor. One of the Republican candidates agreed to a series of debates and these attracted large crowds in several of the larger cities of the district. How many votes this influenced I do not know, but they did help to acquaint the public with my virtually unknown name and some of our southern California political "observers" declared afterward that the debates were the thing that finally gave me the nomination.

The outcome of the primaries was none too encouraging. The Republican nomination went to Fred Houser, a man approximately my own age, but a veteran of several successful campaigns for the state assembly. I won the Democratic nomination with only a little over eleven thousand votes. Mr. Peeler, the Townsend candidate, had nine thousand, the incumbent more than six thousand, and the rest of the field divided about sixteen thousand votes between them. Thus I was nominated with only a little over a quarter of the votes cast in the Democratic primary. To make matters worse, only three of my Democratic opponents gave me even so much as their formal endorsement for the final race against Houser, and only one of them gave me any active help. All the rest endorsed my Republican opponent, as did one of the district-wide Democratic organizations. I have been told that the Democratic National Committee itself came within an ace of disapproving my candidacy, influenced no doubt by my lack of a longer record in the party and by the rather disturbing "independence" of my past political record. The earnest intercession of several influential "old line" California Democrats with whom

I was well acquainted forestalled any unfriendly action by the National Committee and won its tacit if not its active support.

But another formidable obstacle to my election arose in the fact that, although he was supposed to be the conservative candidate, Mr. Houser obtained the official endorsement of the then powerful Townsend Old Age Pension organization. Both of us were called before their district board. We were asked certain questions. I gave unhesitating support to the basic principles of a national old-age pension system, in which principles I still earnestly believe. But I stated frankly that I did not believe a $200-a-month pension was possible of attainment and on that statement I lost the endorsement. Just what my opponent said I do not know, except that it was sufficient on this and other points to secure the endorsement of the Townsend organization.

For these reasons I still do not quite understand how we ever won out in that election. I had hardly any organized support. My opponent had the entire Republican party organization, the only formally organized Democratic group, the Townsendites, and most of the erstwhile Democratic candidates.

We did put on a good campaign, however, consisting of such direct mailing as we could finance and physically put out, a modicum of newspaper advertising, continuance of a weekly radio program I had been carrying on for more than a year, and speeches anywhere and everywhere that I could get anyone to listen to me. I well remember one occasion when I personally arranged for the use of a schoolhouse in one of the towns in the district, placed an ad in the local paper, distributed some handbills to the stores and houses, and then showed up at the appointed time, ready to address the "crowd." But not one single solitary person except myself came near that schoolhouse on that evening. This, fortunately, was not exactly typical and by November I had got my story over to a good many people. By dint of great effort on the part of Mrs. Voorhis and some of the other ladies we gave several picnics at our school, in the course of which a considerable number of new friends were made.

Election Day came and went. Early returns that evening showed us running neck and neck. At noon the next day Houser was reported to be leading. By midafternoon we were almost exactly even again. But by nightfall with late returns coming in I began to pull ahead and finally won by about nine thousand votes.

It was a Democratic year, the year President Roosevelt carried everything but Maine and Vermont. And I would be the last to deny that this trend was a major factor in my own success.

At any rate, the next thing was to get ready to leave for Washington.

Naturally, I was profoundly challenged by the opportunity which lay before me. I was also, I confess, a little frightened as I contemplated the task of making a place for myself in the House of Representatives of the United States.

Chapter 4

I LEARN ABOUT CONGRESS

"I feel sorry for you, Jerry, going back to that den of iniquity in Washington."

"Watch out for those lobbyists!"

"Don't let that bunch of crooks back there in Congress influence you."

These and other similar warnings were given me by many people in our district after my first election.

"I believe there is a great lack of integrity in Congress. Members are controlled by one pressure group or another."

"The old type of statesman seems to have disappeared. There just aren't any in Washington any more."

Such opinion is, I am afraid, widespread in the United States and has been for some time. And little wonder.

I recall reading in a very widely read national magazine about the time I first came to Washington that "the House of Representatives is a degenerate body." Even more vividly do I remember the words of Westbrook Pegler, castigating all members of Congress alike without the slightest attempt at discrimination, and stating that "when the flag of the new order is unfurled it should contain a broad yellow streak in memory of the men who sold their country out for a few lousy jobs." Through the years humorists like the·beloved Will Rogers had written about Congress. Their quips and jokes were moderate and therefore of wider influence than the effusions of the self-righteous Mr. Pegler. Constantly the Congress of the United States was held up to ridicule and depicted as a group of self-seeking officeholders playing political games with the welfare of the nation and possessing few if any of the basic virtues of the people who elected them.

I took none of these ideas too seriously. But they lay in the back of my mind as I left the school with Robert Burns and Harold Herin, my first two secretaries, and drove to Washington in late December 1936.

The United States is a great country. All Americans will agree to that. B. there is no experience which can give greater content and meaning to that belief than a drive across the nation in an automobile. From this point of view Western congressmen have a great advantage over their Eastern colleagues. In jou. leying to the national capital a Western member must pass through the orange or other fruit groves of his own state, over the deserts with their glorious still nights, through the mountains and their mining towns, across the great plains with their seemingly limitless distances. Then he feels the landscape and the atmosphere slowly change as the grazing country merges gradually into the fertile farming country of the middle Mississippi Valley. He crosses that mightiest of rivers—and many more. He travels through the cities and past the smaller farms of the old South or the Ohio Valley. At last he comes to the Appalachians, to the sources of coal and iron, to the smoky cities where American industry still is all too highly concentrated.

And out of all these impressions he gains some conception at least of what the word "America" represents.

It was a cold December day when our road led us to the top of a Virginia hill. There ahead of us on its own hill across the Potomac we saw the Capitol of the United States. The city of Washington lay all about it. The Washington Monument pierced the sky in the foreground. But none of the rest of that picture made much impression on me right then. It was the Capitol building that I saw standing there as it has stood through the decades, one of the few capitols of the world that has not been damaged or destroyed by a foreign enemy in the last hundred years, the central symbol of the vigor of the world's oldest constitutional national legislature in a republic. I wondered whether I could be worthy of that Capitol's best traditions. I wondered how long it would take me to make a place for myself in the work of the Congress that met there to pass laws for the greatest nation on earth.

I shall never forget Tuesday, January 5, 1937. It was the opening day of the Seventy-fifth Congress. Some of the events of the day are now blurred in memory but I can still feel my arm rising above my head and recall the members of the House repeating together these words: "I do solemnly swear that I will support and defend the Constitution of the United States against all enemies, foreign and domestic, that I will bear true faith and allegiance to the same, that I take this obligation freely without any mental reservation or purpose of evasion and that I will well and faithfully discharge the duties of the office on which I am about to enter. So help me God."

When John Garner, of Texas, was Speaker of the House he used to advise new members that there were only two relationships about which they should be concerned: first, their relationship to the people of their districts; second, their relationship with their colleagues (fellow members) in the House. Some of us might want to add a concern about the welfare of the United States or even the world. But there is no doubt that the success of any congressman in his job depends in very large measure on the breadth of his acquaintance with all other members and the depth of his friendship with as large a number as possible.

I should have known beforehand that congressmen are friendly souls. One of the reasons they are able to be elected is that they like people, which is the best way yet discovered to win affection for oneself. So it proved considerably less difficult to become at least superficially acquainted with the members of the House than I had feared it would. And I received some very valuable help. Fortunately for me, the representative from the First

District of Iowa, Mr. Edward C. Eicher, was a law partner of my wife's father. Hardly an hour after my arrival in Washington I called him on the telephone and he very warmly urged me to come to his office right away to attend an important meeting which was then in progress. It is difficult to describe the lift I received from that meeting. It gave me opportunity to meet a considerable number of older members and to listen to their discussion of plans for the election of Sam Rayburn, of Texas, as majority leader. Speaker Byrnes had died and it was a foregone conclusion that the then majority leader, William B. Bankhead, would be elected Speaker. There were two major candidates to succeed Mr. Bankhead as majority leader: Mr. Rayburn, the chairman of the Interstate and Foreign Commerce Committee and Mr. John J. O'Connor, of New York, chairman of the Rules Committee.

As a member-elect I had been generously bombarded with letters asking my support of one or the other of these men. I had made up my mind to vote for Mr. Rayburn since he was regarded as the more progressive of the candidates and was the author of such constructive laws as the Rural Electrification Act, the Federal Communications Act, the Securities and Exchange Act, and the bitterly contested Anti-holding Company Act. There was also a California angle to the situation since, if Mr. Rayburn were elected majority leader, he would automatically give up the chairmanship of the Interstate and Foreign Commerce Committee and, under the seniority rule, would be succeeded by Clarence F. Lea, of California. California held no important chairmanships in the House at the time and this was considered by many members from our state as a determining consideration in voting for majority leader.

When a few days later the Seventy-fifth Congress was officially organized, the Hon. Sam Rayburn was elected majority leader by the Democratic caucus. On Speaker Bankhead's death he was elected to the Speakership and held that position until January 1947. I have never had cause to regret that I supported him for majority leader as the first act of significance in my congressional career.

I made it a point to call on some of the members old and new about whom I had read and with whom I felt I might have logical points of agreement. All of them were cordial. Several of the older members gave "fatherly advice" to me as a freshman congressman.

Certain of the customs of the House changed perceptibly even in the short ten years between 1937 and 1947. Today new members are quite readily accepted as full-fledged participants in the business of the Congress. Considerable effort is even put forth by older members to assist new members in getting started smoothly with their work. As late, however, as 1937 such cases were the exception rather than the rule. New members, like children, were supposed to be "seen and not heard." They were made to feel, in a number of ways, that they belonged to an inferior category of congressmen and that they must labor through a number of re-elections before they could hope to play a full part in the work of the House. Such was not, as I later learned, the attitude of the most worthwhile of the older members or of the real leaders. But it certainly was the general atmosphere in which a new member had to operate.

For what seemed to me a very, very long time (actually it was only a few weeks) I managed to observe the "freshman rules." Day after day I listened, without participating, to debates on subjects in which I had a most active interest. At the close of the sessions I would return to my office with every organ of my body feeling as though it had been tied in knots. It was as if the thoughts I had felt impelled to express had somehow congealed within me and reposed like heavy stones all through my physical being.

Such experiences were not confined to those first few weeks. From time to time through my congressional career I heeded the counsel of friends who told me I was inclined to speak too often and on too many subjects. At times I persuaded myself that I was not adequately prepared to enter actively into a certain debate or to make a statement on the floor on some subject even though I had a deep conviction that it was somehow my duty to do so. But always I suffered profound regret and the almost physical pain which I have just described. I learned that for me, at least, the role of the comparatively silent men who move about the chamber with calm assurance, speak but seldom and are heard, therefore, with presumably greater effect was an impossible one. For better or for worse I had to do the job in the only way I could do it and live at peace with myself. When there was something I believed ought to be said in the House I had to say it. When there was an amendment to a bill which I believed ought to be offered and which I knew would not be presented unless I did so, then I had to offer the amendment.

The first such experience was not without its painful aspects. A bill for employment of the unemployed was being considered by the House. It seemed very clear to me that the amount of money carried in the bill was insufficient to meet the existing need. An older member, "Billie" Connery, of Massachusetts, then chairman of the Labor Committee, saw me writing out an amendment, asked me to let him see it, and assured me he would support the amendment if I would offer it. I told him I would. When the pertinent paragraph in the bill had been read I rose, with some trepidation, to my feet and asked recognition by the Speaker for the purpose of offering the amendment.

I made my five-minute speech in support of the amendment —a better one than I had expected to be able to make—and took my seat. Thereupon Congressman Fuller, of Arkansas, arose, obtained the floor and for five long minutes, as it seemed to me, delivered a speech attacking new members who presumed to try to "legislate on the floor of the House." Not only did he contend that members, especially new ones, should follow the guidance of committees and accept bills just as reported by them, but he also sarcastically denounced new members who apparently believed that they "were bigger than the President" since they proposed amendments to bills stamped with his approval. Needless to say, the occurrence I least expected was that I, a fledgling member of the House, would be compared to Franklin D. Roosevelt, President of the United States and at the height of his popularity. I only felt I must follow my own convictions. Mr. Fuller's speech was, to say the least, hard for me to listen to. It disturbed me much more deeply than would have been the case had I had a more accurate idea of Mr. Fuller's own standing in the House.

Congressman Maury Maverick, of Texas, followed Mr. Fuller. He was one of the members I had called on during my first few days in Washington. I had followed and admired his record. I wondered what he would say. He spoke briefly but very directly. He said new members had as much right to speak as anyone else, that they represented the same number of people as older members did, and that their constituents' voice obviously had a right to be heard. Furthermore, he defended my amendment. I can still recall the way he closed his speech: "I am going to vote with the gentleman from California, because he is all right, and what he said is all right, and a lot better than what the gentleman from Arkansas said."

The first difficult and somewhat frightening plunge had been taken. A feeling of profound concern and nervous excitement always troubled me whenever I was about to speak in the House —or anywhere else, for that matter. Probably it always will. But after that first memorable experience I was not afraid to speak my mind whenever I believed I should.

I was very grateful to Maury Maverick, and out of this and other events of my early months in Congress there developed a friendship between us which I shall always value as highly as any I have ever known. In the course of time an organization of progressive members was formed, known to the newspapers of the time as the "Young Turks." Maury Maverick was the moving spirit and chairman of the group, and I was elected secretary. We met, on the average, about once a week—usually in a rather dingy room over one of the second-rate restaurants that cluster about the Capitol. We discussed pending legislation, heard speakers on almost every phase of congressional work, and drew up a number of statements and programs which we released to the press and inserted in the *Congressional Record*. Probably our most distinguished member was David J. Lewis, of Maryland, affectionally known as "Old Davy" Lewis and nationally known as principal author of the Social Security Act. Mr. Eicher was a regular attendant at our meetings. So was Congressman Ed Izac, from San Diego, California, a Congressional Medal of Honor naval officer of World War I and one of the most conscientious members of the House I ever knew. To a new member of the House, meetings of this sort were a great assistance. We did not always vote alike. But we did have the opportunity of threshing out among ourselves the pros and cons of controversial questions before they came up in the House. Through our Young Turks meetings, through my committee meetings, through contacts on the floor and elsewhere I was learning about Congress and about congressmen as they actually are—not as they are reported to be by the columnists or the humorists of the country.

In the course of time I was to find that some of the unfavorable things that are said and believed about Congress are, in a limited measure, true. On a very few occasions I have seen the House act more like a crowd than like a legislative body. I have seen it in a mood which doomed to defeat the wisest and most salutary amendment to a bill which members were in haste to pass. I have seen it in the opposite mood where almost any amendment, however impractical and ill conceived, was virtually certain to be adopted because the bill before us was one which members did not like but which they were afraid to vote against. I know that there are some members who frequently vote no on controversial bills even though they know defeat of the bill will be of the most serious consequence to the nation. They depend on more conscientious members to carry the burden of passing it. And once or twice I have seen the House swept off its feet by a clever phrase. I recall one such occasion when a member offered an amendment striking from the Agriculture Department Appropriation bill the entire amount for the control of Japanese beetles. About all he said was, "Let us fight the Japs, and not the beetles." The difficulty was that the beetles were on the "Japs' " side and it was necessary in subsequent years to appropriate considerably more for their control than would have been the case had the House acted with judgment instead of emotion in the first place.

It was hardly surprising to me to find that Congress, like the country it represents, is made up of all sorts of people. Very early I discovered that, like New York, Keokuk, and Centerville, Congress has its "select circle." It consists of a number of highly prepossessed members, who have considerable influence in the Congress and who are well aware of that fact. Practically always they are members of long service. A few of them seem to make a point of failing to note the presence of newer members or those not belonging to the select influential group. As a rule these members come from "safe" districts in which one party or the other is so predominant that there is almost no chance of their being defeated. This means that their positions are secure and that if they are not already committee chairmen it is only a matter of time until they will become so. Most of these highly influential members are conservatives; almost without exception they are people of admirable character. I confess to having had a deep desire to have the friendship and understanding—if not the agreement—of certain of these men. I have experienced the hollow, empty feeling of having others of them turn away, almost deliberately, and begin a discussion with another of their circle when I was attempting to speak to them.

But in most cases where it really mattered to me I did succeed in gaining their friendship. There were times when encouragement given me by certain of these year-in-and-year-out congressional stalwarts was of great help.

As time went on and I gained confidence in my own work I naturally laid less store by what others, whoever they were, might think of it.

At the other extreme in both the House and the Senate are certain members who "play" regularly to the galleries and to the press. I soon learned that their influence is vastly less than would appear from a reading of either the *Congressional Record* or the morning papers. Generally they are men who have selected some particular "hates" and objects of attack which they never tire of assailing. They seem to care little what their colleagues think of them—which means they are not likely to be effective congressmen. Nothing pleases them more than to have some attack made on them over the radio or in some special magazine or paper. For then they can make a "point of personal privilege" and virtually compel recognition for an hour by the Speaker. In this time they are supposed to answer the charges made, but they usually employ it to make a good many charges of their own.

Some of the "personal privilege" group are Republicans and some are Democrats; some are from the North, some from the

South. Like the influential group, they come from "safe" districts —else they couldn't carry on as they do. I was constantly impressed with the apparently limitless sense of self-righteousness which these members possessed. Otherwise they could hardly have passed such final and devastating judgment on so many groups of human beings. Their field of responsibility is consequently narrowed to include only those people who are, in race, creed, and circumstance quite like themselves. As I listened to them it seemed to me their work as congressmen must be greatly simplified, since there are so few people about whose problems they need worry. Luckily for the United States, the number of members with this convenient point of view is not great—at least it never was during my term of service.

The membership of the House includes, of course, men and women from every corner of the United States. There is a widespread belief that members group themselves quite clearly and definitely according to the section from which they come. I learned that this is true to only a limited extent. There was, on certain issues such as forestry, reclamation, and the like, a tendency for members from the "eleven Western states" to vote together. But on other issues they split apart as widely as the poles. I had heard a good deal about the "Farm Bloc" and the "Labor Bloc," largely, I now suspect, because these words greatly simplify newspaper copy. Of course, members from rural sections tend to vote for legislation favorable to farmers, whereas members from certain city districts are strongly inclined to support measures which it is believed will benefit wage earners. But in neither case is there any "leader" of the bloc, any actual organization, or even any membership. To add to the confusion, there were many occasions when the majorities of both these rather nebulous groups were found voting exactly alike. I learned that congressmen don't like to be classified and that, except in a comparatively few cases, it is very hard to classify them.

The closest approach to a geographical bloc is, I suppose, the Southerners. Most members from that section can be depended upon to rally for united action whenever an issue is raised which affects the particular interest or the traditions of the South. Racial questions form but one group of such issues. There are many others. And the South is stronger in Congress than the mere numbering of its representatives would indicate. Southern districts have a habit of returning the same congressman or senator to office at election after election. A large number of them are, in fact, re-elected without opposition. Thus, particularly when the Democratic party is in power, Southern members exercise a very great influence, because of their positions of seniority on all the committees. Furthermore, most Southern members have far more time to devote to legislative work than do members from other sections of the country. This is because the volume of their mail is generally much smaller. That, in turn, is due to the difference between the Northern and the Southern idea of what a "representative" should be. The people of most Northern and Western districts feel that their congressmen ought to do whatever the majority of the people in the district want done, whereas the people of the South—at least those who vote in that section —appear altogether willing to elect a representative and depend on him to make the decisions for them. Finally, the Southern delegations contain some of the most likable and winning personalities in the entire Congress and unless Northern and Western members are decidedly on the alert, they awake to find that Southern magnetism has again been used at just the right time and in exactly the right way to protect the interests of that section.

It is but one illustration of Southern persuasiveness that of the six "basic commodities" which receive the lion's share of benefits under the government's agricultural program, no less than four are Southern crops almost exclusively—cotton, tobacco, rice, and peanuts.

The popular designation of the Southern members as "conservative Southerners" is generally correct. But I learned that there are in every Congress some Southern members who are thoroughgoing and courageous progressives—even on questions which are politically dangerous in their section. Moreover, judged on the basis of support of constructive measures with regard to farm tenancy, monopoly, public power, monetary policy, and foreign relations, the voting record of the South is almost as good as that of any other part of the nation.

Over against the Southerners stand the members who have

"come up through the organization," either in some Northern city or some Midwestern semirural constituency. I learned that the operations of a Republican machine in Iowa or Michigan are not so very different in net political effect from those of a Democratic machine in Boston or Chicago or New York. In either case the member owes his seat not alone to his personal qualifications (though these do usually play a part) but to the organized political support which he has received. Such members usually are not very active in debate. They introduce few bills. They follow very closely the program of the political party to which they belong. But they are eager to do a personal favor for a colleague anywhere and at any time. One suspects that this characteristic has a good deal to do with their political success at home.

In recent years an increasing number of women have been elected to Congress, particularly to the House. As I watched their work I could see how difficult is the problem which they face, for they must steer a course midway between two fatal mistakes. The woman member must take care that she does not base her appeal for the cause in which she is interested on the fact of her womanhood. She cannot expect chivalry from the male members when it comes to casting their votes. Neither, on the other hand, can she hope to gain a strong position for herself if she attempts the role of a hail fellow well met and tries to be like the men. What she has to do is to be simply a member of the House who quite incidentally happens to belong to the female sex. This has been accomplished with excellent effect by a number of the women members. In other instances the results have been less encouraging. But there is no reason at all for believing that the proportion of women members will decline. The contrary seems more likely to prove the case.

Among all these types and kinds of members I found at least one point of complete agreement. All of them want to be re-elected. The methods which some are willing to employ to gain that end would not for a moment be countenanced by the more conscientious members. But the latter, generally speaking, hope for re-election just as fervently as the former, and there is nothing unworthy about that hope.

Members of Congress talk very freely among themselves about their campaign experiences and their plans for future elections. Sometimes I found this talk a little discouraging. For example, there is a fairly wide acceptance of the idea that the way to get re-elected is to make few if any speeches, to introduce no bills, to remain as silent as possible on all controversial issues, and to spend one's time cultivating personal friendships with influential people, taking care of the requests of constituents, and working primarily to accomplish things which will be a benefit to "the district." The trouble is that this formula has been proved to work. In case after case it was shown to me that the members who have followed this formula have been able to survive nationwide trends and sweeps, whereas their more active colleagues have gone down to defeat.

Some members of the House and Senate deliberately select important—if possible predominant—organized groups in their districts and make it an inviolable practice never to vote or act contrary to the wishes of such a group. This is what organized groups really want—congressmen and senators who are absolutely "dependable," whose records will be not ninety per cent or ninety-five per cent, but one hundred per cent "good" votes. I found for example there were members of both Houses of Congress whose office staffs were hand-picked by the PAC, whose speeches were written by the very able if sharply biased PAC "experts," and whose position on every question could be depended upon to follow the PAC line. Much less publicized in our "free" press is the fact that other members have placed themselves in a position where they dare not have anyone associated with their offices who is not acceptable to certain business interests, such as the major oil companies, the railroads, the insurance companies, or others. Certain members' voting records, if critically examined, will reveal that they have very consistent "progressive" records on all issues except where oil is involved, but that wherever petroleum does appear in the situation those members' votes are, with equal consistency, always on the "right" side from the viewpoint of the big companies. Again, there are members who have the general reputation of being arch conservatives but who regularly get aboard the labor bandwagon wherever the railroad brotherhoods are interested in the question.

As time went on, I realized that there is an understandable human reaction about all this. Everyone desires the inner warmth that comes from the knowledge that he has friends who can be counted upon. The members of the organized groups desire this. So do the congressmen. It is, again, a formula for re-election. And I confess that there have been times, particularly in the midst of tough campaigns, when I have had more than a tinge of loneliness. It has arisen from the knowledge that there was hardly a single organized group, at least none of great consequence, to whom I could show a "one hundred per cent record." I never quite belonged anywhere. I worked very hard indeed in the interests of agriculture, particularly the farmers of my own state and section. But there were times when I didn't "go along." There was the time, for example, when I could not conscientiously vote for the Elliott rider, removing all acreage limitation under the reclamation laws. I usually voted for what was considered the "best interest" of labor, but I could not cast a vote against the Hobbs Anti-racketeering bill, nor could I bring myself to vote to continue consumer subsidies in peacetime. I wasn't even "regular" as to questions in which California was regarded as having a special interest. I voted for mandatory joint income tax returns for husbands and wives, though this was widely advertised—falsely so, as I believed—as a blow at the community property law of our state. Thus I have been able to understand why members sought a kind of political "home" in the bosom of some strong group, whose interests they would always protect and who could then be depended upon to go all out for the candidate for re-election whenever the need arose.

But it was plain to see that such practices make for bad legislation—not so much because they predetermine how a man is going to vote, but more especially because they tend to reduce what should be debates into mere arguments between people who have already had their minds made up for them. Fortunate it is that there are so many members who insist upon being completely free men. They speak their minds and save the situation for America as a whole.

All this and somewhat more could be said about the faults and weaknesses of congressmen. But the worst things that are said simply are not true—not of the great majority of members of the House and Senate. There are, in my humble opinion, some pretty thoroughly bad members of Congress. But they are "spotted" after a few short weeks of membership and thereafter are tolerated out of respect to their having been elected—nothing more. The majority of members of Congress are very far from the corrupt, cowardly lot which some sensationalists would have the country believe them to be. On vital issues of great consequence to the nation it is my belief that from two thirds to three quarters of the membership would rather be sure that they are right—if only they can discover in their own innermost minds what *is* right—than to be sure of re-election. And there is one group of congressmen of whom I have not yet spoken. They are the people who make one Congress different from another one. They are the members who owe their elections to difficult personal struggles unaided by tradition, large sums of money, or the support of political machines. They come to the House or Senate unencumbered with obligations and they know that the record they make will be the only ground on which they can stand for re-election in case they desire it. Obviously this group, upon whom so much clearly depends, is the most insecure one in the entire Congress. It contains the members most likely to be eliminated from membership in the next or subsequent elections. Furthermore, such men almost always come from districts where party strength is fairly equally divided, and where political interest and activity are likely to be at a high level. This increases correspondence and in a great number of other ways adds to the burdens of the job. Laboring under the handicap of having comparatively little seniority, this group of genuinely free members must carry the major burden of the work of the Congress, except of course for the functions of leadership exercised so largely by the first group described in this chapter.

The members of Congress are men and women, as much the products of their environments and experiences as anyone else. They must possess somewhat more than average "drive" and self-assurance. They must be, and are, on the whole, above the average of their constituents in ability. But they are, as I said in the beginning of this chapter, essentially like the people they represent. They possess the strong points and the weaknesses of the average run of American citizens, which is one of the main reasons why I never allowed the prefix "Honorable" to be placed before my name in the *Congressional Record*. It was always very clear to me that having been elected to Congress did not make me one whit more "honorable" than any other citizen of the Twelfth Congressional District of California. Either all of us should be called "honorable" or none of us should, for the question of one's honor is not to be answered by a title but by the quality of his life and work.

But I like to believe that, confronted with the profound meaning of their oath of office, most members of the Congress of the United States find themselves lifted somewhat above the level of thought and action of which they would otherwise be capable. At least it had better be so, if America is to be safe in the possession of her free institutions and her favored position among the nations during the uncertain tomorrows that lie ahead of us.

Chapter 5

I LEARN ABOUT
THE AMERICAN PEOPLE

A lady wrote to me one day in the midst of the war,

> MY DEAR CONGRESSMAN:
> My daughter likes eggs. In fact we have them for break-
> fast every morning. But this morning, while they weren't
> exactly spoiled, they certainly weren't fresh. And my
> daughter just couldn't eat them. Now after all the eggs I
> have bought from this big dairy company, I should think
> they could at least bring me good ones. I live in Maryland
> and am not in your district, but please do something to
> help me.

I answered the lady's letter. I advised her to call up the "big
dairy company" and tell them what had been the state of their
eggs. She was kind enough to write to thank me for my answer.
It hadn't occurred to her to call the dairy, she said.

But it had occurred to her to write to a congressman. Not to
her own congressman, but just to most any old congressman.
I happened to be "it."

This lady's letter is decidedly not typical of a congressman's
mail. A few such letters, containing utterly trivial and purely
personal matters, arrive from week to week. But not many.

The significant thing about the letter was that this lady was
reacting to her egg problem just as millions of other Americans

have learned to react to their problems—by writing to a congressman.

This is a very new habit. Old-timers among the congressmen sometimes spoke to me with yearning in their voices of the "good old days" when only a handful of letters would arrive each week. Apparently it was not until the coming of the Great Depression of 1929 and of President Roosevelt's New Deal that the American people decided to "write to their congressman"—or somebody else's.

In some sections of the country the habit of writing to Congress hasn't developed even yet. One Tennessee congressman told me, to my complete astonishment, that during all the excitement and fervent debate over OPA in the spring of 1946 he did not receive a single letter from one of his constituents telling him what to do or how to vote. I know of one Middle Western congressman's office where the receipt of as many as fourteen letters in one day was considered a remarkable event.

But from all the districts along both coasts, from the mountain states and the Northwest, from the Great Lakes area, and from some parts of the Southwest there has come a stream of letters to members of Congress. Sometimes that "stream" has seemed more like a deluge to the senators and representatives who were on the receiving end of it.

The letters deal with almost every conceivable subject of human interest. They are from all sorts of people; they contain all sorts of enclosures; they request all manner of jobs to be done. Reading them is a liberal education, a course in psychology, a continuous newsreel of what is going on in the American people's minds.

There has always been something almost sacred to me about a letter—especially a longhand letter. Here is a piece of white paper with some peculiar-looking black lines on it. It has traveled, in many cases, clear across the American continent. Sometimes it has come from foreign lands. Some other fellow human being has made those lines. And when I see them I understand the thoughts, ideas, emotions, and feelings that were in his mind when he made them.

Accordingly when a letter came in the mail addressed to me

it was very hard indeed not to answer it—even if it came from North Dakota or from Maine or from Louisiana, from Canada or Mexico or Jamaica or England or Australia or the Philippines. Yes, it was hard not to answer it even if it asked questions with which a congressman is in no way obligated or prepared to deal. In fact it was so hard not to answer a letter that no more than a handful of the tens of thousands of letters received in my office while I was a congressman went unanswered. And most of those either came to us without return addresses, were identical products of mass "pressure" campaigns which came from outside the Twelfth California District, or were letters so bitter and unreasonable that they made me angry and I could not, with self-respect, make anything but a sharp reply. So I would dictate the reply and then we would all feel better and throw it into the wastebasket.

There was only one real problem about the mail. This was not the reading of it nor even the actual job of answering, but what had to take place between these two events. Hours and hours of someone's time were required to gather the information, to work out the problems, to investigate the claims, to do the hundred and one jobs that were required before we would be ready to answer even so much as one day's mail. And always there was tomorrow, with more mail coming in and more jobs to do in connection with it. Sometimes we would feel like three or four people trying to hold back a waterfall with our bare hands.

I say "we" because, of course, I didn't do by any means all of this myself. I couldn't possibly have done so. I did read all the mail, and when it was time to answer I either dictated the answer myself or went over the answer written by one of the other workers in our office. However, what I would have done without the kind of loyal, willing, efficient, and tireless assistance of the people who worked with me I simply cannot imagine. For some reason which I cannot explain, I was blessed all through the ten years with as earnest, interested, and capable a staff of coworkers as there was on Capitol Hill.

At the beginning the staff consisted of Robert Wayne Burns, then a newspaperman from Covina, California, who had been among the first to urge me to run for Congress in 1936, and Harold Herin, one of the graduates of our Voorhis School and one of the most rapid and accurate takers of dictation that I have ever seen. Ben O'Brien, another Voorhis alumnus, who was studying law in Washington, helped us out during all his spare time. In later years his brother Edmund did the same thing, although neither of them ever received a cent of pay for the work they did. When Mr. Burns found that he couldn't carry on both his newspaper work and the work in Washington, Duane de Schaine, another of my former students, came on to replace him. But the war was coming and when it broke upon the nation Harold and Duane went to the Army. Stanley Long, with whom I had become acquainted when he was office manager for a small manufacturing firm out in our district, and Mrs. Kathryn Farmer, of Washington, took their places. When the war was over Duane and Harold came back and took their old jobs again.

Always out home in the district there was V. R. (Jack) Long, who managed my first campaign—and later ones too—and who was our "field secretary" during all the hours he could spare from his poultry business. To him went special "cases" that had to be handled on the home ground. From him and from my father came firsthand reports about how things were going with the people in the district, what the people were saying, what new problems had arisen. Except at the very close of my tenure, when the "clerk hire" was increased sufficiently to enable congressmen to pay three good salaries out of it instead of two, our regular staff consisted only of Mr. Long, two people in the office in Washington, and myself. But there were months, even years, when there were additional workers, some of them paid out of my own salary, some of them volunteers like Mrs. Catherine Blaisdell. I remember one period shortly before the end of the war when only three of us tried to get along in the Washington office and when our work piled up so that we were three weeks behind with the mail. There was nothing to be done but hire a third secretary to help us out. It would require an entire volume to tell all these people did. Nor have I even attempted to name them all. Suffice it to say that without their help the job simply could not have been done and that whatever I may have accomplished was due in large part to the faithful and efficient services of the people who worked with me through the years.

They never liked it much, I think, when I insisted upon reading all the mail that came to our office. They wished I would let them take a considerable proportion of the letters as they arrived, read them, work out the answers, and reply to them without my being "bothered" with them at all. Many congressmen follow this practice. I never could. I felt it was part of my job to read all the letters that were addressed to me and I always did so.

I seldom got any of this done during the daytime. There were too many other things to be done then. But every evening when I left the office one or more large envelopes full of mail were part of what I carried home with me.

I always read the mail after all the other "homework" had been done. The mail was interesting, and it consisted of other people's ideas—not my own. I could keep awake going through the mail, even if it was very late, whereas I might have fallen asleep over some other sort of task.

Usually it was after midnight when I finally came to the last letter. But I never went to bed until I had read the mail. Tomorrow there would be more.

There were many times during those midnight hours when I felt like cursing the efficiency of the Post Office Department. I used to complain, as do many congressmen, about the work the mail entailed. But down deep in my heart I was thankful it came, thankful people cared enough to write, even thankful their letters came in batches of 50, 80, 100, sometimes 250 a day. Over the ten years I expect our office averaged 150 letters received and as many mailed per day, which makes 54,750 letters a year and 547,500 letters in ten years. When I made too big a fuss my wife would say, "You'd feel a lot worse if you only got a couple of dozen letters a day." And I would have to admit that she was right.

One night in 1942, I finished the mail about eleven o'clock, and I decided to make a list of the subjects with which the letters received that day had dealt. I still have that old list, and here is part of it, just as I wrote it out that night:

> Letter describing an invention made by the writer and urging me to help him secure its adoption by the Army—with due compensation.
> Letter sending me a long article in manuscript and ask-

ing me to read it and help the writer get it published.
Letter giving me hades for not having written a letter of
character reference for a man I simply cannot remember
and who lives 1000 miles from our district.
Letter telling me it was "un-American" for me to resign
from the Dies Committee.
Two letters telling me I should have resigned from the
Dies Committee long before I did, and one of them saying
it was "un-American" for me to go on the committee at all.
Letter from the Library of Congress offering to send
abstracts of all books and articles written on problems
likely to face our government at the conclusion of the war.
Several communications urging favorable vote on a bill
to increase the pay of postal workers.
Letter urging that I read several articles in a certain maga-
zine.
Fifteen letters urging that I secure an increase from OPA
and Dept. of Agriculture in the ceiling price on oranges.
Letter asking me to write a paragraph statement for a co-
operative commenting on its purchase of an oil refinery.
Letter urging that I do something to save the small news-
papers of the country from being forced out of business.
Letter urging the enactment of national prohibition.
Eight letters urging the adoption of the pay-as-you-go plan
of taxation.
Letter urging that I do something to provide employment
for older people and also vote in favor of the Townsend
plan.
Letter requesting that I secure a rating for a second-class
seaman on a United States destroyer.
Letter bawling me out for not having answered a recent
communication more promptly.
Letter urging that I secure additional clerical help for
a ration board.
Letter protesting the proposal of the Ways and Means
Committee for a pay-as-you-go tax plan.
Letter stating that I talk 'like Washington' and it sounds
like a lot of words and lacks "Americanism."
Letter urging that more meat be bought from South
America and less be shipped out of our country for Lend-
Lease.

Letter urging improvement in the Social Security system.
Letter from a disabled veteran enclosing numerous documents regarding his claim against the government.
Letter from Illinois urging me to secure an old-age pension for a lady in northern California.
Letter urging that all of the credit agencies of the Department of Agriculture be consolidated.
Letter urging adoption of a world perpetual calendar.
Form letter protesting the number of government forms that must be filled out.
Letter requesting copy of *Agriculture Yearbook*.
Letter protesting against 'the conscription of women.'
Letter urging that the drafting of manpower and property be immediately enacted.
Letter requesting that I make a gift of my book recently written to 'Liberty, Freedom, and You, Inc.'
Letter requesting that I send copies of six bills to Wendell Willkie.
Letter asking that I secure position for the writer as shoemaker instructor with the government 'someplace.'
Letter asking that I secure a loan for the writer so that he can start farming in Oregon.
Letter urging that I do something to get the production of Ramie started in the United States immediately.
Several letters expressing support of my resolution on postwar planning.
Letter thanking me for introducing H.R. 375 to provide for relief for the blind.
Letter urging the immediate dismissal of a certain employee in the Office of War Information.
Letter urging that the Department of Agriculture take up vigorously the production of *Cryptostegia* as a source of rubber.
Letter concerning legislation introduced on the problem of the physically handicapped.
Two letters from a young man asking information on entrance requirements for West Point.
Letter from a man asking, first, assistance in getting a job, and, second, my opinion of an essay he has witten on airplane hydraulics.
Letter protesting against the construction of a dam in New

Mexico which would interfere with certain rights of Indian tribes.

Telegram protesting the OPA price order on rayon hosiery.

Letter stating that the New Deal is jeopardizing the writer's freedom and the freedom of the American people and protesting against the proposed expansion of the Social Security Act.

Letter protesting certain action by labor unions and asking what I propose to do to correct these matters.

Several letters urging that I secure federal aid for the schools.

There are a few of the above that will sound foolish. Some of them probably were. A good many of them covered matters that were hardly a congressman's business. But it was the voice of the American people, a voice of many tones and variations, a voice that could be angry and demanding and even unreasonable, but one that could also be kind and earnest and concerned about the future. A great part of the drama, the human emotion, the joy and the sadness, the comedy and tragedy that are part of a great society passed before my eyes each night as I read my congressman's mail. Thousands of those letters are worth quotation. A few passages selected at random are all this volume can contain:

FROM A MOTHER

You are my representative in Congress and as such are my only voice in National Government. You and your fellow congressmen are bearing grave responsibilities these days.

We mothers at home have our grave responsibilities too, to fight for our children's rights and raise mentally and physically healthy children for the sake of the future of our Democracy.

Without our family unit, Democracy is not worth much. Our armed forces are fighting to preserve our family rights. Yet our government, at home, is doing its utmost to tax the family out of its basic necessities for life. Why must the exemptions on dependants be lowered?

FROM A HIGH SCHOOL STUDENT

I am a senior in high school and am preparing a script for a speech on the topic, "Coops—A Solution."

Our country is in a grave situation and not only present thoughts of winning the war are of importance but also the future questions of "What are we going to do after the war?"

I would appreciate it very much if you would be kind enough to send me some literature, and if possible, a statement from you which you think would cover the topic mentioned.

FROM AN OLD GENTLEMAN

I cannot conceive the wisdom of the policy of this government in putting into the army our young men and leaving out men between the age of thirty-eight and fifty when I know from my own personal experience that when I was at that age I was as well fitted to shoulder a gun if not really better fitted than I would have been at eighteen or twenty, and, while I am too old to take any part in this war, I am only wishing that it were not so, for I am thinking that the allies are fighting the most religious war in all history and for that reason I say let the older men have a part in helping to win.

FROM A POULTRYMAN

Not being a constituent of your district, nevertheless, I know your reputation very well. Therefore, I am asking a favor from you. What I want is anything and everything pertaining to the diseases and culture of chickens that you would care to obtain for me. I am starting in the chicken business and whatever assistance I can receive from you will be very much appreciated.

FROM THE ARKANSAS EDUCATION ASSOCIATION

Public Education is soon going to cease to be the basic principle in this Democracy—so far as Arkansas is concerned—if we don't get Federal Aid for elementary and secondary education immediately.

By 1946 the world was at peace again. The war letters were replaced by letters about veteran problems, atomic bombs, hopes for peace. But the total volume was just as great and human nature apparently a good deal the same too.

Here are a few passages from 1946 letters:

FROM SOMEONE WHO DIDN'T
SIGN HIS NAME

Thank you so much for what you've done for the rabbit · raiser. From a struggling rabbit breeder of El Monte. Thank you very much.

FROM A MAN I NEVER HEARD OF
BEFORE OR SINCE

I am in receipt of a letter from Mr. ———, who is Mr. ———'s attorney in his case in the State of Utah. As you no doubt know Mr. ——— became involved in a murder there and was found guilty and sentenced to be executed by a firing squad on the twelfth of last April. However, due to prejudice, false testimony and many errors in the trial, a new trial was allowed on the appeal. Mr. ——— writes me that they need approximately $1,000 to perfect the appeal. Therefore, we all would be very grateful if you would mail to Mr. ——— whatever you can spare in this worthy cause. As you are no doubt familiar with Mr. ——— I am sure you will know what I mean. Speed is essential.

FROM AN IRATE CONSTITUENT WHO DIDN'T
TELL ME WHAT "FORCES" HE MEANT

Please do something about curbing the forces that are trying to wreck America.

FROM A MINISTER

I personally wish to thank you for your recent action relative to House Joint Resolution 325.

In my opinion it is imperative that the production of alcoholic beverages be sharply curtailed to relieve the grain shortages, both for the relief of the starving peoples of the world and the relief of dairy and cattle feed here at home.

FROM A LADY WHO DIDN'T KNOW
ANYTHING ABOUT OPA

Am writing in behalf of the soldier boys who have been working on mail routes. The OPA has them carrying packs of advertisements of store sales weighing forty to fifty pounds.

FROM A LADY CONSTITUENT

Sometimes I think you care about nothing but sitting back there drawing down your salary and wanting more.

FROM A HOUSEWIFE

I surely hope you will cast your vote to retain OPA and price restrictions for one year. What chance has the man with a stationary income if we have inflation? I can't understand anyone with average common sense voting to lift price restrictions. I am sure the people want it kept in force.

FROM ANOTHER HOUSEWIFE

I am of the opinion that if the OPA continues in power many will be prevented from building due to the fact that it is almost impossible to get many essentials needed in building. Too, it is making rogues and hypocrites of really good people.

I trust that you may be convinced that a continuation of the OPA in office is detrimental to the vast majority of the people of California and that you will use your influence to release its strangle hold on reconversion.

A LETTER WHICH I RECEIVED AFTER I HAD CEASED TO BE A CONGRESSMAN AT ALL

I am writing you regarding the sugar situation. The time has come to demand a change in the present New Deal program in the matter of sugar.

We want our sugar to remain at home in U. S. A. and not all be sent across the water while we go without.

We want sugar on our grocers' shelves and to be able to buy it without a *silly stamp*.

Thanking you and trusting you will attend to this at once as it is very important.

FROM A NINETY-YEAR-OLD AMERICAN CITIZEN

Whom the Lord loveth He chastens. Surely the great awakening is upon us now. I had these words spoken to

me one morning not long ago as I was getting out of bed;
old things are passing away; behold all things are becoming
new.

There were some short cuts and our office used as many of
them as we could. For example, there were times when we received hundreds of letters all dealing with the same subject. In
such cases I would prepare a form letter which could be mimeographed in quantity. With hundreds—sometimes thousands—of
them to answer, this was the only possible way we could reply
at all.

Here is an example on one of my form letters:

February 12, 1940

DEAR MR.————:

A petition regarding the low-cost housing project with
your signature on it has come to my office. I can understand why some of our people are against this project
and I know it is going to cause some folks to have to sell
their places. I feel sure that a fair price will be paid for
these places and if the owner wants to he can, of course,
contest the price in a court of law.

So far as the location of the project is concerned, I, of
course, had nothing at all to do with that and, if I can
be of any help to anyone whose property is affected, I'll
be glad to try to the extent of my ability.

Now the petition contains a threat that unless I see to
it that the project is moved there will be a move to recall
me or at any rate that people will vote me out of office at
the next election. That, of course, would be all right with
me. I could ask for nothing that would make me happier
than to go back to schoolteaching and lay down the burdens and the awful worries of this congressional office. If
the people want me to do that, I shall not be unhappy but
rather relieved.

But I think we should look at all sides of this housing
project.

What are the gains and losses from this project?

First, Congress has provided for a certain number of
these projects scattered over the country. *Some* communities will have them and some won't. In the commu-

nities that do have projects, there will certainly take place a rise in property values, and improvement in business, a raising of morale. Also, there will, during the building period, be employment for a considerable number of people and more business for local business people on account of this. Would we rather have these things in our community or someplace else?

Second, in order to comply with the law, a certain number of older houses must be torn down before new ones can be built. In the Marvilla project, 177 houses will be purchased from their owners and 504 new houses will be built. In other words, 177 families will have to move to make possible new and better housing for three times that number. The gain here seems to me clearly much greater than the loss—though the trouble of having to move and in some cases the giving up of a little home are real losses and no one can say they aren't.

If I could change the present law all by myself, I would change it so it would be possible for people to buy these new houses over a period of time and own them. But we must remember that this is an attempt to help out some of our people with small incomes. No one with an income of over $100 a month can live in these new houses. We are all eager to promote Americanism and understanding and devotion to our country among all people. Perhaps this effort to make it possible for some five hundred families to live in better, cleaner, more wholesome homes will help in that direction. I hope it will and I believe it will.

Sincerely,

JERRY VOORHIS

Frequently I have been asked: "Does it do any good to write to congressmen?"

The general answer to that question is an emphatic "yes." Most congressmen certainly do "pay attention" to the mail. Of course they have all been elected by the people of certain districts, and they pay far more attention to letters from those people than to those from other sections of the nation. This, after all, is as it should be. Frequently, also, members of the House and Senate will vote "against the mail," that is, in a manner contrary to the way in which the majority of their letters are urging them to vote.

They know that many letters are "inspired" by interested groups and organizations. They know that people who are against things are at least twice as likely to write letters to congressmen as are people who are for something. And they know that people who are afraid their side is going to lose are many times more likely to write to them than are people who feel reasonably sure that their opinion will prevail.

But, generally speaking, it is decidedly worth while for citizens of the United States to write to their senators and representatives. Stones are gradually worn away by the dripping of water upon them. In like manner, no one who is human can help being influenced to some extent at least by the reading of message after message on a given question, even if the general purport of the messages is contrary to the thinking of the person receiving them. And senators and congressmen are especially "human." It is their primary business to be.

Then there is another question that generally follows the first one. It is: "What kind of letters have the greatest influence with members of Congress?"

I can, of course, only speak from my own experience. But I believe it is fairly typical.

To begin, then, at the bottom, the least effective of all the various sorts of communications that are sent to congressmen are mimeographed telegrams. It is evident on their face that the same message has been sent to all members, or, at least, to a large number of them. Hence, each member feels that the message was not intended especially for him, but, rather, for the Congress as a whole. And he accordingly discounts the necessity of acting upon it personally. Moreover, he knows that such "blanket" telegrams can be sent only by someone who possesses a good deal of money, and this means that they can hardly be regarded as "the voice of the people." Even individual telegrams which have the appearance of being sent especially to a certain member have an impersonal quality about them which makes them much easier to disregard than a letter. Again, when a congressman receives a telegram he has a tendency to ask why this person was so late in realizing what was going on at his national Capitol that he had not time to write a letter about it.

So "Write, don't telegraph" is the first rule that should be followed by those who are in earnest about "winning votes and influencing congressmen."

Then there are the mimeographed postal cards which sometime descend on Congress in such large numbers. They are generally signed by someone. But it is clear that they have originated from one central place, and it is likely that the people signing them have been urged to do so and that their action has not been wholly voluntary. Furthermore, every congressman knows that some of the signatures on such cards are not genuine, for, whenever he answers such communications, a very substantial percentage of his replies are returned to him marked "no such person" or "no such address."

Next to mass-production postal cards the least effective messages to Congress are identical letters, where the writers have clearly been told what to say and have said it without giving, apparently, any personal thought to the matter. More than a few times I became certain, while reading my mail, that I had read the same message in the same handwriting before. Once I found that no less than five such identical letters written in the same hand but with five different signatures had been received. I certainly was not favorably impressed by the methods being used by the writer of those letters.

Though they are easier to read and cost less eyestrain, carefully typed and evidently dictated letters had less influence with me than did those which were written in longhand. In fact the one type of communication which always influenced me most deeply was the handwritten letter in which it was clear from the content that the writer had gone to great pains to tell his congressman exactly what he, himself, as an individual American citizen, was thinking about his country's problems.

Finally, it made a difference if the letter came from someone whom I knew or at least from someone who took the trouble to explain who he was, how he made his living, and a few other details to make him a personality to me. Then I could feel, as I read his letter, that I was fairly close to the person who had written it. And, whether I agreed with him or not, I "listened" and took account of what he had to say.

Chapter 6

POLITICAL LABELS

Democratic strength reached its peak in the Seventy-fifth Congress. No less than 333 of the 435 members who took the oath of office at the opening of that Congress were members of the Democratic party. Almost immediately, however, one of the most controversial issues in modern political history, namely President Roosevelt's proposal for changing the number of justices on the Supreme Court, drew into bold relief the fact 'that the huge Democratic majority was far from a unified group. As time has gone on, one of the larger facts about recent Congresses has become more and more clear. Briefly it is this. Even in the Seventy-fifth Congress there was but a bare majority of progressive-minded members. In all subsequent Congresses the conservatives were actually in the majority, although there were times when advanced pieces of legislation were enacted by Congress under the intense pressure of public opinion.

A certain number of American citizens take their party politics seriously and are devoted members of the Democratic or Republican party. But to most of the people the only thing that matters about Congress is the sort of legislation which it passes. From this standpoint the question is not whether a member of the House or Senate is a Republican or a Democrat, but rather whether he is a reactionary, a conservative, a progressive, or a "united fronter."

To give an accurate picture of the make-up of Congress all four of these categories are necessary. A reactionary is a man who wants to return to the days when "the rich, the well-born, and the able" ruled the world, who distrusts and holds in substantial contempt the great mass of people, and who is so determined to keep the people "in their place" that he is in constant danger of embracing, if he does not actually embrace, an essentially fascist philosophy.

His counterpart at the other extreme is the united fronter. He is a man who believes so blindly in the superiority of the "left" over the "right" that he regards a Communist as nothing more than an extreme radical or extreme "left-winger." Therefore, whether or not he consciously embraces part or all of the communist philosophy, the united fronter is quite willing to collaborate with communists and to defend them against all criticism, however well deserved and however factually based. The united fronters, like the reactionaries, do not have a fundamental primary allegiance to constitutional government, majority rule, minority rights, or liberty in its fullest sense. In both cases the primary objective is power for the "right" people, in which group they themselves are of course always included.

Between these two extremes are to be found the conservatives and the progressives (or liberals). The former are people who realize, in a vague way at least, that the world does move but who want to retard the movement as much as possible. In the United States they believe that "business should not be interfered with" by government; they have little concern about the growth of monopoly; they are opposed to organized labor except when labor is weak; and by and large, though not without exceptions, they lean toward a high-tariff and more or less isolationist foreign policy. The progressives, to which group the writer of this book quite frankly belongs, are people who believe that the best way to preserve the great and true values of the past is by constantly making rapid enough progress, particularly economic progress, to maintain the basic security of the people as a whole and to provide them with reasonable hope that tomorrow will be a brighter day.

The essential difference between reactionaries and united fronters on the one hand and conservatives and progressives on the other lies in their attitude toward governmental institutions and the means to be employed in gaining their objectives. For while the first two groups would, in the last analysis and when all the chips are down, probably yield to an effective appeal to abandon democratic and constitutional methods in gaining their ends, both conservatives and progressives will stoutly say, even in defeat, that they cherish human liberty and the values of government of, by, and for the people too highly to use any but the methods of constitutional democracy to gain their political objectives. To put the matter another way, the middle groups value liberty for its own sake as a possession of the people of at least equal worth with economic well-being. But the extreme right and extreme left believe that if liberty must be destroyed in order for them to keep or establish the sort of economic order they desire or to preserve or place themselves in power, then liberty must go.

The greatest danger to liberty in America today lies in the indefensible political tactics whereby progressives, to gain votes, label their opponents "fascist" and conservatives for the same reason label their opponents "communist" with utter disregard for the truth of such charges. Such tactics inevitably create in the public mind the idea that "communists" and "fascists" cannot be too bad, else so many perfectly good Americans would not belong to such groups. It thus becomes many times more difficult to isolate and effectively combat the real communists and fascists in our midst. And so the very people who vow their most bitter opposition to fascists and communists are busily engaged in providing them with the exact atmosphere in which they can work best.

Needless to say, the overwhelming majority of the American Congress, as of the American nation, belongs and has always belonged to either the conservative or the progressive school of political thought. Therefore while the reactionaries and united fronters have not been without their representation, their numbers have never been so great as the opposition, in either case, has tried to represent them.

No man has a right to sit in judgment on the inner thoughts or motives of a fellow human being. For this reason I shall not name names in this connection. But, basing my judgment on actions alone, the following analysis of the make-up of the Congresses in which I served gives a fairly accurate portrayal.

Reactionaries have sat in every one of those Congresses. A majority of them have been Republicans. But there have been a few Democrats who were as far "over to the right" as the farthest Republicans. The bulk of the united fronters—that is, the so-called liberals who fail to see the irreconcilable difference between a true liberal and a left-wing totalitarian—have borne the Democratic party label. It is my best judgment that the number of such members in the House in both the reactionary and the united-front category has never exceeded twenty at any one time.

Aside from the reactionaries, almost the entire Republican membership of the Congresses in which I served could fairly be described as conservative. The exceptions were anywhere from ten to twenty brave souls who attempted the very difficult role of being progressive Republicans. Almost two thirds of the Democratic membership of these five Congresses consisted of progressives, not counting the united fronters in that number. But—and this is most important—in every Congress about a third of the Democrats have been conservatives. And unlike the progressive Republicans, most of them were members of long tenure in the Congress and hence of greater influence than even their numbers would indicate. By no means all of the conservative Democrats have come from the South. Other sections of the nation have regularly been electing to Congress a number of Democrats who invariably take a conservative position.

Grouped according to the nature of their basic political convictions, then, it is evident that congressional Republicans are a remarkably homogeneous conservative body, whereas the Democratic party name is borne by members who belong in every single category, with the progressives predominating but by no means always controlling.

With the advent of the Republicans to the majority position in the Eightieth Congress, it was to be expected that more disagreement would be evident in the ranks of that party than was previously the case. But, there is no reason to anticipate that, over the years, the rigid discipline which has governed so effectively the votes and actions of the overwhelming majority of Republicans in Congress will appreciably slacken.

This brings us to one of the outstanding differences between the two party groups. The number of Republicans who have been willing to vote contrary to the decisions of the "Republican conference" has been few indeed. (The Republican conference is a meeting of all Republican members of the House. It compares to the Democratic "caucus," which is simply an older and perhaps less savory name for the same thing.) It has been disturbing to note the regularity with which those who did vote contrary to Republican organization decisions have gone down to defeat in the next Republican primaries. This has been due primarily to the opposition of the party high command.

On the Democratic side, on the other hand, there was never, in my experience, any determined attempt to "keep the members in line." It would have done no good, and the older Democratic heads knew it. The efforts of President Roosevelt to defeat conservative Democrats in party primaries ended in smashing victories for the "purgees" in all but one case. Even as blood is thicker than water, so a man's convictions on the issues of the day will inevitably exert a far more determining influence on his votes than will his technical party affiliation. This is why, in contrast to the frequent and regular meetings of Republican conferences, Democratic caucuses have been almost non-existent, except for occasions when it was necessary to choose a majority leader or a candidate for Speaker or to elect a member of the Ways and Means Committee. (The Committee on Ways and Means acts as the committee on committees. Its Republican members are chosen by secret ballot of all Republican members of the House; its Democratic members, by secret ballot of all Democrats. Thereafter the two party groups on the Ways and Means Committee— each meeting separately—assign the members of their respective parties to all other committees of the House.)

Even the appeals of President Roosevelt at the height of his popularity could seldom muster more than two thirds to four fifths of the Democratic membership of the House behind his proposals.

Moreover, it was to be observed all through the Roosevelt administration that there were two kinds of congressional Democrats, and only two, who could regularly gain the ear of the White House. The first of these were the absolutely unwavering followers of presidential recommendations—that is, those members who could be depended upon to vote for or against any measure simply because they were supporting the President, and who required no further reason. Strange but true, the other kind of member who almost always received ready acceptance of his requests was the senator or congressman who, with equal regularity, opposed the President, and who, therefore, was a person to be "won over," if possible, by favored treatment. Since I never belonged to either of these categories, I was in a position to know that it was not enough to support the Administration when one believed it to be right. Something more was required. For all these reasons Democratic members were seldom very deeply concerned if they cast votes contrary to the official party program. Democratic members of Congress have been and are essentially free men so far as "party discipline" goes.

An additional reason for the wide divergence between members of the Democratic party, both in and out of Congress—in contrast to the Republicans—is the fact that only the Democratic party is a national party. To all intents and purposes the Republican party is non-existent in the Southern states.

Furthermore, the sort of people who are Republicans in New York or Pennsylvania are not so very different from the sort who are Republicans on the Pacific coast. But not so with the Democrats! In the South the traditional conservative seventh-generation American will always be a Democrat, though more and more he is finding progressive forces at work in his party in that section. In the Northeastern cities the members of organized labor, some, though by no means all, of the recent immigrant groups, and the men and women who make a business of their politics are likely to be Democrats. In the West, however, the tendency is more and more for liberals and progressives generally to become Democrats. Therefore the diverse make-up of the Democratic congressional membership is scarcely to be wondered at.

One question echoes regularly about the country. Why don't the liberals (or progressives) get together ? Those who, with some impatience, ask this question fail, I believe, to take into account certain facts. Those facts not only explain why a union of liberals is so difficult but why Congress is usually more conservative in its actions than the opinion of the nation would call for.

In the first place being a conservative is a comparatively easy job. It consists primarily of saying no. And, since most human proposals have something wrong with them, it is a comparatively simple matter to bring about united action by those who are against almost any specific or general course of action. But when it comes to proposing a program for constructive progress in the nation or for the solution of its complex problems, then immediately many ideas are advanced and the task of securing agreement becomes many times more difficult. Progressives and liberals are the people who must carry the burden of such proposals. It is their proper political role. Moreover, those of their number who succeed in getting elected to Congress usually do so by advancing certain plans and programs of their own which they naturally feel called upon to push once they have arrived in Washington. Consequently the welding together of the liberals or progressives into a working unit for the purpose of saying yes is a great deal harder than uniting the conservatives for the purpose of saying no. I have seen it attempted over and over—generally with only the most moderate success. We approached the task, I believe, from almost every angle during the five terms I served in the House and while we did manage to work together with reasonable effect in a number of instances, the results on the whole were disappointing.

In the second place, there can never be unity among American liberals or progressives either within or outside the Democratic party until a certain false idea is dead and deeply buried. That idea is that American progressives (or liberals in the true sense of that word) can find common ground or in any degree collaborate with organized totalitarians whose beliefs are diametrically opposite to those of liberalism on some of the most vital phases of human life. I refer, of course, to the communists. As long as the bogey of the united front persists, one promising progressive movement after another will be first discredited and then broken to bits because of infiltration by communists and the impact of their rule-or-ruin philosophy. It must be remembered that neither reactionaries nor conservatives can successfully combat a communist movement. Their policies are likely to add fuel to the Red flames. The only really effective enemies the communists have are the true liberals and progressives who offer to the people a constitutional, decent, truly hopeful way to a solution of their problems and to a better world. Nor need anyone deceive himself that the communists are not well aware of these facts. Witness the present bitter struggles going on in many a European country between the communists and the socialists, particularly the "Christian Socialists." Moreover, either a man believes in liberty or he doesn't. Either he believes concentration of economic or political power is bad or he doesn't. The communist philosophy, like that of the fascists, holds that liberty is utterly unimportant and that concentration of power is necessary and altogether desirable so long as it is concentrated in communist hands. But unless the American progressive or liberal values liberty and unless he opposes with all his strength such concentration of power, he is neither worthy of the name nor will he be able to build a strong, forward-looking political movement in the United States.

Americans are naturally an impatient people. Consequently, when the voters of a district or a state elect a progressive to the Congress, they tend to expect him to produce almost immediate results. After all, hasn't he campaigned on a program of constructive change which he told them he would try to advance? Quite regardless of the odds against him, he must either make evident progress toward his avowed goal soon after he arrives in Congress or else he is altogether likely to suffer defeat at the polls at the hands of a conservative opponent. The net result is that progressives and liberals find it harder to stay in Congress than any other group. Therefore, in view of the importance of seniority, the progressive members always find it difficult to wield a strength even proportionate to their numbers.

Only when deep conviction as to the rightness of certain basic causes once again grips the American nation can there be substantial hope for the appearance in Congress of a strong, determined, and reasonably cohesive group of members devoted to true progress in the American way.

As it was, during the five Congresses in which I served the conservatives were in the position of real control all the way through, with the possible exception of the Seventy-fifth. A few important progressive measures such as the national minimum wage law (Fair Labor Standards Act), the Flannagan School Lunch bill, the McMahon Atomic Energy Control Act were passed, it is true. But these measures were enacted only by dint of the very greatest effort and only when public opinion was strong and vocal. By and large, whenever conservative forces earnestly desired to block a measure they could do so. The explanation of this is fairly simple. The key to it is the general rule that one third of the Democratic membership has been, all along, conservative.

In the Seventy-fifth Congress the Democrats had 333 members. Subtracting one-third, we get the figure 222 progressives, a bare majority of four members in the House as a whole, to which a few Republicans might be added. But that is hardly enough to provide a working "majority," as in most instances it did not. Then in the Seventy-sixth Congress the Democratic membership dropped to 268 and the Republican rose to 162. One third of 268 gives us 89 conservative Democrats, and if we add that figure to 152 (allowing for ten progressive Republicans) we get 241 members as the approximate conservative strength. This meant a comfortable conservative majority. And in the Seventy-eighth Congress, where there were only 222 Democrats and 208 Republicans, the net conservative strength mounted to some 283 members, or almost a 2 to 1 majority, which indeed the record of that Congress reflected. Moreover, we must add to the rough picture given by these figures the simple fact that as the Democratic membership declined it was generally the conservative Democrats who held their seats and the progressives who lost theirs.

How far the postwar reaction will carry our country toward even greater conservatism cannot be predicted. But certain it is that no negative attitude toward the problems and potentialities of the perilous atomic age that lies ahead can possibly provide either safety or hope for our nation.

Chapter 7

THE STATE OR
THE NATION?

Whenever an attempt has been made in recent years to bring the
progressives in the House or Senate into a working organization,
the conservative press (which is most of it) has been quick to
discredit the effort. Only too clearly do I remember one such
occasion. It was at the beginning of the Seventy-sixth Congress.
A letter was prepared, signed by about a dozen members, and
sent to everyone whom we believed would be sincerely interested
in working for the passage of forward-looking legislation.

The first meeting was a dinner meeting in one of the smaller
dining rooms at the Capitol. There were about fifty or sixty members present. We discussed problems and issues, selected certain
objectives to be worked toward and agreed to meet regularly
and pull together for the measures in which we all believed. It
was a unanimous opinion that no "bloc" tactics should be used,
that there should be no binding of members of the group as to
voting, and no attempts to coerce the House leadership by threat-
ening to withhold support from important measures as a means
of gaining our ends. We thought alike and would try to work
together. That was all. One of the last things we did that evening
was to agree that Congressman John Martin, of Colorado, should
be the only person to report our plans and purposes to the press.

In order to avoid misunderstanding and the harm which we knew the wrong kind of publicity would do our group, none of the rest of us would make any statement at all.

After the meeting I went back to my office to sign some letters and to get my "homework" together. After about a half hour the telephone rang. It was a press wire service reporter. Could I tell him anything about the meeting? No, it was agreed only John Martin would do that. Yes, he understood that was the case, but he could not reach Mr. Martin and he needed something for a story for the morning papers. Wouldn't I please "fill him in"? I told him I was very sorry but I just couldn't. Well, would I at least tell him who was there? If I would only do that he wouldn't bother me any more and would contact Congressman Martin in the morning. I thought for a moment (which was not nearly long enough) and concluded that there could be no harm in giving him the names, since there had been such unanimity in the meeting, and I would not be telling any of the actions or decisions of the group. So I read him the list of the names.

That was enough. Rather, I should say it was far too much. Next morning the story appeared. What it said was about as follows: a caucus of "dissident" House members had been held to form a bloc and to plan a campaign of taking control of the House away from the elected leadership. And here were the names of the people who had attended.

I cannot say whether the next few days were the very most difficult of my career in the House, but none, I believe, were much worse. I called John Martin to apologize and explain what had happened. He was very kind and understanding, but several other members were very angry. Obviously, they had a right to be. They had been put in a false light, and it was my fault that this was the case.

Our group carried on, but with a much smaller attendance and not nearly so good a spirit. One mistake of judgment on my part and one newspaper story, "played up" as any reasonably imaginative reporter who knew the kind of story that was wanted would have done, had blocked the possibility of an effective organization of progressives in that Congress.

But if our meeting had been a state delegation meeting the

story would have been different! California papers would have said that the representatives from our state were on the job, that we were going to "fight for California's interests," and that we would act as a unit in so doing, regardless of whose toes we tread upon.

This difference makes the going tough for those who attempt to serve a general national need or to work for a "cause."

In any event state delegations are, or more accurately, *can* be important factors in Congress. In the Seventy-ninth Congress the Texas delegation included the Speaker of the House, the chairman of the Senate Foreign Relations Committee, who was also one of America's delegates to the United Nations, and the chairmen of the House committees on the Judiciary, on Rivers and Harbors, on Public Buildings and Grounds, Elections No. 2, and Elections No. 3. Texas was the only state having two Democratic members on the powerful Appropriations Committee. It likewise was the only state with two Democrats on the Military Affairs and Agriculture committees. The ranking members—that is, the members next to the chairmen—on the Military Affairs and Foreign Affairs committees were Texans. In both cases their influence was far greater than that of their chairmen. The third place on the Banking and Currency Committee was held by a Texan. No wonder press and radio have regularly spoken of "the powerful Texas delegation."

Meanwhile, California had only the chairman of the Interstate and Foreign Commerce Committee and the chairman of the committees on War Claims and Disposition of Executive Papers (sometimes called the wastebasket committee). Both the latter two committees were abolished by the Reorganization bill. Yet California elects two more members to the House than does Texas!

Connecticut's voice could not be a very effective one in the Eightieth Congress. Except for Senator McMahon, elected in 1944, every single member of Congress elected by Connecticut in 1946 was a brand-new member and hence at the bottom of the list of whatever committee he was fortunate enough to be assigned to. The voters of that state did not see fit to re-elect even one member to his old job in the 1946 election.

With the Republicans in control of Congress, powerful delegations are upstate New York, Michigan, Ohio, Massachusetts, and New Jersey. Indiana, Illinois, and Kansas have a considerable voice in the House, as do the northern New England states in the Senate. The main reason for this is that these states have certain specific Republican members of both House and Senate whom they have been re-electing regularly for a long period of years.

There is no mystery as to why some state delegations are strong and others weak. The Senate operates almost entirely on a personal basis, and it is rare that two senators from the same state, even though they be of the same party, lose their individualism long enough to form anything approaching a real co-operating "delegation." However, if a senator establishes close working relationships with the House members from his state, he can not only strengthen his position in the Senate but also greatly increase the power of his state in Congress. As a matter of fact, few senators take the trouble to do this, partly no doubt because of the tremendous number of regular obligations they have as senators, but partly, too, because some senators are inclined to take the designation of the Senate as the "Upper House" very seriously.

It is obvious that the big state delegations are the only ones that have much opportunity to exert important influence in the House. Nevada, Wyoming, Delaware, and Vermont, with only one house member each, can hardly expect to do much as "delegations." The potential power lies with New York, Pennsylvania, California, Illinois, Ohio, Texas, Michigan, Massachusetts, Missouri, North Carolina, New Jersey, and other states having a substantial number of representatives.

But the full strength of these large delegations may or may not be developed depending on other factors. The first of these has to do with the senators and representatives themselves. The majority of members of Congress work hard at their jobs. But not all of them do. And a great deal of very hard work is required if, over the years, a member is to build himself into an influential factor. The extent to which various states elect members willing to do this largely determines the power of that state's delegation.

Leadership within the delegation is also, of course, an important factor. The Alabama delegation, for example, was a very much more important factor in the House when it had the Speaker of the House, Mr. Bankhead, as a member than has since been the case.

The way the seniority rule is applied in congressional committees is this. It makes little difference how long a member has continuously served in the House or Senate. His position on the committee depends upon how long he has been a member of that particular committee. If a new member can be assigned to an important committee immediately and then stay on it, he will, in the course of time, outrank other committee members of longer total service in Congress. This will be due simply to the fact that these men had to wait one, two, or three terms before receiving from the Ways and Means Committee the committee assignment of their choice. Therefore if a state delegation can secure for its new members good committee assignments which are related to the nature of those members' districts, these new members will immediately start on the road to a committee chairmanship or the position of "ranking member." This is why positions on the Ways and Means Committee, by whose action at the beginning of each Congress all committee placements are made, are so coveted and so important. It is also why a delegation which includes the Speaker, the majority or minority leader, or an unusually influential representative is likely to build up its power. Such men naturally can have influence upon Ways and Means Committee decisions.

But there are other factors in the situation quite beyond the control of members of congressional state delegations. First and most important are the political complexion and voting habits of the state in question. If it is a state where one political party is in a substantial majority, the position of its delegation will be the stronger whenever that party is in control of Congress. Its members are then likely to be of that party and the full strength of the delegation can be brought to bear.

On the other hand, where the two parties are nearly equal in voting strength in a state or section, the delegation will usually be split, some Democrats, some Republicans, so that united action is difficult. What is more important, in such districts the turnover is likely to be rapid and few members will be able to hold their seats for many terms in succession, thus rendering it most difficult for members of these delegations to attain positions of seniority in the Congress. It can almost be laid down, therefore, as a rule of the operation of the Congress, that the very states or parts of states where the most intense and vigorous campaign battles are carried on are the ones having least to gain from the outcome. If, for example, the Democrats carry Pennsylvania, Illinois, and California and thus win national power, the power of the South in Congress will become very great—the power of Pennsylvania or Illinois or California markedly less so. If the Republicans, in gaining control of the government, can carry these same three states and, let us say, Missouri and Kentucky in addition, it will, again, not add appreciably to the power in Congress of these five state delegations but will rather place control of the government in the hands of upstate New Yorkers, Michiganders, New Englanders, and, normally, Iowans and Kansans, since these are the sections which send Republicans to Congress year in and year out.

The final factor is the character of the various districts within the various states. If a state chamber of commerce wanted to enhance the power of the congressional delegation from that state, one of the most effective things it could do would be to gerrymander the boundaries of the congressional districts in such a way as to make all of them include approximately the same proportions of city people and farmers, rich people and poor people, conservatives and progressives. In this way all the members would be responsible to the same sort of constituencies. As a matter of fact this is one of the reasons the state of Texas has been so influential. Only two districts out of twenty-one in Texas are predominantly urban and even these contain a strong rural element. In all the other Texas districts there is a high degree of similarity in the general mixture of life and economic interests included among the people. Therefore the sort of measures that will be popular in one Texas district are likely to be popular in others as well.

Contrast this situation with California. In that state there are eight districts which consist entirely of city streets and two others of which almost the same thing could be said. There are at least four districts which are completely dominated by the agricultural groups within them. One district is primarily made up of people engaged in mining or forest industries. Several of the state's districts have strong maritime interests, whereas others are, economically at least, as landlocked as Nebraska. Three or four California congressmen represent districts whose general temper is as conservative a one as could be found anywhere in the United States, whereas at least two others come from sections which are progressive almost to the point of radicalism. When, therefore, certain segments of the California press complain that the state's delegation does not in all instances act as a complete unit (and incidentally in complete accord with the wishes of such newspapers) they completely overlook a basic fact about representative government. If members of Congress are supposed to represent the people of their districts, it is hardly reasonable to expect members from wholly urban districts and members from almost completely rural ones to see eye to eye on every issue.

During my term of service I was a member of the California delegation, referred to in newspaper dispatches as "Jerry Voorhis, (D.—Cal.)." As such, I attended meetings of the delegation and took part in its deliberations and its work. I will remember happily the personal associations thus developed.

But for the reasons already given in this chapter the influence of the California delegation has never been as great as the population of the state deserves. In southern California particularly the turnover of members has been very great in recent years. The state delegation has been divided, in varying ratios, between Democrats and Republicans. It has included, as has been explained, members from very different kinds of districts and hence with widely divergent general points of view. Under the circumstances, and despite repeated stories to the contrary in certain sections of the California press, the delegation has worked together well.

But though it is the fifth largest delegation in the House, it has, during the period of Democratic control, had but one chairman of an important committee (Lea of Interstate and Foreign Commerce) and one chairman of an Appropriations subcommittee (Sheppard of Naval Appropriations) in its membership. And when the Republicans came into control of the House in 1947, California had only one chairmanship (Welch of Public Lands). Significantly enough, it is never referred to in the press as "the powerful California delegation."

Some of the results of this situation can be illustrated from my own experience. When I was first elected (Seventy-fifth Congress) I exerted every effort I could as an individual new member to secure a place on the Committee on Agriculture. It was then and remained, all through my ten years of membership in the House, my first choice for a committee assignment. Nor did California, the nation's first or second agricultural state, have a single member on the Committee on Agriculture in the Seventy-fifth, Seventy-sixth, or Seventy-seventh Congresses.

Meanwhile, I was serving on four so-called "minor" committees. These were Flood Control, Rivers and Harbors, World War Veterans Legislation, and Public Lands. I enjoyed this work despite the fact that the committees seemed to have a diabolical habit of nearly always all meeting on the same day. Furthermore, I was gaining experience and seniority on these committees, so that by the time the Seventy-eighth Congress opened I was the ranking member of the World War Veterans Committee and well up on Flood Control. However, I was still anxious to serve on the Agriculture Committee, and so expressed myself. From a purely political point of view, I was probably unwise in so doing, especially in view of my good position on the Veterans Committee. Nonetheless, since farming has always seemed to me the very basis of America's national life, since I have always believed protection of the family-sized farm one of the primary duties of the Congress, and since I was intensely interested in farm credit, the school lunch program, and other legislation which the Agriculture Committee handled, I went ahead and made formal request of the Ways and Means Committee for transfer to the Committee on Agriculture.

This time I got it. And landed, of course, almost at the bottom of the list on my new committee. The fate of Jerry Voorhis in this connection is, of course, of no importance at all. But from the standpoint of the farmers of the Far West it was unfortunate that the member representing them on the committee should have been so long delayed in obtaining membership. For when I finally did so, I found that I ranked below three members from other state delegations, with from two to four years less congressional service than I had had and that those committeemen who had been first elected in the Seventy-fifth Congress, as I was, so far outranked me as to be almost out of sight. As the months passed, I believe I made my place on the committee a worthwhile one, but, since most of those of longer committee membership were from the South, I would have had to be re-elected for a period of many, many years before I could have even approached the chairmanship.

There was a time in the year 1944 when, had circumstances been different, I might have been elected to the Ways and Means Committee. The California member of that committee (Mr. Buck) had passed away and it was generally agreed that whoever the California Democratic delegation nominated would be elected by the Democratic caucus without opposition. No one on the delegation wanted the place very badly, for the reason that no one wished to give up the committee assignments he then had with the sacrifice of seniority and the loss of experience in the committee work which would have been entailed. When it came to voting within the delegation for our nominee for the Ways and Means position, some of the members voted for me. I shall never cease to appreciate those votes—certain of them in particular since they were cast by men who disagreed with me on many issues. But there was one factor which persuaded me and, ultimately, I believe, the delegation that I should not be the person chosen. That factor was my position on the question of mandatory joint income tax returns for husbands and wives. I knew there were hundreds of millions of dollars in additional taxes that would be paid by wealthy families if such a law were in effect. I knew, therefore, that hundreds of millions of dollars of just tax obligations were shifted to other shoulders by these wealthy families each year. For these reasons I had voted for mandatory joint returns to prevent the practice of dividing large incomes between husbands and wives for tax evasion purposes only. This was regarded as a blow against the California community property law, which provides that half the income and property of every husband belongs legally to his wife and vice versa. I am frank to say I have never been able to see how a requirement that each family should nonetheless pay its taxes as if it were, in fact, a family unit would constitute any violation of the community property principle.

But while I had not only a right but a duty to vote my sincere convictions on this or any other question, it was another matter for the California delegation to present my name as a candidate for the Ways and Means Committee, the very committee that handles all tax legislation. Under those circumstances the other members of the delegation, none of whom took the same position on the mandatory joint returns issue that I did, would have appeared to be, indirectly at least, endorsing my stand. And this, as I myself pointed out, would have subjected them to unjust and undeserved criticism from powerful California groups. Thus, for good and sufficient reason, I think, our delegation decided not to present my name, and I was not elected to the Ways and Means Committee.

The seniority rule is one of the principal reasons why some state delegations are able to exert a very powerful influence in Congress while others and sometimes larger delegations are unable to do so. But the seniority rule is, in the last analysis, nothing more or less than practical recognition of the importance of experience in congressional work plus a natural tendency on the part of Congress as a whole to build its structure around the members who are most certain to continue to be re-elected over a period of years. No doubt some substitute for or modification of the seniority rule should be worked out. Until this is done a great premium will continue to be put on political conservatism of the sort that avoids change even in mediocre representation. But, to my knowledge, no better system has as yet been proposed. Until it is, the greater power in Congress will lie with those districts which do not frequently change their representatives or senators.

However, the most important fact about state delegation politics in Washington is that it is concerned primarily, if not exclusively, with special interests rather than with the general national welfare. Generally speaking, insofar as state delegations act "en bloc," they become a divisive force in the government of the United

States. It would be different if their action were directed toward the general welfare of all the people of the states in question. But most often it is in behalf of a certain group: the shipping interests —both management and labor frequently—or a certain agricultural commodity interest, or a particular industry. There is nothing reprehensible or illegitimate about this. But it represents the sort of action which tends to obscure and force into the background the general problems of the people as consumers, citizens, farmers, city workers, or just plain Americans. Moreover, it tends to make the work of congressmen a compartmentalized proposition directed at the advancement of the particular interests of particular groups at the expense of others. Sometimes the California delegation meets to consider such matters of general concern as the housing shortage or West Coast transportation or the all-important question of water supply. But the other type of thing takes far more time, not only among Californians, but in other state delegations as well.

I cannot remember more than one or two isolated instances when our California delegation met to agree upon a course of action which would help in solving a problem facing the whole American nation or affecting great numbers of people throughout the country. I believe we should have done so regularly. For if state delegations are not going to contribute to this, the main and basic task of the Congress, the United States might well be better off if congressional state delegations, as such, never met at all.

Chapter 8

THE NEW DEAL

Franklin D. Roosevelt made two great contributions to American political thought. First, he laid down the principle that mass unemployment is a national problem and that the federal government owes to the people the duty of attacking and, if possible, solving it. Thus he broke fetters which throughout the previous history of our country had bound the hands of the government of the United States and prevented its dealing with the most dangerous social malady of the modern world. He broadened the conception of governmental functions to include the curing of that malady.

Second, President Roosevelt told the people of the United States that if cruelty, aggression, war, and the violation of weaker peoples were allowed to run unchecked in the Eastern Hemisphere they would eventually span the oceans and involve the Western Hemisphere as well. He said that the peace of the world is, in times like these, indivisible. Thus he broke an isolationist tradition which, except for the brief interlude of World War I, had kept America from assuming the position of world leadership which was her destiny. He broadened the conception of America's world position to include that leadership.

I was not in Congress during the famous "hundred days" of

March, April, and May 1933, when the New Deal was hailed on all sides as the salvation of America and when more far-reaching legislation was enacted by the Congress than had been passed in any previous decade. Of the events of the first term of Mr. Roosevelt's presidency I knew only what any other interested citizen of the nation knew—what I read in the papers.

By the time the members of the Seventy-fifth Congress arrived in Washington to take their places, the New Deal "honeymoon" was over and the contest between the President and the Supreme Court was in full swing. It was not the first such contest in American history: Andrew Jackson and Abraham Lincoln and Theodore Roosevelt had had similar conflicts with the high court.

The Court had declared unconstitutional what were widely regarded as two of the major New Deal measures, the National Recovery Act and the Agricultural Adjustment Act. In retrospect it is clear that in neither case was any real harm done by the Court's decision. The NRA, whatever may be said of the "lift" it gave the country at the time of its passage, contained features which would have encouraged monopoly and might have forced our national economy into a sort of strait jacket. It was not a measure calculated to bring about expansion and growth. The same may be said of the original AAA, helpful as it was as an emergency measure to save our agriculture from bankruptcy in the dark days of 1933.

The roots of the conflict between the President and the Congress and the Court grew much deeper than the provisions of the particular acts of Congress which the Court invalidated. It was a question of the direction in which our nation and its government were going to move.

The danger, if there was one, lay not in what *had* happened but in what *might* happen if measures were not taken to adjust the relationship between the Congress and the Court.

I believed then, as I do now, that in times of crisis Congress must have the freedom and the authority to establish new national policies, to meet new national needs, and that the Supreme Court should not be left in a position to block all such efforts by reference to the dicta and precedents of the past. In my first major speech, delivered on February 16, 1937, and entitled "The Needs of the People and the Court Issue," I expressed that belief. I said, "I am interested in legislation to take the profits out of war. I favor the passage of a law which will make it mandatory that whenever America drafts men for war she must also draft finances and capital and essential means of production. I can see no shadow of justice in paying well for the use of money, in permitting profiteering in orders for war supply, and at the same time sending our manhood out to be shot and mangled at thirty dollars a month.

"But I am convinced that, should we pass such a law, it would, under present circumstances, be declared unconstitutional on the ground that the owners of the money or the factories so drafted would be deprived of property without due process of law. Against such an argument, of course, a liberal judge might point out that such a law as I have suggested would certainly provide for the common defense and promote the general welfare as opposed to the welfare of the profiteers. But I believe in the present Court he would be voted down and our attempt to take the profit out of war would be blocked. So, I am for the President. . . . I would prefer trying to define the relationship between the Congress and the Court in some other way. . . . But in the end I have been driven to admit that there is no other way except the President's way in which the legislation which the preservation of our democratic life requires can be given a fair hearing in the next three or four years. . . . Let us understand that not alone the precedents of the Supreme Court but also the fate of needy children, unemployed men, insecure old folks, and underpaid mothers hang in the balance and await our action."

I believe today, as I did in February 1937, that the needs of the people are primary, the precedents of the law secondary, though of very great consequence. I confess, however, that if I could rewrite that speech I would change it in one important respect. I would not say, as I did then, that the President's proposal was the "only way" the needs of the people could be met. I now believe I should have said that the issue of the relationship of the Court to basic legislation passed by Congress had to be faced squarely, but that the straightforward way to do so was not the one proposed by President Roosevelt. I believe I should have said that I would support a constitutional amendment to require at least a two-thirds vote of the justices to invalidate an act of Congress, that I would support an amendment to provide that, in the face of an adverse Court decision, Congress could maintain a statute in effect by passing it by a two-thirds or three-fourths vote, but that I could not support the President's bill.

For the proposal of the President, as I now look back upon it, was indelibly stamped with the characteristic which was Mr. Roosevelt's greatness as a politician but sometimes his weakness as a statesman—his cleverness. We were dealing with a fundamental problem of all democratic governments. Such an issue can never be met rightly by oblique proposals which conceal their real objectives under a cloak of arguments that, failing to go to the root of the problem, attempt to solve it by raising secondary if not extraneous issues.

I continued to be worried and troubled over the whole matter, and I confess that, when the Senate voted to recommit the President's bill and thus to kill it, I felt that this action probably was for the best. I wished even then that I had taken the position outlined in the preceding paragraphs.

As events turned out, of course, President Roosevelt achieved, by retirement of some justices and the death of others, his real objective—a more liberal Supreme Court. But the defeat of his bill by the Senate marked the high tide of the New Deal as popularly conceived and the beginning of its recession. By the methods he had proposed, more than because of the objective he sought, the President had overreached himself and the Congress had rebuffed him.

In a few short months Franklin D. Roosevelt began his last and perhaps his greatest work—the marshaling of the forces of democracy against the forces of dictatorship around the world. But his influence upon domestic legislation was never again so great as it had been before his Supreme Court proposal was advanced, nor, in my opinion, as it would have been had he chosen a more direct road toward his objective in that great contest.

Was this, then, the beginning of the end of the New Deal?

That depends altogether on one's definition of that much-bandied phrase.

Few political movements in American history have been the subject of so much oratory, pro and con, as the New Deal. But the orators have failed to reveal any accurate conception of the meaning of those two words. If the New Deal were the NRA or the original AAA or the Supreme Court bill or all three of them put together, then it would be a thing of the dead past. But it is not. The New Deal was not killed with the Supreme Court bill. It was not "dead" in January 1944, though President Roosevelt himself so pronounced it. It is not dead today because the "New Deal" can only be sensibly defined as the body of legislation passed during the presidency of Franklin D. Roosevelt, who coined the phrase on the day he accepted the Democratic nomination in July 1932.

What was that legislation and what does it mean to the future of the United States? On March 4, 1933, America was without any national provision to protect its aged or disabled citizens, or its dependent children, against the unavoidable hazards of life in this modern machine age. We were without any means whereby the purchasing power of these people could be maintained in the face of advancing age disability or the death of a family's bread winner. We had no system of unemployment insurance. The Social Security Act was, and is today, the New Deal's provision for these national needs. Incomplete and inadequate as it still remains, that act stands for a principle of American life which the most violent opponent of the New Deal would not strike down. On the contrary, even some conservative politicians compete with the progressives in advancing proposals for its expansion and its rounding out.

It was a New Deal measure which we passed in Congress when we wrote into the law of the United States the principle that there is a certain point below which wages paid to workers in interstate commerce cannot be allowed to fall without violating the policy of this nation. Prior to the passage of the Fair Labor Standards Act, an American worker who was not a member of a strong labor union had no way of protecting his standard of living against the cutthroat competition of even more needy or less encumbered workers than himself. Neither was there any means of curbing the action of employers who attempted by wage cutting to gain advantage over other employers who sought to pay their workers well. Though conservative Congresses may attempt to weaken its provisions, the New Deal's Fair Labor Standards Act marks so definite a milestone in the progress of the American nation that no one but a reactionary would advocate its repeal.

Before the coming of the New Deal no Congress and no national administration had raised a finger to check the continuous and profligate waste of America's basic wealth, namely her soil. Only the forest conservation measures passed in the administration of an earlier Roosevelt can be said to have even skirted the critical problem. Yet the hope of the United States to remain a great nation depends directly upon the maintenance of the fertility of her soil. The Soil Conservation Act is part and parcel of the New Deal. But "soil conservation" has become almost a national slogan and never again will America return to the suicidal habits of an irresponsible youth.

For years politicians as well as sociologists have been pointing with alarm at the increase of tenancy on the land. It remained, however, for the New Deal to take the first practical step against this trend in the Farm Tenant Purchase Act.

Only a few years ago it was said by every private utility company in the country that it was impractical to bring electricity to our farms. They said that if electricity were brought to the farms the cost per kilowatt-hour would range between forty and seventy cents. Today, thanks to the extension of government credit, thanks to the growth of co-operatives among farmers, thanks in short to the New Deal's Rural Electrification Act, America's farms are being electrified, their production increased, the life of the farm wife made brighter. And the day will come soon when the debts to the government will be paid and the farmers themselves will own and control through their co-operatives the electric lines which the REA helped make possible.

The TVA, the Grand Coulee, Bonneville, and Shasta dams, and a good many others, were built under the New Deal to belong to the people whose homes, farms, and factories it furnished with electricity. Every one of these projects was carried through against the bitterest kind of opposition. Year after year while I was in Congress we fought attempts to stop their construction or, failing that, to capture their benefits for private interests. Indeed, in the case of Shasta, the failure of the California delegation to stand as a unit for the public interest may yet mean that a giant monopolistic corporation will carry off the lion's share of the economic benefits from the expenditure of a quarter of a billion dollars of public funds. But wherever the people of an area have found themselves paying a fraction of the former rates for electricity, they will not readily relinquish these advantages from public generation and distribution of electric power, even though they stoutly declare themselves opposed to "the New Deal" and all its works.

There was a time not so many years ago when it was an open question whether or not wage earners had the right to join together into labor unions and bargain collectively with their employers. That time has passed. The New Deal said to the workers of America: "You have a right to organization, for it is recognized that without it you are at the mercy of economic forces wholly beyond your control and in a position where it is impossible for you to meet your employer on equal terms." Fundamentally, this statement meant just what it said and no more. It did not presuppose closed shops. Certainly it did not presuppose any loss by the rank and file of workers of control over their own destinies or their own organizations. It simply meant, and it simply means today, that the right of organization is as fundamental a right of workers as it is of stockholders who come together to form a corporation.

The basis for a co-operative farm credit system was laid before the United States had heard of the New Deal. But that system was strengthened and expanded in the New Deal years until the goal of farmer ownership and farmers' control of their own sources of credit seems likely to be reached. The day of ten per cent interest rates on farm mortgages is gone.

It may be that the words "New Deal" have been so misused, distorted, and misapplied by friend and foe alike as to render it impossible to restore to them their true and proper meaning.

But names and labels are unimportant. It is the substance which matters—and the substance of the results of the legislation I have just described will remain a part of America for a long, long time to come. It will remain to make this a happier country. And when tempers are cooled and bitterness forgotten, the historian of the future will, I confidently predict, call it the "New Deal."

But that historian may also point to another and less shiny side of the New Deal coin.

Deep in the structure of our country economy there lodges a maladjustment upon the correction of which depends the future of freedom of mankind in this and other parts of the world. That maladjustment is the chronic tendency of man's productive powers to outrun the ability of existing monetary and distributive machinery to move the goods produced into the hands of consumers. Out of this maladjustment grows the economic disease called unemployment.

During a crisis in our country's history, which had its roots in unemployment, the New Deal was born. The administration of Franklin Roosevelt was the first in our country's history to acknowledge the responsibility of the federal government for the solution of this problem. It recognized that freedom and constitutional democracy could not stand for long side by side with bread lines of willing workers. It recognized also that the key to the solution of the problem lay in increasing the purchasing power of the people, thereby making the demand for goods more nearly equal to the potential supply.

It is, therefore, one of the ironies of history that, great as were its achievements, the New Deal never developed an effective or lasting answer to the central problem with which it sought to deal. As some of us who were labeled "New Dealers" repeatedly pointed out, the methods used were not such as to offer much hope of correcting a fundamental and chronic social malady. These methods sought to deal with a fundamental maladjustment by means of temporary or "emergency" agencies of government to which Congress was asked to give wide discretionary power. In all too many cases these agencies were not even created by act of Congress but by executive order, nor were their powers and duties defined by Congress except as an incident in the passage of large appropriation bills. While the objectives of such agencies were deliberately limited to partial ones and while all the emphasis was upon "relief" rather than cure, nevertheless officials guiding the agencies were given sweeping latitude in making decisions which, in many cases, involved the very sustenance of American citizens.

The New Deal did much for America. Its constructive accomplishments are nearly all embodied in definite, understandable, statutory laws, some of which this chapter has briefly outlined. And some of these, such as the Social Security Act and the laws regulating the stock exchanges, will protect our country to some degree whenever deflation and depression threaten us. Moreover, censure of the New Deal cannot, in justice, be too sharp, for it at least ventured to attack the problem from which previous administrations had only shied away.

But the cold simple fact is that the New Deal did not solve the unemployment problem: it only managed to "relieve" it. And the measures of "relief" opened the way to those abuses of ill-defined governmental power which provided the principal factual basis for the flood of propaganda against the entire progressive program of the Roosevelt Administration.

Two types of fundamental corrective action might have made the difference had they been vigorously pressed.

The first was the freeing of the nation's economy from the deadening influence of monopoly. Despite the sincere, earnest, and devoted efforts of Thurman Arnold and his tiny staff in the Anti-Trust Division, the power of monopoly was never broken or even seriously threatened during the Roosevelt regime. True, Arnold's efforts represented the first real attempt at enforcement of the Sherman Anti-Trust law in all American history. But they were never supported either by the Administration or by Congress to anything like the extent necessary to make them successful. As in every depression, the power of monopoly waxed greater and greater. Financial and industrial concentration extended its roots deeper into the structure of American economic life. Bank holding companies reached their tentacles into many a formerly free community. With the coming of the war these trends were allowed to develop into a headlong rush. Monopoly spells the deliberate restriction of production, the deliberate maintenance of artificially high prices. Under its stifling hand neither full production nor true economic "recovery" was possible—except under the forced draft of a war emergency.

The other type of fundamental corrective action neglected by the New Deal was adaptation of the monetary and fiscal system of the nation to the needs of the age of dynamic production in which we live. In place of curative reform measures which might have prevented inflation and deflation for all time, "deficit financing" was continuously resorted to. The banks of the country, at first reluctantly, then with a keen eye to riskless earnings, transformed themselves from business enterprises to manufacturers of "checkbook" money for the government of the United States. Since the creation of demand deposits on their books was a costless process and since the banks were paid dollar for dollar in interest-bearing United States securities for every dollar they created, this "deficit financing" program had its appeals to the financial powers of the country.

But it was a poor substitute for what might have been done. There might have been a new departure in taxation which would have definitely favored small competitive enterprise and encouraged active investment. It might have offered incentives for the taking of risks in productive, labor-employing enterprises. It might have included penalties against hoarding, or holding out of use, the medium of exchange of the nation and thus reduced the need for so much "new money."

We might also have come to grips with the fact that, as the productive capacity of the nation increases, so the credit of the nation must expand instead of its debt. But all through the disastrous years of the deflation that followed 1929, all through the period of the New Deal, and even in the face of war, our government compelled itself to borrow into circulation at interest from private banking institutions every dollar of the new money so vitally needed to balance increasing production, to overcome depression and unemployment, to forestall agricultural price declines, and to defeat our foreign foes.

Here we find the principal reason for the astronomical increase in the national debt of the United States in recent years.

But the New Deal leadership did not move against this problem. Other methods were chosen. They relieved some of the suffering, but in the larger sense they failed. It remains for the statesmen of the future to develop for their country the basic cure for unemployment.

The America of tomorrow will not be built by the hesitant hands of conservatives. Neither, certainly, will we allow it to be shaped in the rigid pattern of a totalitarian state by the hands of fascists or of communists. Nor, indeed, can it be built in another period of one-man leadership like that of the New Deal. The America of tomorrow can arise only if it is founded on institutions built by the people for their own salvation.

Chapter 9

FAIR LABOR STANDARDS

It is a tribute, I believe, to the membership of the Seventy-fifth Congress that the Fair Labor Standards Act was ever passed. No bill in recent years had a more stormy time of it or was beaten down more often only to rise again in amended form. I like to believe that the essential rightness of the measure was the reason for this.

I entered Congress with an old-fashioned American idea in my head. The years have deepened and strengthened it. It is that the aim of all good government is to promote the general welfare of all the people. Therefore a good government must concern itself primarily with efforts to raise the standard of living and broaden the opportunities of those groups of citizens who are poorest and whose need is greatest. Usually they will not be the ones with the loudest voices. Part of the job of Congress is to find out who they are.

The unemployed certainly. From them is taken their right to support their families or make their contribution to the economic well-being of their country. Only worthwhile work of economic or social value at least equal to its cost can restore to them their full status as citizens. Such employment is a by-product of general economic health. Only to a limited extent can it be provided directly by government, unless indeed the government enters fields of productive industry to a much greater extent than was ever done by the New Deal. To have done so might have had the effect of further reducing the amount of private employment being offered. So the choice lay then, as always in time of depression, btween four alternatives: (1) continuing unemployment of millions of people; (2) invasion of fields of essentially "private enterprise" employment by the government; (3) resort to "made-work" programs; or (4) the stimulation and motivation of an expansion of general employment by measures tending to increase the volume of active consumer purchasing power but not involving governmental control over or undue interference with the production system of the nation. The fourth alternative offers, in my opinion, the one sound cure for unemployment in a free economy.

As it was, we got through the thirties by means of a program involving a little of all four of these alternatives but relying largely upon the third one. The WPA never offered employment to more than one fourth of the unemployed. Indeed, some supporters of WPA appropriations in Congress frequently used this fact as an argument in defense of the program! There was no "danger," it was said, of actually getting everyone to work.

The volume of unemployment was reduced from a high point of some fifteen million to about eight or nine million at the time of the outbreak of the war in Europe. From that point on there swelled up a made-work program of such proportion as the most irresponsible advocates of such measures had never dared to dream. From an economic point of view it was not WPA at its best. It was what the WPA would have been if it had been as useless as its enemies claimed.

The work had no economic value. It added nothing to the wealth of this or any other nation. It was carried on with lavish disregard of the cost. It employed in many cases far more people than were really needed to get the job done. Yet it was part of the sacrifice of the American people to the cause of freedom, part of the cost of the most terrible war in history. What we thought we could not afford for peacetime rehabilitation we readily did afford many times over when the war came upon us. Thus and only thus did unemployment vanish temporarily from the United States.

There were other people in the United States in the 1930s beside the unemployed who fell within the group which must be a first concern of government "of the people, by the people, for the people." There were the so-called "low-income" farmers. There were those on enforced "retirement," the aged, the crippled, the widowed mothers of dependent children. And there were several million employed wage earners.

In the year 1937 there were some twelve million workers employed in industries affecting interstate commerce who were receiving wages of less than forty cents an hour. About fifteen per cent of *all* common laborers employed in the most prosperous industries were receiving less than that amount. In textiles, the service trades, and a good many other lines the percentage was much higher. In not a single type of occupation in the cotton-goods manufacturing of the South were the wages as high as forty cents per hour. The average earnings of all persons employed in the boot and shoe factories of New England amounted to only $853 per year. Forty cents an hour means $3.20 a day; it means $19.20 a week if the worker works eight hours a day, six days a week. It means $998.40 a year if he works every single day of the year, Sundays alone excepted. Small wonder then that a considerable group of members of the Seventy-fifth Congress were determined that a national minimum wage law, such as the President had repeatedly recommended, should be passed.

The bulk of organized labor had no direct monetary interest in such a law. With the exception of two or three industries, the members of labor unions were already in receipt of wages substantially higher than any figure which had been suggested as the national minimum. Indeed, most of the millions to be benefited by such an act were unorganized and had no direct spokesman in Washington. They do not have today.

For many years organized labor in the United States had been opposed to the passage of general minimum wage legislation. It warmly supported such laws if applied only to women and it consistently favored both state and federal measures against child labor. But the old-time leaders apparently feared that the enactment of a law establishing a national minimum wage might cause workers to rely less on their unions and more and more on the government for the protection of their living standards. There may, indeed, have been some validity in this fear. But the difficulty was, of course, that the unorganized workers paid the price in miserably low wage standards for the absence of some such legislation on the statute books. It is, therefore, a tribute to the greater vision of the labor movement of more recent times that most of organized labor supported passage of wage-hour legislation when it was proposed in the Seventy-fifth Congress. It was by that time clear that, although direct benefits to members of organized labor would not be great, the indirect benefits to the entire nation would be substantial. These benefits would result from raising the standards and the buying power of millions of workers then unable to buy even enough food and clothing for their families' needs.

The old fear still lurked in some labor leaders' minds, however. This partly accounts for the fact that the law that finally passed contained not only a statutory *minimum* below which wages could not legally fall, but also a "ceiling" provision to the effect that the legal minimum could not be fixed at *more* than forty cents per hour. All the work of raising wages above that point was left to collective bargaining.

Some of the strongest supporters of minimum wage legislation were employers in highly competitive industries. West Coast garment manufacturers, for example, saw in the passage of the bill some protection against the competition of those Southern companies which were paying wages far below the West Coast figures. The more farsighted employers located in regions where organized labor was strong supported the bill for the same general reason.

But opposition to it was bitter, deep-seated, and powerful. It ran the gamut from misguided low-paid workers who had been told their jobs would cease to exist if such a law passed, to those in well-heeled alarmist circles who, sincerely or otherwise, contended that passage of a wage-hour act would signify the beginning of totalitarian dictatorship in America. The opposition included, naturally, practically all of the conservative forces in the country, ably represented by the overwhelming majority of Republicans in Congress. Many farm groups came out against the legislation despite the fact that one of its principal effects was certain to be an increased demand for food on the part of people who had not had enough of that rather basic essential of life. Stranger still, the South, while by no means unanimous, generally opposed the bill. Southern employers, of course, saw in it a threat to the competitive advantage they had enjoyed from their lower wage scale. This was understandable. But it was much more difficult to understand why so many senators and representatives from the South should have agreed that this point of view was good for their section. Many of the "Southern" mills are owned outright by "Yankee" capital; and one of the greatest injustices which the South has suffered ever since the Civil War has been the siphoning off of the bulk of the profits from Southern industry into Northern financial centers. Wages paid to Southern workers on the other hand are, every dime of them, spent in the South. Any increase in these wages is certain to mean a better market for the products of Southern farms and businesses. Some Southern members of the House pointed this out in the course of the debate.

Although most Southern senators and representatives opposed wage-hour legislation, it was due largely to the skillful handling of the measure by the then senator from Alabama, Hugo Black (now Supreme Court Justice Black), that the Senate passed the bill, S. 2475, on July 31, 1937, by a vote of 56 to 28.

The principal battleground, however, proved to be the more conservative House. The Senate bill was taken up by the House Committee on Labor, which meanwhile had been unable to agree upon a measure of its own. The committee reported the Senate bill favorably to the House on August 6, 1937. But before a bill of this importance can come upon the floor of the House it is necessary for the Committee on Rules to pass a resolution setting forth the time and circumstances of debate and the rules to govern the taking of votes upon amendments and the bill. This the majority of the Rules Committee refused to do. And when the Congress adjourned on August 21, the Fair Labor Standards Act was still reposing in the Rules Committee's pigeonhole.

But the fight had only just begun. Back to their home districts went the members—but not for long. The wage-hour bill was not the only piece of legislation, deemed important by the Administration, which had failed of passage. Consequently, in early November President Roosevelt called the Congress to meet in special session on November 15, 1937, for the consideration of four pieces of legislation, one of which was the wage-hour bill. Now there is a remedy which is at all times available to members of the House when either a legislative committee or the Rules Committee refuses to act on a bill. A petition can be placed on the Speaker's desk by any member and if a majority of the House members (218) sign the petition, the bill automatically comes upon the floor for consideration.

Accordingly, on November 16, 1937, such a petition was placed on the Speaker's desk. The necessary 218 signatures were affixed within a few days' time and on December 13 Senate bill 2475 became the order of business in the House. But it did not pass. After a week's stormy debate and after opponents had succeeded in amending the bill until it was changed almost beyond recognition, a vote was taken on a motion to recommit the bill to the Committee on Labor. That vote carried 216 to 198 and the wage-hour legislation was dead at least until the third session of the Seventy-fifth Congress should assemble in January 1938.

Criticism had been made of the Senate bill on the ground that too much discretionary authority was bestowed on the administrator of the act. This was particularly objectionable to those Northern employers who had been supporting the legislation. Consequently a new bill, which allowed very little discretion or flexibility, was worked out by the Labor Committee early in the third session. It provided for a minimum wage of forty cents per hour after three years and for maximum hours (unless overtime were paid) of forty after two years of operation of the act.

Technically the bill was still "S. 2475," for it would have become necessary for the Senate to act all over again had the House passed a differently numbered bill. Since it was still the Seventy-fifth Congress, the action of the Senate taken in the first session of that Congress was still valid and would continue so until the Seventy-fifth Congress finally adjourned and a new

Congress took office. For these reasons it frequently happens, as in this case, that though a committee may rewrite an entire bill and propose completely new language, no new bill will be introduced. Instead the old number will still be used and the new language will simply be offered as a substitute for the entire bill as passed by the other house of Congress.

The new, substitute bill was even less acceptable to the membership of the Rules Committee than the old Black-Connery bill had been. Weeks passed and no rule was granted for consideration of the bill, nor was there any prospect of such action. At last, along in the spring of 1938, a group of us got together and decided upon another drive to petition the bill out of the hands of the Rules Committee and onto the floor. Several meetings were held under the chairmanship of Congressman Arthur Healy, of Massachusetts. We conferred with every member of the House whom we believed at all likely to favor wage-hour legislation. We secured promises to sign the petition—or received refusals—and then met again and again to compare results. I still have my old lists of members to whom I talked, together with notes on their attitudes.

At last we believed we were ready. On May 6, 1938, a petition was placed on the Speaker's desk at the very beginning of the session while supporters of the bill lined up around the House chamber behind the "rail" ready to sign. It took about two hours for the line to do its work. But at the rate of about one a minute our signatures were affixed and before two-thirty that afternoon we knew that on May 23 the wage-hour bill would come before the House once more. Of those who signed the petition that day, 196 were Democrats, 8 were progressives, and 5 were Farmer-Laborites (all the membership of those two minor parties in the House). Only nine Republicans signed the petition.

Signing or not signing this petition was a far better test of the attitude of members toward wage-hour legislation than was the final vote on the bill. Without the petition there would have been no bill at all. And by the time we got to the final vote the "wise thing to do politically" was to vote for it.

May 23 came. All that day and all the following day the debate on the wage-hour bill went on. A host of amendments was offered but this time we were prepared to meet them and almost all of them were beaten. At last the vote was taken late in the afternoon of May 24, 1938, and the House of Representatives passed by a vote of 314 to 97 the Fair Labor Standards Act. After conference with the Senate and signature by the President the bill was law. In simple language it means today that no worker in interstate commerce can be employed for longer than forty hours per week without payment of overtime (except for certain "peak season" employment in plants processing farm crops) and no such worker can be paid less than forty cents an hour.

Such a standard afforded, of course, no more than a bare living when the act was passed. And it became tragically and indefensibly low as the postwar inflation caused severe shrinkage in the buying power of the wage earner's dollar. Perhaps, therefore, the outstanding failure of the Seventy-ninth Congress was the refusal of a majority of the House to pass legislation which would have increased the statutory minimum wage.

To a large number of the nation's workers the Fair Labor Standards Act makes little difference. The theory of Karl Marx that all wage earners would always belong to the poorest group in society has been proven false by events. Even before the coming of World War II, with its unprecedented demand for labor and the consequent increase in dollar wages in many industries, the pattern had changed. The days of the free land frontier, the days of America's youth when almost anyone with "a little gumption" could start a business of his own had long since passed. With the development of the great financial and industrial monopolies the door was closed tighter and tighter against the entry into a self-employing business of anyone without substantial capital. Except for retail merchandising, farming, and a few other lines, membership in a co-operative became about the only way the average citizen could participate in the ownership of any part of our great complex industrial system.

Meanwhile, behind the growth of capitalistic monopoly there followed the growth of the labor movement, stimulated in later years by the legislation and governmental attitudes of the Roosevelt period. Millions of America's ablest citizens began to deliberately choose to be hired employees. And two World Wars taught the nation that there are times when its very life depends on there being enough *human beings* to make our much-vaunted capital and machinery work at all. Stories of fabulous incomes flowing to the workers of America have been exaggerated beyond all reason. Many a war veteran who tried to find one of the "hundred-dollar-a-week" jobs he had been told about while in service can testify to that fact. It is true that a considerable percentage of organized American workers receive yearly incomes substantially higher than those of a great many farmers, salaried workers, teachers, ministers and other professional workers whose economic bargaining power is much weaker than that of trade union members. But what is true of some American wage earners is decidedly not true of all of them—popular misconceptions to the contrary notwithstanding.

In the closing weeks of the Seventy-ninth Congress some of us tried our best to secure action in the House on the bill, already passed by the Senate, which would have increased to sixty-five cents an hour the statutory minimum wage. We found that more than four million workers in interstate commerce occupations which were covered by the Fair Labor Standards Act were at that time receiving wages of less than sixty-five cents an hour. How many more millions were working for similarly substandard wages in occupations not affected by the act no one knew exactly. But almost certainly it was at least another four million. And we had the figures to prove that of the "job openings" being offered to returning veterans, forty-three per cent were at wages of less than sixty-five cents an hour. Despite the tight "labor market" of the war and its aftermath, four million American workers were in a position where passage of a simple bill increasing the legal minimum wage would have increased their pitiably small incomes. Had the coverage of the act been broadened to include some of the traditionally underpaid "service" groups, the number benefited would have been correspondingly greater. We made speeches; we held meetings; we filed a petition on the Speaker's desk and signed it. But there just weren't enough of us and the bill died.

Thus, as the new Congress met in January 1947, one of the

greatest needs of the nation in general and of its unorganized wage earners in particular was the passage of a bill to increase the minimum wage standard. But the Eightieth Congress moved in exactly the opposite direction, for, in passing legislation ostensibly designed to quiet the large number of portal-to-portal pay suits filed by labor unions, the Congress included provisions calculated to make effective enforcement of even the existing wage and hour standards extremely difficult. Only 56 votes were cast against this bill in the House of Representatives and only 5 of these came from the majority (Republican) "side of the aisle."

The hope is probably forlorn, therefore, that any Congress elected during the postwar trend toward conservatism in the United States will pass a bill raising the minimum wage above the forty cents per hour fixed in the original act. But someday such action must be taken, since it is no more than a matter of elemental justice.

Chapter 10

LABOR AND MANAGEMENT

Every time a wave of strikes hits the country the press demands that Congress "do something." So does congressional mail. So do many congressmen.

A much smaller number of people, either in or out of Congress, suggest exactly *what* should be done. But the demand that a better relationship than constant conflict be developed between management and labor becomes ever louder, angrier, and more insistent. A good many people regard this as the nation's most pressing problem. It goes to the very roots of man's economic life and involves the basic questions of how the division of the fruits of industry is to be made and how control and responsibility are to be divided.

It is hardly to be wondered at, therefore, that no domestic issues have been debated in Congress with greater bitterness than those arising out of labor-management relationships or that, a decade after its passage, no law on the statute books is more vehemently discussed than the Wagner Labor Relations Act.

The popular idea is that the membership of Congress can be divided into pro-labor and anti-labor groups. To be sure, there have been considerable numbers who could with fair accuracy be classified in one of those two ways. There have always been members who, regardless of the merits of a given issue, would find out first what the leaders of organized labor wanted and then vote accordingly. And there have been other members, in numbers larger than the pro-labor group, who stood ready to strike at labor from any possible vantage point and by almost any available means. But, judged by their actual point of view rather than by the votes they were compelled to cast, a number of members of the Congresses in which I served could not be classified as belonging to either of these groups. We were in the middle, and it wasn't always a very comfortable place to be. We recognized that management-labor relationships are absolutely central to the economic welfare of America. We recognized the indispensable positive values in the labor movement. But we saw at the same time that abuses of labor's power are possible and that they have sometimes taken place. We knew that efficient management is the essential counterpart of efficient labor. But we viewed with profound alarm moves by capital to attempt to severely weaken or destroy labor unions. We wanted to correct what was wrong and to do it without destroying the positive values or crippling the labor movement for the job we knew it had to do. We hardly received even a decent hearing.

In the eyes of the pro-labor groups it was rank heresy and evidence of "not being for labor any more" whenever it was suggested that it would be a positive service to the labor movement itself if certain measures to correct abuses were passed. To the anti-labor bloc we were hopelessly "tied to labor's apron strings" because we were unwilling to vote for bills we believed to be extreme or positively unjust to labor or for those which we knew had never been exposed to the critical analysis of the representatives of either management or labor.

During quiet periods of apparent labor-management peace nothing was done. In times of public excitement the Labor Committee, reluctant to act at all, would sometimes bring to the floor a bill containing comparatively mild but generally rather carefully considered provisions. Or someone would manage to work out such language for a more drastic labor bill that it would be referred to another committee less "friendly to labor" such as the Committee on the Judiciary. One of these bills would be reported for the House consideration. The anti-labor bloc would then proceed to amend it. They had the votes to do so. Amendment after amendment, bearing on almost every facet of the activities of labor unions, would be written into the bill. After this process had gone on for a while the pro-labor group would decide that their best strategy was to "make the bill as bad as possible so it would be easier to vote against it." Thus there would be only a handful of the middle group opposing the amendments. And when the final vote came it was almost impossible for a conscientious member to support the bill, principally because neither he nor anyone else could have any clear idea what its practical effect would be. Many of these bills carried provisions which the moderates would have liked to vote for had it been possible to isolate them from the rest of the bill. But since this was impossible and the whole "shotgun" measure had to be voted up or down, most of us voted no. Thus we were regarded by our constituents as well as by many other members of the House as "unwilling to vote for anything which official labor leadership opposed."

Actually this was not the case. One bill was handled in a very different way from the foregoing description and gave some of us a chance to prove that where a simple straightforward issue was presented, calculated to correct an obvious abuse in the operations of labor unions, it would have our support. This was the Hobbs Anti-racketeering Bill.

The federal Anti-racketeering Act makes it a federal offense to use force or intimidation or threats of force to exact money from another person. A Supreme Court decision of a few years ago exempted from the operation of this act any activity carried on in connection with labor union operations. The Hobbs bill was drawn simply to amend the Anti-racketeering Act so as to make it plain that in the eyes of the law racketeering is wrong by whomever and under whatever circumstances carried on. Some labor officials countered by saying that abuses which they agreed were all wrong were being curbed and were no longer a matter requiring legislation. But though it was true that progress had been made, that did not seem to be an argument against making actions which clearly were wrong a crime in the eyes of the law. Indeed, it was my belief that it would be no aid to the labor movement to allow the Supreme Court exemption to stand but that, on the contrary, labor's position would be far stronger if it were known to all that labor union members were, and wanted to be, subject to such laws as the Anti-racketeering Act. I knew many union men who felt the same way.

The Hobbs bill was passed by the House twice during my membership. Both times I voted for it, despite the opposition of official labor.

There were few occasions, however, when any phase of the problem connected with organized labor was considered in the simple direct form of the Hobbs bill. Indeed, I cannot recall a single parallel. Every other vote on a bill affecting organized labor came on an omnibus measure containing a large number of unrelated provisions, many of which had not even been exposed to the criticism or analysis of labor leaders or, for that matter, employers.

For example, there was the famous War Labor Disputes Act, popularly known as the Smith-Connally Act. It was precipitated by the wartime coal strike and it was understandable, certainly, why Congress felt called upon to take some kind of action. Labor leaders argued that reliance on the voluntary "no-strike pledge" would as a practical matter come closer to keeping all workers on the job all the time than legislation could do. But it was too late for those arguments to deter Congress from action. It was only a question of what was going to be done. I told the House: "I am prepared to vote for the Ramspeck bill or a measure similar to it. But I know it would be a great mistake for us to have an anti-labor field day here. . . . It is our job to consider what the real *results* of what we do here today are going to be."

The original bill, however, was drastically amended on the floor and when the House came to the final vote it contained these main provisions. It extended the power of the President to take over any plant, mine, or facility equipped for the manufacture, production, or mining of articles or materials required or useful for the war effort. It specifically permitted such seizure whenever there was an interruption of operations caused by a strike or other labor disturbance. No one could quarrel with this provision. It was part and parcel of the necessities of war. The act provided that this power should end upon the cessation of hostilities.

Then the bill provided penalties against anyone encouraging or "coercing" any strike, lockout, or other interruption of work in any plant so taken over by the President. Since such a strike would be a strike against the government of the United States—and in wartime at that—this provision was no more than logical.

The logic of these provisions and their possible effectiveness against "wildcat" stoppages was clear enough, so that in my opinion the act would have been accepted by labor with fairly good grace had it stopped at this point.

But it didn't.

It proceeded to forbid political contributions by labor organizations—a matter hardly pertinent to "war labor disputes" whatever the pros and cons of the question. And it contained another requirement which the very authors of the act were to sincerely regret. This was the requirement that, before any strike could be called, thirty days' notice must be given and a secret ballot election conducted by the National Labor Relations Board. In other words, the act started out by trying to prevent wartime strikes and then said, "But if you are going to have a strike, this is the way to do it." Moreover, what actually happened was that the labor leaders, in order to protect their bargaining strength, proceeded to put themselves in position to call strikes if need be. They began as an almost regular practice to call for strike ballots by the National Labor Relations Board. It was no use from the labor leaders' viewpoint to have such a vote unless it came out in favor of a strike. So, in order to secure a favorable vote, it was in every case necessary to emphasize the grievances of the workers. This was done by the very men who in most cases were the least anxious to actually have a strike. What they were after was bargaining power with the employers and before the War Labor Board. They were afraid the Smith-Connally Act would deprive them of that power unless they protected themselves in this way.

One result of these unwise provisions was to enable John L. Lewis to say, later that he had called his coal strike in accordance with the requirements of the War Labor Disputes Act. And what he said was perfectly true.

Had the War Labor Disputes Act stopped where it was supposed to stop—with the provisions aiming to prevent wartime strikes in vital industries, it might have passed with little opposition. But it attempted instead to reform labor union practices with respect to campaign contributions and strikes at the very time when strikes were supposed to be "out for the duration." Events proved how unwise this was.

So I voted against the Smith-Connally Act, voted to sustain the President's veto, and lived to see the day when the very men who had most strongly supported the act originally were the loudest in their demands for its repeal.

The most difficult decision, I confess, was on the Case bill, passed in the spring of 1946, and vetoed by President Truman. As any social or economic institution grows in power, there comes a time when some standard for the relationship of that institution to the whole of society must be set up. Organized labor can expect to be no exception. The standard probably must be established by the passage of what may be termed a labor union code. Such laws cannot be properly framed in an atmosphere of anger or vengeance. They cannot be successfully drawn unless labor helps to draw them. Neither can they have the required salutary effect, in all likelihood, without containing some provisions to which some leaders of labor will object. As the House approached a vote on the Case bill, I faced the question whether this was a measure temperate enough and well enough directed at real ills so that, on balance, and despite the arguments of labor against it, it should receive an affirmative vote.

I believed then, as I have always believed, that jurisdictional strikes are indefensible. No labor man attempts to defend them. All deplore them. The best that is ever said by way of excuse is that they are "unavoidable." Evidently, when a jurisdictional strike takes place the general public is called on to undergo inconvenience or even hardship not because a group of workers have a grievance against their employers, nor because they are seeking to improve their wages or working conditions, but only because two labor unions have been unable to agree on which should enroll as members a certain group of workers. Obviously some other method beside the strike must be devised as a means of settling such disputes.

The Case bill contained an attempt to prohibit jurisdictional strikes.

Again, all labor leaders to whom I have talked are agreed that nothing does quite so much damage to the labor movement as does a breach of contract by a union or an official of a union. They never attempt to argue against the principle of "equal responsibility for the carrying out of contracts." They only say that they are now responsible and that in most states it is possible at present for a union to be sued for violating a contract. So it would seem that measures aimed to prevent *either employers or unions* from breaking contracts would be good legislation from everyone's point of view.

Well, the Case bill provided that, if a union broke a contract, suit for damages could be brought in any federal court.

Undoubtedly there have been cases where labor unions, following the example of corporations and other much better-"vested" interests, have by making large financial contributions to political parties or candidates placed these parties or candidates in a position of embarrassing obligation. The outstanding example of such practice, ironically enough, is John L. Lewis's $500,000 contribution to the campaign of President Roosevelt in 1936. This one, of course, backfired with a recoil which the nation still feels, since Mr. Roosevelt failed to listen to him as attentively as should, in Mr. Lewis's opinion, have been the case. Nonetheless, the practice could obviously become dangerous to the functioning of democratic government—less dangerous, no doubt, than large contributions from corporations and financial interests because more certain to be widely known, but dangerous nonetheless.

The Case bill had a provision in it forbidding contributions to political funds by either labor unions or corporations.

Yet I voted against the Case bill. I voted to sustain President Truman's veto of it. Just after the latter vote was cast I had to go to Philadelphia to make a speech. As I looked out of the coach window or read the newspaper accounts of the action of Congress

I was troubled—troubled by the thoughts just outlined regarding some of the Case bill provisions. Had I perhaps been wrong? Had I missed the chance to vote, even against labor's wishes, for a measure that would correct some of the things that sooner or later would have to be straightened out? Politically, my vote against the bill would be a heavy liability. The "smart" political vote, considering the make-up of my congressional district, would have been to vote for the bill. I knew that. As always, just after I had cast a difficult vote, I seemed able to remember only the arguments against the position I had taken. All the reasons I had found so persuasive in deciding to vote as I had done seemed to vanish from my mind.

But as the days passed I remembered them. I remembered that the Case bill had also contained a prohibition against employers paying into workers' "welfare funds"; that such a provision would in all probability have thrown certain long-established industrial insurance programs into confusion; that in the garment industry, for example, the unions and the employers had for years operated such a welfare fund that neither of them wanted to give up.

I remembered, too, that the mediation and "cooling-off" provisions of the Case bill had been carelessly drawn, their penalty clauses unwise if not unworkable. I remembered that, while these provisions would have attempted to punish those participating in a strike after mediation was begun, nothing would have happened if the strike was called first. So "quickie" strikes would have been positively encouraged.

Again, was the Case bill's answer to the jurisdictional strike the right one? Would a flat prohibition against such strikes work? Can we any more pass a law against interunion competition than against tuberculosis or some other troublesome factor in our national life? No. It isn't so easy as that. What is clearly required is to recognize that such disputes will take place but to set up an alternate method of settling them and then require that it be used instead of the strike method.

And would the oversimplified proposal that all contractual disputes be threshed out before the ordinary courts of the land have produced the desired results? Probably not. The courts once had pretty complete control over labor-management relations. It didn't work. It worked mostly against the human interests and for the property interests involved. Something better than the Case bill answer would have to be adopted before this problem would be solved.

I had tried to do exactly that, too. In the course of consideration of the labor legislation in which the so-called Case bill was involved. I had offered a substitute myself. The problem Congress was supposed to be facing was not that of reforming the labor movement. It was the problem of reducing strikes, of attempting to find a formula that could assure more continuous production at a time America badly needed it. Accordingly, I had prepared a bill aimed to accomplish that purpose. It contained two main provisions. The first was for a unified and strengthened mediation, conciliation, and voluntary arbitration service in the government, as a means of facilitating the collective-bargaining process and settling what we may call "disputes of interest" between employers and unions before work stoppages took place. I had worked out the language of the bill with greatest care. Much of it had been obtained from the Senate Committee on Education and Labor which had heard the most experienced and able men in America in the field of labor-management relationships. Generally, my bill followed the recommendations of William M. Leiserson, former member of the National Labor Relations Board and the National Mediation Board and, perhaps, the most realistic, able, fair, and fearless thinker on this subject that our country boasts. I had also drawn upon a Minnesota law, which had worked well in practice. I had provided for the appointment of fact-finding boards to present the facts in the disputes to the American people for their judgment, in case all else failed. Meanwhile, it was simply required of both parties that "no change be made in the status quo existing at the time the dispute began" during the process of collective bargaining, conciliation, mediation, voluntary arbitration, or fact finding. My bill laid upon both employers and labor the positive obligation that both of them bargain together in good faith before calling upon government agencies for help. This the Wagner Act should have provided in the beginning but did not.

The second part of my substitute bill dealt with the problem of what may be termed "legal disputes"—disputes affecting contractual rights and duties between employers and labor unions. That is, it aimed to deal with the "equality of responsibility" for the observance of contracts about which everyone was talking so much. But the provisions of my bill recognized the complexity and difficulty of this problem and foresaw that to throw such matters into the ordinary courts would lead to confusion and probably to injustice, since, in the nature of the case, the regular courts are not equipped to deal from day to day with all the specific, detailed phases of management-labor problems.

Now it is obvious that a dispute over the interpretation of a signed contract is an entirely different sort of thing from a dispute over what the wage scale ought to be. In the latter case there is no absolute right and wrong. Two *interests* are in conflict and both may claim that they are "right." But, in the case of contractual questions, it is possible to determine what is correct action under the terms of the contract. It is possible to determine whether the contract has been violated, by whom it has been violated, whether it was done under provocation or not, and what, if any, damages have been sustained by the aggrieved party.

Sometimes labor-management contracts are violated. Those who know most about the problem tell us that employers, wittingly or unwittingly, violate them every day. Sometimes labor unions violate them—generally in a way that attracts much more attention and affects the general public much more directly than do employers' violations.

Therefore the first essential in the settlement of contractual disputes is to have an experienced, specialized tribunal decide whether the contract has in fact been violated. Second, it must be decided whether there was provocation for the violation and whether the provocation was or was not deliberate. Only after these questions are decided is it possible to assess damages or impose penalties.

So my bill provided for appointment by the United States Board of Arbitration (the voluntary arbitration board which the bill would have created) of special labor-management adjustment boards similar to those created by the Railway Labor Act.

These boards would have acted like courts for the hearing of cases of disputes over contracts between management and labor. Their decisions, if approved by the United States Board of Arbitration, would have been final and binding upon both parties. They could have imposed penalties for contract violation and required offending parties to make amends. Thus, in an orderly, workable manner, the problem of legal disputes, of avoiding strikes in connection with such disputes, of maintaining equal responsibility might have been solved. At least some of the most able students of labor-management problems in America so believed. Writing in the Catholic magazine *America* for March 2, 1946, Rev. Benjamin L. Masse, S.J., commented on my proposed bill in an article entitled, "The Law That Wasn't There." He imagined that my bill had been passed and summarized his argument for it as follows:

> In the short time the Voorhis Act has been on the books —in the pleasant world of fantasy, I mean—there have been a few major strikes and a number of small ones. But more frequently than in the past, industrial disputes are being settled in an orderly and peaceful way. Anyhow, the Act was not intended to outlaw strikes, since only a totalitarian government can do away with strikes completely. The most encouraging aspect of the situation is the great change in the attitude of labor and management. When the bill was before Congress, not a single leader of labor or industry spoke in its favor. Most of them were adamant in their opposition to anything like it, and predicted the most dire consequences if such legislation should be passed. If you were to talk to them now, they would admit, privately at least, that their fears had been somewhat exaggerated. Only a few of them would confess a willingness to return to the "good old days."

As is evident from Father Masse's article, my substitute bill was not adopted by the House. There were two reasons. Those members who were angry with labor thought it too moderate; and those members who wanted no legislation at all believed it too reasonable: they felt that if it had been adopted as an amendment by the Committee of the Whole, it would have passed both the House and Senate, been signed by the President, and become the law of the land.

Now there are a number of facts which anti-labor forces in the United States would like to have the people forget. Some of them I couldn't—and can't—forget.

I remember back in 1933 when Los Angeles was an "open-shop" town. I remember seeing checks for as little as $5.41 for a girl's week's work in a garment factory. I remember when the International Ladies Garment Workers Union called these workers to go on strike for better wages and recognition of the union. Only a fraction of them belonged to the union at the time. I helped to interest people in the community in that struggle. I remember the headlines in the Los Angeles papers: LOS ANGELES MINISTERS JOIN PICKET LINES IN GARMENT STRIKE. I was there too. It was a desperate human struggle for something like a decent livelihood. And it was only fourteen years ago.

Ever since that strike of 1933, I have been an honorary member of the International Ladies Garment Workers Union, which organization, incidentally, I believe to be one of the most effective influences against totalitarianism in the whole United States. I was proud to be given a life membership in the summer of 1946 in Local No. 1507 (El Monte, California) of the International Brotherhood of Carpenters and Joiners of America and to promise as a member of that organization to protect this nation against any forces seeking to destroy it.

Organized labor is too basic an institution in any democratic society to be lightly harmed. Why otherwise has every dictator— Nazi, communist, or fascist—gone about destroying the labor movement in his country as one of his very first acts upon gaining power? All too much of the propaganda hostile to organized labor flows originally from powerful interests which seek not the constructive reform of things which are clearly wrong but rather the destruction of the power of the American worker to protect himself and his fellows by united action.

Like most other human institutions, however, organized labor has suffered from abuses of power. The secondary boycott as sometimes used is an example. Others were pointed out by former Assistant Attorney General Thurman Arnold when he headed the Anti-Trust Division of the Justice Department. Powerful labor organizations have no more right to levy tribute upon the nation for services which are not performed than has any other group in our society. Nor can labor in the long run afford to resist improvements in production techniques which, if applied generally, would yield great benefit to all the people of the nation. All union members should be furnished, as most of them now are, with full financial reports from their local and national officers. No man's dues should be used for political purposes without his direct consent. And it is certainly no help to the cause of organized labor for any agency of government to fail to enforce with utmost vigor every law against violence, extortion, racketeering, or dishonest practices.

The most difficult problems, however, center about the closed shop. A point of view on this problem can be summed up in one sentence as follows: wherever a closed shop exists, there devolves upon government a responsibility to see that that closed shop does not defeat the purpose for which labor unions exist or undermine their necessarily democratic character.

There have been and there now are many closed shops where, because of the excellent leadership of the union or the unusual vigor of its membership, no serious problem has arisen. Furthermore, there are arguments for the closed shop which are difficult if not impossible to refute on grounds of sound logic or justice. It is unfair to expect the majority of men in an industry to contribute of their money, time, and strength to the building of an organization and the establishment of fair standards of work and wages and then to require that a minority of men in that industry be allowed to enjoy these same advantages without turning a hand to make them possible. This of course is the basic argument for the closed shop. And at the very least, it leads to the conclusion that whether or not a worker in an organized industry belongs to the union he should help pay the cost of the collective bargaining machinery which maintains the standards of his job.

But once a closed shop has been established, certain very real dangers arise which can undermine the democratic character of labor organizations, unless wisely dealt with either by labor itself or, failing that, by government.

It is clear that in a closed shop, since men's jobs depend on continuing union membership, the power of union officials over the rank and file becomes very much greater. Employers themselves may be called upon to enforce union discipline and compel union loyalty. Independently-minded union men may find that unpopularity with union leaders means dismissal from their jobs.

It is under the closed shop that practices aiming to limit entrance into a higher-paid craft or trade are most likely to arise.

Finally, if membership restrictions or a high schedule of initiation fees and union dues is added to the closed shop, a condition approaching a "closed" union is also created.

I certainly do not believe that the closed shop should be prohibited by law any more than I think it should be established by law or required by any act of a government agency. Comparatively few people are aware of the fact that the Railway Labor Act, which has been pointed to as something of a model of labor legislation, not only forbids employers to attempt to *prevent* workers from belonging to a labor organization, but also forbids them to take any action which would *require* them to do so. In my opinion, this is one of the reasons why the railroad unions have for so many years enjoyed the reputation of being among the most constructive organizations in America, not alone in the labor field but also in other fields of our economic life. Very nearly one hundred per cent of the men who work on the railroads of the nation belong to one or other of the labor unions in the field. But they belong because of what the organization has to offer them and not because the employer says they must do so. Vigorous and constructive action and growth on the part of labor unions can be had only if, on the one hand, they are protected against discrimination by the employer and, on the other hand, union leadership is under the necessity of winning the voluntary allegiance and membership of the workers and is subject to democratic control by such members.

Under the Wagner Labor Relations Act a union can secure redress from an employer who seeks to interfere with the right of the men to organize and join a union of their own choice. This is absolutely fundamental and should be regarded as one of the permanent features of American law. And as long as labor is protected by the Wagner Act in this way, the whole closed-shop question can be considered in a much more realistic manner than would otherwise be the case.

One possible solution would be to pass legislation placing upon closed-shop unions certain obligations to their own membership which would not be imposed (at least not by law) in any situation where a closed shop did not exist. Some of the requirements might be: regular and frequent elections of officers, full financial accounting to the membership, establishment of a means of appeal for members from expulsion from the union, limitations on dues and initiation fees, and reasonable entrance requirements. Such a law would not attempt in any way to forbid the closed shop. It would simply say, "If you do have a closed shop, then, in view of the increased power of the union over the individual worker, the government is constrained to protect that worker's interest."

With such a law on the books it is hard to see how the closed shop, where agreed upon by the employer and the union, could have any bad effects. Democratic control over union policy would be assured and no union could logically be accused of "denying men the right to work."

We now come to the final and insistently recurring problem— namely, that of strikes in industries absolutely vital to the continued health and life of the average citizen.

Does the right to strike include the right to shut off the electric power of whole communities, to cut off the water supply, to stop the telephones, to cause basic transportation to cease, or to deprive the people of fuel to heat their homes? And in like manner, does the right of business management to "run its own business" include the right to make decisions which will cause strikes to take place with the foregoing results?

The right to strike is the other half of the principle of the freedom of the employer to run his business without governmental interference. The American idea has been to let management and labor work out their differences by means of collective bargaining, and for the nation to take not only an impartial but a passive attitude in case collective bargaining proves unsuccessful and a strike ensues. When, during the war, it was evident that strikes could not be tolerated, the War Labor Board was set up and disputes between labor and management were settled once and for all by the decisions of that board. This was recognition of the fact that when the right to strike is taken away other means of securing justice must be provided by action of the government. Otherwise the workers are in the position of being told that they have to go on working under any conditions which may happen to exist in their industry without any hope for redress of those conditions. Manifestly, such a situation would be contrary to everything America stands for.

There are groups of workers in the country who never strike and who freely recognize that a strike among them would be illegal. They are the public employees such as policemen, firemen, forest rangers, post-office workers, and the like. But, as to such workers, we assume that public agencies will be responsible for their working conditions. That responsibility is discharged through Civil Service legislation, either national, state, or local.

If, in such vital industries as water systems, electric light and power, gas, transportation, communication, and possibly basic fuels, the nation is so dependent upon continuous operation that the freedom of labor and management must be curtailed, then similar responsibility must be taken for the welfare of these workers too. Some long steps, some new steps, some difficult steps are implied in those words "continuous operation," for, spelled with other letters, they read either "public ownership" or "compulsory arbitration." If we turn to compulsory arbitration, then along with any such requirements in public utility industries would have to go provisions governing the type of labor-management contract to be made in such industries. Something resembling the status of Civil Service workers would have to be given the employees in any industry where compulsory arbitration was required. Impartial and speedy machinery for the settlement of grievances, boards of appeal from arbitrary dismissal, systems of retirement, and payments of adequate compensation in the event of accident, sickness, or death, and similar provisions would have to be made as the only means of dealing justly with groups of workers who were being told that, in the last analysis, they could not take action to protect themselves.

The history of compulsory arbitration in such countries as Australia has not been one of universal success by any means. But if backed by determined public opinion and coupled with provisions protecting the workers, it might be that where others have failed our country could succeed with such a plan for public utility industries.

But it is possible, I think, that we have not yet probed deeply enough to find the root of the trouble. It may be that management-labor conflicts are inherent in a situation where owners and non-owners attempt by bargaining to bring industrial peace. It may be that so long as this condition prevails no law can be written that will "assure continuous operation." Perhaps the only ultimate answer lies in some form of co-operative sharing of ownership where motives and points of view can be changed and where all who work in an industry will acquire a greater responsibility and a greater interest in continuous full production for the simple reason that they have something of their own for which to be responsible.

For what they may be worth as food for thought, two simple rules about strikes can be laid down: (1) there is no way under the American Constitution in which strikes against private employers can be forbidden; and (2) there is no way under the concept of the American nation to justify a strike against the government of the United States.

The soul of the labor movement has, historically, been its struggle to raise the oppressed and the underpaid. All through its early years the union movement stood almost alone as a means of restoring some measure of economic strength to otherwise helpless individual workers who could hope to own no tools of modern industry and whose very sustenance depended upon securing employment at some kind of wage. That worker and the union that struggled to protect him were, all thoughtful people knew, the underdogs in an uneven economic battle. Some public sympathy was forthcoming for this reason. And as for the workers—union or non-union—there was hardly ever a question but that the union's battle was their battle. The labor movement was a crusade for basic human decency. Its shortcomings were not hard to forgive. Except in a few industries its hold was tenuous, subject to the ever-present possibility of a successful "union-busting" drive by employers.

The American labor movement gained a new position in the United States when the Wagner Act was passed. It was made the law of the land that workers could organize and bargain collectively with their employers and the United States Government was obligated to protect that right with all its power and prestige.

Organization proceeded far more rapidly than ever before. The power of the unions grew despite the split in the movement between AF of L and CIO. Industry after industry signed contracts with its men. With the coming of the war the need for workers became unprecedented. It was impossible to find enough people to do all the work America had to get done. In this situation, and despite the no-strike pledge, the power of organized labor again grew until today the labor union is one of the great institutions upon which the economic structure of America is raised. Its power and position cannot be destroyed without wrecking the entire national economy.

But the Wagner Act and the power that flowed from it into the hands of union leaders were not without their price. Something was lost along the way. Few people seem to have noticed it; fewer still seem to have realized its significance. The labor unions of America are no longer recognized, either by the general public or by a great many workers, as "underdogs in an uneven economic struggle." In some industries the unions are, in prosperous times, (though never in time of depression, be it remembered) even stronger than the employing companies, from an economic point of view. Coal and railroads are good examples of this. The union representative speaks with power, if not with positive authority.

It is very important that all of us recognize the change in the feeling of the American public which this has brought. The old sympathy can no longer be counted upon. Labor's case will no longer be accepted by any considerable number of people as right "because it is labor's side." The case has to be proved—and proved moreover in the teeth of publicity in the daily press which is almost never prolabor, seldom neutral, usually procompany.

All this might be of no great consequence, except for the fact that it leads to one additional result. The stronger the labor movement becomes, the more closed-shop agreements that are signed, the more generally accepted the position of the unions in industry becomes, the less clear it is to the industrial worker that he has need of a labor union to protect his interest. This is why the closed shop may spell weakness rather than strength to the labor movement. It is why reliance upon government is dangerous to the labor movement. It is why true friends of labor will not be afraid to support well-considered and fairly framed legislation in the field of labor-management relations—particularly such legislation as will make it clear that neither management nor labor can any longer "run its own affairs" without regard to the effect of its actions upon the whole American nation. Had organized labor itself proposed some such legislation during the period when its friends were strong in the Congress, the whole temper of public opinion would, in my opinion, be a very different one today. And so would the personnel of the Congress.

Chapter 11

"A BOLD PEASANTRY,
THEIR COUNTRY'S PRIDE"

The best hope of America for tomorrow, like her hope of yester-
day, lies in the soil. It lies in the regeneration of the healthy point
of view toward rural living which made strong the America of
earlier centuries. It lies not only in the protection and preservation of such family-sized, owner-operated farms as we still boast
but in an increase in the numbers of that fundamental economic
unit of any good society. It rests on the chance that we can prove
wrong the prophecy of Goldsmith:

> Princes and lords may flourish or may fade;
> A breath can make them, as a breath has made;
> But a bold peasantry, their country's pride,
> When once destroy'd, can never be supplied.

"Never" is too long a time.

I first read those lines in the spring of 1920 on a railroad train,
traveling through southern Wisconsin. I remember vividly every
detail of that experience—the word picture of the deserted English village which the poet painted, the tragedy it represented,
and, by contrast, the deep live green of the pastures and of the
young corn in the American fields. I wondered to whom the land

belonged. Tenants and hired laborers frequently grow good crops on the deep soil of the Mississippi Valley. And men who own their farms sometimes face hungry children around the supper table in other areas of America. But through the years, if our villages are not to become "deserted" too, the land must be a homestead for people to whom it belongs, not a mine to be stripped of its richness and abandoned as has already happened with so much of our country.

I remember as a little boy how every spring I would turn over with a child's spade a plot of eastern Kansas loam and plant my vegetable seeds with never a question in my mind but that they would germinate and grow and bring health to our table. I have cultivated California hillsides with the boys at my school and found the almost unbelievable difference between the yield from the eroded upper portions and the more gently sloping lower ones, where the good soil had been washed. And I tried each year while I was a congressman to make a little crop of vegetables from the outworn clay of eastern Virginia, only to find how meager was the yield.

And yet I confess that until more recent years I took the bounty of the soil, its fertility, its unending productiveness, quite for granted. I assumed, like most Americans, that God's greatest natural gift, the reproductive powers of our land, accumulated through ages of the life and life-giving death of plants and animals, would always be ours to exploit as we saw fit.

It is not so. One of the very great contributions of our generation to the future of America is that it made America for the first time soil-conservation conscious, erosion conscious, potash conscious, superphosphate conscious. Except for Theodore Roosevelt's bitterly contested forest conservation bills, the first legislation aiming to keep America a great nation by husbanding and rebuilding her soil resources was passed in the New Deal period. For that, unborn generations will bless our times.

Now farmers don't destroy the soil if they can possibly avoid it—not men who own their land—unless they own too much of it. Which is to say that, insofar as the small farm is the unit of American agriculture, our soil will be saved if only the necessary information is supplied and agriculture is reasonably prosperous.

But for too long, economic forces have been allowed to work which are as destructive of human values as erosion is of land values. We should have started decades ago to check the trend away from ownership and toward tenancy upon the land, to prevent the swallowing up of family farm after family farm into huge baronial corporation estates farmed by machinery and hired gangs. We should have seen that the figures on geometric increases in tractor sales and combine sales spelled no unmixed blessing, that they meant bigger holdings, fewer fences, more former owners' and tenants' families wandering the roads of America. We should have understood then that the practice of co-operative ownership of such machinery by groups of small landowners must come very quickly to the rescue.

All these thoughts I took with me to Congress in January 1937. They were why I wanted the place on the Committee on Agriculture, for which I had to wait six long years.

I had some other reasons too. It was as true in the middle 1930s as it had ever been that when Americans got into trouble they moved West. It was one of the characteristics of which we were most proud. We didn't "take it lying down." We moved on to a better place and started over. In his biography in a California Who's Who the editor of one of the state's outstanding conservative dailies had boasted of how he rode into California on the rods of a freight train, friendless and penniless.

But that was different. At least, judging from the comments of that gentleman's paper, it was different. For what business had these equally penniless and much more friendless folk from Oklahoma and Texas and Kansas and New Mexico and Arkansas to come to California at such a time as the middle 1930s? The state numbered its unemployed in the hundreds of thousands. There were "too many people" there already. The federal government ought to take them back where they came from. (To piles of drifting dust or barren mountain "farms"!)

Some California legislators attempted to devise laws to bar immigration into the state. But what about the tourists who even in the depression were coming with fat pocketbooks to spend their money in California's much advertised warm winter sunshine? We didn't want to discourage them. We'd spent a lot of money inviting them. It was just the poor people California wanted to stop, the descendants of the very rugged Americans who had gone into another and earlier "West" in accordance with the nation's very best tradition.

California had good reason to be worried. Her farms could employ only so many people; her own farmers were in great distress and unable to hire even a normal number of workers for the harvests. Her hospitals were overrun with sick people, her highways clogged with miserable, temporary shelters where homeless people congregated. America was a big country. Surely there was some other place.

And still they came, in their broken-down Fords, by thousands and tens of thousands, homeless, ill, stricken, people mostly unlearned, but earnest and religious and remarkably free from bitterness. By mid-1937 some seventy thousand of these refugees —for such they were—had congregated in the San Joaquin Valley alone. They lived along roadsides, behind billboards, or in squatters' camps in shacks built of rubbish. Sanitary provisions were non-existent. So in many cases was good drinking water. Here, indeed, were some of the "one third"!

Most California communities did the best they could. But they couldn't meet the problem. It was too big.

Indeed it was not only too big but too fundamental. The nation had millions of unemployed in its cities. There wasn't any place but the roadsides for dispossessed farm folk to go. And agriculture suffered from deeply distressing problems too.

Of all the jobs I undertook in my first term in Congress I believe I worked hardest and worried most about the "transients," as they came to be called. I introduced a bill to provide for federal aid to the states in meeting their relief needs, and also a bill to prevent one state from canceling the state citizenship of a person until he had acquired legal residence in another one. This bill also would have set up more adequate means in the United States Employment Service of guiding and informing migratory workers as to where job openings existed or were likely to exist and where on the other hand there just weren't any such openings. My bills didn't pass. Even in California they received only mild support. The issue was too "hot." And the other states, except Florida and New York, were against the bills since they were on the sending rather than the receiving end of the migration.

I spoke in Congress repeatedly and over the radio at every opportunity about the plight of these people, the plight of the areas to which they had gone. I wrote to the President, the Secretary of Agriculture, everyone else I could think of. I believe I had something to do with pushing forward the building of migratory labor camps by the Farm Security Administration in California and elsewhere. Most of them consisted only of some tent platforms clustered around a little central building where there were clean running water and toilets and a place to inquire about jobs. But they were a Godsend, for they were clean, decent places where homeless people had a right to be.

With the sale of these federal camps, responsibility for the housing of migratory farm labor will fall once again on the shoulders of local people. They'll have a hard task at times. But I believe the value of this action by government will never be lost. For I doubt that our people will again tolerate the sort of living conditions for farm workers which the migrants of the thirties found all over the country.

The homeless migrating people for whose assistance these camps were originally established weren't from the cities. They were "off the land." As I studied more about their problem it took on all the aspects of a great and terrible tragedy. Their plight was a visitation upon them of the wrongs of a nation. For centuries it had been an American characteristic to exploit the resources of this great continent without regard to the interest of future generations. There was bitter resentment at any "governmental interference" with the right of any citizen to use the gifts of God for his own gain as he saw fit. The tragedy of the "dust bowl" came as a direct and inevitable result. It was the faulty judgment of certain men that they plowed land which never should have been broken. But theirs was not the basic wrong.

The basic wrong was national—in our blood. The dust bowl was only a final dramatic chapter to a very long book that began to be written at the time of Columbus. It is the book of soil destruction. It is written upon some 253,000,000 acres of what was once the fertile soil of this great nation. This is sixty-one per cent of the total acreage now under crops in the United States. It has, in the course of cultivation, been either completely or partly destroyed, or it has lost a substantial part of its fertility. Of the 415,000,000 acres now under crops in our country, only about 161,000,000 acres can safely be farmed by present methods. But if the best soil practices were used we could safely plant to crops some 450,000,000 acres of American land. These facts and figures are from the United States Department of Agriculture Yearbook for 1938.

It may well be that the pages of history record nowhere so profligate a waste of national wealth by any people as that of which the American people through the years have been guilty. We have been guilty partly because great areas of our land have been farmed not as family homesteads but as quick-profit ventures, partly because we have not understood, and partly because our farm people have, in millions of cases, been too poor to take the needed measures even if they had understood the danger. And for all this the migrants of the thirties were paying the price.

With the outbreak of the war in Europe and the rise of a greater demand for labor than America had ever known, the "transients" of the middle thirties became the war workers, the soldiers, and the farm workers of the later period.

But the root causes of their migrancy remained—every one of them.

There were plenty of times during the ten years when I voted and even worked hard for measures only because I believed they were "better than nothing" or better than some alternative. This was the case with most of the bills affecting foreign relations during the period before the outbreak of the war. It was the case with several of the bills affecting organized labor. It was certainly the case with the WPA bills. Every time a new grant of power to an executive agency was proposed it was a problem of deciding whether such action was really necessary in the circumstances, and I was seldom absolutely certain.

But on any bill which I believed would contribute to the protection of the small farm, there I was *sure* of my ground. On such bills the issue was the preservation of the rock-bottom foundation of American democracy. On such farms rests the hope of revival of the sturdy character and virtues that made America great. And from them, we could hope, would continue to come the most vigorous of our new generations of children.

In this field I could work with the confidence that comes from the assurance that one is on the right road, for the values sought to be preserved and strengthened are fundamental, earthy ones good for the long, long future. But they are also the values most difficult to rebuild, if too long neglected, just as Goldsmith said.

While it was six years before I finally gained my place on the Agriculture Committee, it was barely six months after I first took my seat before I had opportunity to vote for a measure bearing upon those very values. It was the Bankhead-Jones Farm Tenant Act, which became law on July 22, 1937. The bill proposed that direct government loans at four per cent interest and with forty-year maturities be advanced to selected tenant farmers in each county in the United States. A local committee must approve each loan, both as to the farm to be bought and the character of the man being enabled to buy it. It was a small start at one of the most basic problems of American life. Some of its enemies repeatedly attacked it on this very ground. But it established a principle which was and is as right as anything can be. And at last we are today in a position to broaden the application of that principle and to make substantial progress in "planting owners where only tenants used to grow."

I remember the debate on the bill very well indeed. Opponents claimed that the plan was "another New Deal experiment" which was bound to fail and which would cost the government untold sums of money. As a matter of fact it has to this hour never cost the government of the United States a single cent, since the tenant-purchasers have been consistently repaying their loans, not only on schedule but, on the average, a little ahead of it. This bill was one of the very few which brought Speaker Bankhead down from the rostrum to take part in the debate. It passed the House by a substantial majority.

The 1920s have gone down in history as a period of considerable prosperity for the United States. It was not so with agriculture. Farm income was halved in the deliberate deflation of 1920 and it never substantially recovered until the coming of World War II. I remember when I was a senior in college reading an article about the farm problem in a Sunday issue of the old New York *World*. The article pointed out how farmers produce their crops in competition with thousands of other farmers, how almost universally they are compelled to go into debt to finance the planting and harvest of their crops, how therefore at the time of harvest there is an absolute necessity that farmers sell what they have produced in order to meet their debt payments and how, in the absence of some protection from co-operatives or government, this places them in the weakest possible position relative to the middleman purchasers of the crops. Those purchasers, on the other hand, have had facilities and resources which enabled them to wait for a better price.

Except for the effects of some of the legislation that we passed during the thirties, and except for the influence of farm co-operatives, that picture is still an all too accurate one.

The extent of the farmers' distress was the measure of the middleman's opportunity for profit—until the coming of the co-operatives, whereby the farmers themselves can own together the marketing facilities upon which they all must depend.

The farmer produces in co-operation with nature and must decide months—even years—before harvest what and how much he will, God willing, produce. Thus, to a very much greater extent than any other producer, he becomes subject to the winds of economic fortune. If a depression comes, he is certain to be its victim: first, because he is usually in debt; and second, because the very bounty of his yield is bound to force down the prices he will receive.

And so it is clear why the establishment of a co-operative farm credit system was a basic necessity if our agriculture was to be saved. Long-term, low-interest loans have removed some of the economic pressure and hence the economic helplessness from the farmer's shoulders.

It is equally clear why some means was necessary to enable farmers to take their crops to market with some chance of finding there a reasonable balance between supply and demand. There is a good way and a decidedly second-best way to accomplish this.

The good way is to sustain the demand for farm crops at all times. That, for some reason, meets with terrific opposition, since it implies that dread situation called an "economy of abundance." But in the crisis of 1933 the other way, for better or for worse, was taken and the Agricultural Adjustment Act was the vehicle employed. It aimed to enable farmers to regulate the production and marketing of their crops in accordance with the "effective" demand. Which means the "demand" of people who have money enough to pay for what they need.

But the Supreme Court declared the AAA unconstitutional. Therefore President Roosevelt called a special session of the Seventy-fifth Congress in November 1937 to pass among other things a new farm bill. The old patterns of agricultural distress were certain to come back otherwise. While the whole idea of crop regulation, acreage allotment, marketing quotas, and, above all, penalties for overplanting did not, to say the least, appeal to most Americans, it was the only available alternative to either far-reaching measures to increase demand for farm products or the very rapid growth of co-operatives.

The result was the passage of H.R. 8505 in early 1938. This bill had to avoid the measures, such as the processing tax, which the Supreme Court had held invalid. And it did one other thing which marked, in my judgment, a fundamental improvement over, and a fundamental departure from, the old AAA. In the act of 1938 the main emphasis was upon the principle of soil conservation. Payments were to be made not as compensation for crop reduction but for the planting of soil-conserving crops in place of soil-depleting ones. Perhaps there was some subterfuge in this. In the minds of some, the real objective may have been regulation of production rather than soil conservation. But the possibility of developing the legislation into something economically defensible and indeed absolutely essential to the nation's future welfare certainly was present in the act of 1938, whereas this was, I believe, not the case with the original act. It so happens that the so-called five basic commodities—cotton, corn, wheat, tobacco, and rice—are all severely soil-depleting crops. The idea behind the farm bill of 1938 was this: it is very foolish to grow soil-depleting crops only to sell them at a loss either at home or abroad and it is logical, especially at times when demand is inadequate, to shift production to soil-building crops.

In a really rational economic situation any limitation on production is indefensible. During the war we wished most earnestly that we had bought from our farmers and stored against that "rainy day" all the non-perishable foods they could possibly have grown. It has been my growing conviction that it is possible to meet our agricultural problems without the imposition of any production regulations except those which are actually part and parcel of the voluntary co-operation of farmers in a soil conservation program. But I know this will be possible only (1) if we consistently maintain throughout our whole economy a balance between the producing power of the people and the buying power of those same people as consumers, and (2) if we encourage the growth of co-operatives as a vastly more satisfactory means of enabling the farmer to market his crop in an orderly and advantageous manner than governmental action can ever be.

Even in the conservative Seventy-eighth and Seventy-ninth Congresses there was little opposition to a national soil conservation program. But certain members of the Appropriations Committee of the House regularly made a fight against the appropriations for soil conservation payments. I wondered whether they could be really serious—whether they would have done it if they had thought that they would win.

But there were millions of American farmers who stood to benefit hardly at all, except possibly in the most indirect way, from soil conservation payments or the farm credit system or the expansion of foreign trade or the "Agricultural Adjustment" legislation or from much of the rest of the general farm legislation. Most of it was, after all, directed at helping what may be called the "commercial farmers"—that is, the men who raise substantial cash crops for sale. But half the agricultural income of America, measured in monetary returns, goes to about fifteen per cent of the farms of the country. At the other extreme we find almost half the farms of the nation receiving less than twelve per cent of the agricultural income. Some of these are little more than subsistence farms, where the family efforts produce as much as possible of their own meager living, generally on outworn soil. More of them produce a bale or two of cotton or a little wheat or corn for sale. Thousands of these are tenant farms where only one crop is produced and where frequently much of the crop goes to the landlord as rent. The average yearly cash income of these farm families in many states is about equal to the monthly pay check of a secretary to a city businessman. Throughout the nation their incomes average substantially less than those of common urban laborers. Their children receive the poorest schooling of any group of children in all America. Their teachers are paid but a pittance because there is only a pittance with which to pay them. It is these "low-income" farmers who try to work the eroded, outworn lands.

Yet they are the stuff of which the strength of America once was made—and can be made again. By and large they have probably contributed more men to the fighting forces of the United States throughout her history than any other group in the population in proportion to their numbers. From families such as these came Andrew Jackson, Abraham Lincoln—probably more American presidents than from any other group in the population.

The depression meant disaster to hundreds of thousands of these families—especially if they were in debt at the beginning of it, as most of them, being farmers, were. Thousands of them were forced to abandon their farms and join the roving bands of migrant laborers. For them the Bankhead-Jones Act had come too late and done too little.

The Resettlement Administration created at the very beginning of the New Deal by executive order of the President was designed to make a start at dealing with the problem of poverty on the land in America. Its accomplishments were considerably greater than the barrage of criticism to which it has been subjected would permit anyone to believe. But primarily because of mistaken choice of personnel, blunders were made and a number of foolish projects undertaken, along with some very good ones. In an attempt to improve matters, several of the most extreme members of the staff were dismissed.

Then in 1935 the whole agency was reorganized and given the new name of Farm Security Administration. This agency continued to function until the closing days of the Seventy-ninth

Congress, when the Farmers' Home Administration Act abolished it and provided for the taking over of its functions by the Farmers' Home Administration.

No New Deal agency sailed a stormier course than did the Farm Security Administration. It made mistakes. It loaned too much money to some people in circumstances where there was no chance of their ever being able to pay off the debt. It embarked on certain government-sponsored projects where numbers of farm families were to own the lands jointly. All of these, regardless of some merits which they probably had, eventually fell into bad odor. In the later years particularly, there was some evidence of efforts to persuade farmers to borrow from the agency whether they really needed a loan or not—a practice clearly indefensible. Some types of work were given to FSA to do and were done by it without any kind of congressional authorization. But this was more the fault of the office of the President than of FSA. Apparently, too, there were some on the staff of FSA in certain regions who frankly sought to make of the agency's borrowers a sort of political organization to elect or defeat candidates for public office. There were instances, too, where men were told that if they received their loans from FSA they must become members of a certain co-operative. No true co-operative can be built that way.

But all these things, widely as they have been advertised, were not the real FSA. At its core the agency had a job to do that was as close to the heart of America as any activity in the whole government, for it was the one agency in government which attempted to lift out of a condition of hopelessness and into a condition of economic soundness and physical health a great and deserving segment of America's farm population. Its efforts can be measured by this one standard: are there or are there not numbers of farm families in America who today are working their farms successfully, gaining a good if modest living from their land, and gradually paying off their debts, who but for the help of FSA would have lost their farms, their homes, and their place in the ranks of American landowners? And the answer to that question is an unequivocal yes.

If some of us fought hard for the Bankhead-Jones Tenant Purchase program because it would help farm tenants to become farm owners, we fought equally hard for the Farm Security program because we believed it was absolutely necessary to prevent thousands of farm owners from becoming tenants or wandering laborers.

Through the years this was one of the bitterest fights of all. In the early years there was a deep enough concern over the survival of our very basic institutions to keep opposition to "rehabilitation" programs at a minimum. Grants were made to destitute farm families, especially in the drought areas, with no requirement that they be repaid. Camps were built for the migratory farm workers, and FSA shouldered the unpopular task of becoming a sort of defender of their basic citizenship rights. But most important was the program of rehabilitation loans to families that still clung, though often tenuously, to their land. Two hundred dollars were loaned here, fifty dollars there, two thousand or more in a few cases, at interest not to exceed four per cent, and always to people who could not borrow anywhere else. With the loans went the advice and help of FSA field men in developing farm plans and budgets which included more vegetable gardens, a little livestock to balance the farm operations, a mule perhaps, a piece of equipment, or repairs to some of the buildings.

How much money did it cost? Well, for the year 1939, for example, President Roosevelt recommended an appropriation of $175,000,000 for these purposes—and got it.

Always there was an attempt to reduce the appropriation, first in the House Appropriations Committee and then on the floor. Sometimes cuts were made in the House only to have the money restored in the more liberal Senate, with a resulting compromise in the 'conference committee and in the final bill. For the year 1943 this process provided $120,000,000 all told for the production and rehabilitation loan program, its administration and some minor activities of the agency.

Those of us who supported Farm Security would meet together just before the appropriation bill was to come on the floor. The group contained a number of members of both parties who took little interest in WPA appropriations or other New Deal measures, but who were ready to do anything they could for the rural rehabilitation program.

With the coming of the war and the general increase in prices for farm commodities, the situation of the low-income farm people of the nation was somewhat improved. But the improvement depended directly upon whether or not they had their farms going well enough to produce any considerable surplus for sale. And as the facts became known, it developed that a surprising number of them did.

The demands of the war for food and more food brought to thoughtful people the realization that it was not from the most efficient and prosperous farms that the greatest increase could come, but rather from the formerly inefficient and comparatively non-productive ones. And to a remarkable extent these farmers provided such an increase. In 1942, for example, more than one third of the nation's increase in milk production was accounted for by 463,000 Farm Security borrowers—people who had been considered such poor risks that no one but FSA would lend them money. Ten per cent, again, of the nation's increased production of eggs, chickens, and beans came from FSA borrowers' farms, and so on. One fact about these figures that meant most to me was that they represented increased production of animal products. And that spelled fertility going back into the soil and better hope for tomorrow on these farmsteads.

Another thing was happening too. The FSA borrowers were graduating—not all of them, but substantial numbers. Once when I stopped off at Columbia, Missouri, to see my daughter, who was in college there, I got a call from one of the bankers in that city. He wanted only to tell me that for his part he hoped Congress would keep the Farm Security going because of the number of farm families in that area who were now considered eligible for loans from his bank. They had decidedly not been eligible, he said, before they had received their FSA loans and guidance.

The story of Farm Security can be summed up in a few simple figures. From 1935 to 1943, 1,500,000 farm families received some kind of FSA help—most of it in the form of loans. By December 31, 1942, out of $712,000,000 loaned by the agency, $338,000,000 had been repaid and this was ninety-one per cent of the maturities to that date. In other words, the poorest credit risks of America's farm population had failed by only nine per cent to repay all they owed. But more important than that were some more modest figures. In a Texas county some two thousand families were FSA borrowers in 1937. As a result of the planned expenditure of their borrowed money these families, on the average, increased their net worth from $268 to $407 in that one "hard-times" year. By 1941, for all FSA borrowers in the nation the increase was from a net worth of $871 to $1242. That is to say that the value of what these families owned minus the amount they owed was $371 greater. That $371 represented, we knew, a few head of hogs or a small flock of chickens or a new small building or a piece of badly needed machinery or a tighter farm home against winter. If American farming is in fact a way of life and an art as well as a means of making a living, these things, small as they were, seemed to me of almost immeasurable value to the nation.

However, the story was not all so encouraging as that. There were, as I have said, things wrong with the FSA. Its opponents were busy finding out about this. Its supporters were, I suspect, too hesitant about criticizing and insisting upon correction, though some of that we did. Furthermore, in all the years from 1935, when the agency was established, to the very date of its abolition, Congress never passed a bill authorizing its existence nor did it in any careful way set standards for its operations. The fault lay partly with the Administration, whose general point of view undoubtedly was that an executive order was as good as a law of Congress any day. But it lay mostly with the Congress which, while complaining about the assumption of authority by the executive, still permitted a number of important agencies to go on with their work without taking the trouble to pass a bill authorizing them to do so. The regrettable part of this situation was that, had such a bill been passed, it could have been used to correct the things that were wrong and to bring the program into line with the intent of a majority of Congress with regard to it.

While the fights were going on for and against Farm Security's rehabilitation program, the same sort of thing was happening with regard to the Farm Tenant Purchase program.

Whatever justification there may have been for criticism of the former, it was hard indeed for me to understand how anyone could attack and even attempt to destroy the Tenant Loan program, unless indeed he was actually in favor of tenancy as opposed to land ownership by working farmers. From the very start the tenant borrowers kept their payments more than current. The Bankhead-Jones Act had provided for a maximum of $10,-000,000 for loans in 1938, $25,000,000 in 1939, and $50,000,000 in 1940 and the years thereafter. Every time the appropriation bill came on the floor its opponents would make two main arguments. The first was that the national debt was already very large and that the nation "could not afford these expenditures." This point we were able to meet without trouble for the reason that no "expenditures" were being made since the money was for loans and the loans were proving very safe ones. The second argument was that it was "only a drop in the bucket," and that so few tenants could benefit from the whole affair that it was useless to carry it on. The trouble with this argument was that the first part of it at least was true. In fact defenders of the $25,000,000 appropriation for 1939 (an amount which we obtained only because of the insistence of the Senate, having lost our fight in the House by a vote of 154 to 149) made the very same point. Mr. Pace, of Georgia, told the House that the $10,000,000 had been enough for only two thousand loans in the whole country and that meanwhile the number of tenants was increasing by some forty thousand every year. So we were actually falling behind. Yes, it was true that the attack on farm tenancy was only a drop in the bucket of the need. But we wanted to keep the drop in the hope of eventually getting at least a rivulet.

In 1941 someone conceived and, amazingly enough, the Congress adopted the ridiculous idea of providing that the Department of Agriculture should borrow from the Reconstruction Finance Corporation the funds for farm tenant loans. This meant, practically, that RFC would issue some of its own notes or debentures and sell them to private banks; that the banks would create the money with which to buy them (by writing up deposits on their books for that purpose in favor of RFC) and RFC would then pay the banks interest on this newly created money. Then the Tenant Purchase program would pay interest to RFC on the $50,000,000 loaned to it and would reloan to the tenant borrowers. If Congress had simply appropriated the money for the loans as it had previously done, the full amount of interest paid by the borrowers would have come back to the government. So the net effect of this ingenious device was, first, to pay a subsidy to the banks for their costless act of money creation and, second, to cut down the income of the Tenant Purchase program by the amount of interest paid to the RFC. It was a clever way of trying to make the Tenant Purchase program look less favorable by reducing the income from the loans.

The most dramatic fight came on the very eve of the resignation from Congress of Congressman Marvin Jones, the author of the Bankhead-Jones Act. On that occasion an amendment was offered from the Republican side to cut out the appropriation for tenant purchase loans entirely. Mr. Jones argued against this with tears in his eyes. We defeated the amendment by a very narrow margin. But during the war years, despite our efforts, the program was cut down by congressional action to a point considerably below the $50,000,000 per year maximum allowable under the act. For 1943, for example, the amount allowed—through borrowing from RFC—was $32,500,000.

For some reason which is hard for me to understand it is always much easier to get things done in Congress for people who are already well off than it is to provide some help for the poorer people who need it most. RFC loans to great corporations have aroused little criticism. Even the advancement of $65,000,000 at no interest to the Aluminum Corporation's Canadian subsidiary caused protest from only a few people on Capitol Hill, of whom I am proud to have been one. Measures to benefit the more prosperous farmers went through Congress without difficulty. But it was like pulling teeth to keep alive these efforts to save the small farms and to enable tenants to become owners.

Out of the rising criticisms of the Farm Security Administration as well as the attacks on the Tenant Purchase program came the Cooley Committee, which took its name from its chairman, Harold D. Cooley, of North Carolina. It was a subcommittee of the House Committee on Agriculture commissioned to investigate the charges against the FSA and to bring in recommendations for remedial legislation. For many months this committee traveled about the country, held hearings, asked questions, and discussed their findings. At first many people had assumed that the committee would recommend the abolition of the whole program for the low-income farmers. But the committee was composed of thoughtful men. What they did was to separate in their own minds the good features of the FSA program from the bad ones and to recommend legislation which would correct the abuses and set up the program on the proper foundation of a congressional law. With all the committee's conclusions I have never agreed. I believe on the whole it was inclined to be "tough" on FSA. But, precisely because of that fact, it was possible to win a great fight which otherwise might have been lost. It centered around the Cooley bill, which was the end product of this subcommittee's work.

With the beginning of the Seventy-eighth Congress I was at last elected to the Agriculture Committee by the Committee on Ways and Means. Until I took my place near the bottom of the committee table I had not realized certain significant facts about the make-up of the committee. On the Republican side, out of twelve members all but three came from the Middle West. One was from New York, one from Pennsylvania, one from California. On the Democratic side, out of fifteen members only two of us, Walter K. Granger, of Utah, and myself, were from any other section than the South. In other words the committee represented the "five basic commodities." The main interests of the overwhelming majority of the committee were—and still are—summed up in "cotton, tobacco, wheat, corn, and hogs." One member of the committee owned, with other members of his family, a whole county in the state of Texas, and faithfully represented the interests of cattlemen, of whom he himself was one of the largest in the world.

It was soon apparent that the temper of the committee, like the temper of the Congress as a whole, was decidedly conservative. Even in our committee, measures for the benefit of the low-income farmers were hard to pass. That, however, they could be passed by dint of earnest effort was to become clear before I was through.

There was in our committee deliberations abundant evidence

of a fundamental understanding of the place and problems of agriculture in the economy of the nation which was most encouraging. Had the committee been equipped with a staff of people even half so able in the field of agricultural problems as the smallest section of the smallest bureau in the Department of Agriculture, it could have accomplished even more than it did. As it was, most of the information upon which we were able to base our action came either from representatives of farm organizations or from officials of the Agriculture Department. Both these sources are, of course, entirely proper and valuable ones and should be used to the greatest possible extent by any congressional committee on agriculture. To do otherwise would be to violate basic principles of democracy. But our committee needed its own staff of "experts" whose testimony and advice could be used as a check upon other testimony and as a help in devising, on the motion of Congress itself, the best possible legislation.

There was another interesting thing about the Agriculture Committee, at least from the standpoint of a Democrat. Every congressman looks forward to the time when he may become the chairman of a committee. So Walter Granger and I used to make calculations as to how long we would have to wait—and meanwhile keep on being re-elected—before we might hope to reach that position. Our calculations were, to say the least, discouraging. For there ahead of us sat members from South Carolina, Virginia, North Carolina, Georgia, Alabama, Texas, most of them as young or younger than we were, most of them able men; all of them virtually assured, by the traditions of .the South, of repeated re-election; none of them possessed, so far as we could determine, of senatorial aspirations; and all of them—we honestly did not regret this—in very good health.

During the Seventy-eighth Congress our committee functioned none too well. The chairman was, as we later learned, a sick man, seldom able to give real direction to the committee. He requested the ranking member to be acting chairman in his absence. But he was just active enough so that we were never quite sure exactly who the functioning chairman of our committee was. Little vital legislation was passed out of our committee during the Seventy-eighth Congress.

But with the coming of the Seventy-ninth Congress the situation changed. John W. Flannagan, of Virginia, became chairman of the committee and we began to consider legislation of vital importance. Not only that—our committee held frequent hearings on problems growing out of the impact of the war upon our agriculture. The OPA, the draft, the farm labor supply, and many other matters were discussed, and these hearings had undoubted effect upon the action of the wartime agencies as they affected the farmers of the country.

Our committee handled and passed the bill providing for United States membership in the Food and Agriculture Organization of the United Nations. We passed a number of bills in the field of farm credit, the most far-reaching and controversial of which provided for bringing all government agricultural agencies together under one bipartisan board outside the Department of Agriculture. This bill passed the House but was never acted on by the Senate.

The two bills, however, in which my own interest was deepest were the School Lunch bill and the Cooley bill. Both of them were finally approved by our committee and enacted into law, which was quite enough to make me feel that my service on the Agriculture Committee, brief though it was, was eminently worth while. The Cooley bill was a measure providing for the continuance of the basic program of aid to low-income farmers and for the expansion of the loan program for farm tenants.

The Cooley bill was revised a half-dozen times. Our full committee held three or four separate sets of hearings on it, in addition, of course, to those held already by the subcommittee. Bills to extend quota restrictions on tobacco acreage or to renew the sugar subsidies went through without much discussion. But not the Cooley bill. Time and again, after we thought that all possible objections and suggestions had been presented, new letters would be received from this or that organization asking for new revisions. Then the committee would meet to discuss the bill, to read it, to amend it. I am afraid I shall never forget the contemptuous, almost sneering attitude which certain members of the committee took toward this bill. Always when we should have been ready to take final action on the bill, something would happen, a new objection would be raised, an important committee member would be out of town. Powerful financial interests—yes, and some big farming interests—wanted to kill completely any program of low-interest loans to low-income farmers. For the family-sized, owner-operated farm, particularly the reasonably self-sustaining farm homestead, is the enemy of big-profit corporation farming, the enemy of the conditions that create great numbers of drifting farm laborers forced to work for a mean wage, the enemy of helpless tenancy. Some people have profited from such conditions. Those people did not want a program to help the low-income farmer keep his land, improve it, or enlarge it. Least of all did they want a good program. A well-thought-out program run in accordance with a law passed by the Congress would be harder to kill than would the old battered Farm Security Administration, which had existed only by executive order of the President and only because points of order were waived by special rule on agriculture appropriation bills.

So the delays went on and when, late in the first session of the Seventy-ninth Congress (1945), we finally got the bill reported out of our Agriculture Committee, it was so close to adjournment that the Rules Committee, which was none too sympathetic to the measure, forestalled action during that session.

We started early in 1946. We held some more hearings at the request of some of the committee members. Mr. Cooley and his subcommittee had exhaustive analyses of the bill prepared so everyone would understand it. Still it was objected that "undue haste" was being used. But at last, with some of the tempers of those of us who had worked so long and hard for the bill pretty badly frayed, we secured an agreement that we would vote on reporting the bill. And it was reported favorably to the House. However, there was still the task of obtaining a rule. This was somewhat complicated by the fact that some members of the Agriculture Committee wanted Mr. Cooley and the supporters of his bill to promise that we would not try to bring the Cooley bill to the floor until after the Flannagan bill to consolidate all farm credit agencies under one bipartisan board had been passed by the House. This we would not do, but it was agreed that all members of the committee would appear before the Rules Committee to ask for rules on both bills. We did so. And the Rules Committee did grant the rules.

I had expected a bitter fight on the floor of the House against the Cooley bill. But the long-drawn-out battle I had feared did not develop. There was bipartisan support for the bill and it could be argued that it was calculated to correct practices of the Farm Security Administration about which there had been complaint. All too little was said in that debate, considering the profound importance of the bill. For the law that resulted from it marks a milestone along the very difficult road of proving that Oliver Goldsmith was wrong—that even where a "bold peasantry" has been despoiled of its ownership of land, even where poverty has prevented the development of a good life for farm families, it is still possible to change the course of these sinister trends.

The Cooley-Bankhead bill, as finally enacted into law, places all *direct* lending to farmers by government agencies under the Farmers' Home Administration in the Department of Agriculture. This corporation will perform two main functions. First, to the extent that Congress appropriates funds, it can make loans of not longer than five years' maturity at five per cent interest to farmers who cannot obtain credit elsewhere. Every such loan must be approved by a local county committee. Such loans can be obtained to help finance the planting of a crop or the raising of livestock. But their principal purpose is to enable the farmer-borrower to improve his farm plant, to obtain badly needed equipment, to put in livestock which is absolutely essential to a balanced farming operation. One of the five major policy recommendations of our subcommittee on agriculture of the Post War Planning Committee was: "The development of a broad program to enable farmers to enlarge their family farm unit, where necessary for efficiency; to adopt modern techniques of farming; and to purchase the necessary equipment." These provisions of the Farmers' Home Administration Act were a step toward its practical realization.

The second function of the Farmers' Home Administration is to help worthy farm tenants to become farm owners. It administers the Bankhead-Jones Farm Tenant Act as amended by our legislation of the Seventy-ninth Congress. And those amendments may turn out to be the most important part of the Cooley bill. Not only may the Farmers' Home Administration, with the approval of the local committee in the county, make direct loans to farm tenants or laborers for the purchase of farms; it can also guarantee loans made for this same purpose by private banks. The rate of interest to be paid by the borrower is two and one half per cent in the case of direct loans and three and one half per cent in the case of the guaranteed loans. In both cases the loans run for forty years. In the case of the guaranteed loans, the government of the United States through the Farmers' Home Administration assumes one hundred per cent of the risk and must pay to the bank the entire amount of any default by a borrower. One half of one per cent of each loan is paid into the insurance fund of the Farmers' Home Administration each year for this purpose. Two and one half per cent goes to the bank, which takes no risk whatsoever. Thus, when a bank writes up one of these guaranteed loans, it is acquiring for itself what really amounts to a United States Government security drawing two and one half per cent interest. While most of this interest seemed to me an utterly unjustified gratuity to the banks, nevertheless I agreed with those of our committee who argued that if we could at last achieve a really broad attack upon farm tenancy it was worth it.

The Cooley bill was not perfect. Neither is the law that resulted from it. But they are good legislation. Beyond a shadow of a doubt they represent a hard-won victory for the people. That victory was long delayed. It came none too soon. We found in the agricultural census of 1945 that the percentage of America's farmland in farms of over 1000 acres each had increased from twenty-five per cent in 1920 to no less than forty per cent in 1945. Those figures meant more corporation farming, more tenancy, fewer individually owned small farms. But with the passage of the Cooley bill it became for the first time possible for genuine progress to be made in the long hard task of reversing these trends and bringing more and more of the soil of America under the careful tillage of an owner's hands. To what extent that possibility will be realized depends, of course, on able, dynamic administration of the act and full congressional support of its objectives by appropriations and otherwise. A determined people must see that these two things are done.

Through the recent decades of our history the cities have been draining our farms of their wealth, their strength, and their people. Only in times of deep depression is this trend reversed. Only then, when agriculture can with greatest difficulty support more people, do we seem to realize that real security is impossible except in close association with fertile soil.

There are signs of a change in our diseased national outlook. A literature in praise of rural life is beginning to appear. A few people are seeing the perilous parallel between recent trends in our own country and those which led great civilizations of the past to destruction. The drive for "federal aid to education" has its roots in the clear injustice of our rural areas paying for the education of twice the number of children per capita as the urban areas and then having these same children when grown migrate to the cities, carrying with them a part of the wealth of the community which reared them. But the underlying danger remains. It is symbolized by a thoughtless attitude which regards farming and rural living as appropriate subjects of jokes and city life as the goal of the more able and enterprising among the people.

Even farm people share in this. How often is the most capable child of such a family selected as the one to be educated and prepared to "go to the city," while the less promising children carry on the fundamental work of America and all mankind—on the land?

It was not always so.

The hope of early America was in the land. It was the land giving its increase that built the colonies and bred independence in them. It was the ninety per cent of the population who were farmers that carried the day for Thomas Jefferson in his fight against the reactionary interests of his time. It was, above all, the free land of the West that made it possible for the United States to become in truth and in fact one of the very few free democratic nations the world has ever known. The farmer owns his land and therefore owns a part of the nation to which he owes allegiance. He works the land and hence he shares the experience of every worker. He produces and consumes. He encompasses in his experience the problems of every other group in society. He is the nearest approach to a free man that modern society knows. And in America he has pioneered the development of the co-operative as a means of enabling people of few resources to remain free even in this highly industrialized world.

The conscience of the nation is at last awake to the necessity of soil conservation. Its importance is stressed at every meeting of farm organizations. Other citizens' groups such as Friends of the Soil have been organized specifically to promote it. Conservative cries of "socialism" have thus far failed to check the outstanding soil-building work of the TVA or its production of the almost invaluable "triple superphosphate" fertilizer. Co-operatives on their own account are producing sufficient volumes of fertilizer to have broken the monopolistic practices which prevailed in that industry for so long. The co-operatives, that enable the farmer to stand as a free man in the market place when he sells or when he buys, continue to grow and flourish despite attack and abuse by forces of greed and voices of ignorance. The Farm Credit system, essentially a co-operative system of credit for farmers, stands stronger today than it ever has. Great progress has been made in paying back to the government its original capital investment, and we can look forward to the time when this whole system will be co-operatively owned by the farmer-borrowers. These things are good.

The sometimes bitter battles and the constant hard work of the past ten years have not been lost. Here, in the very place where it may mean most to the future of our country, real success was achieved. I believe our work has made it somewhat more likely that America's "last, best hope"—in her soil, saved and rebuilded, and in her people, owning and loving that soil better than before —will one day be realized.

Chapter 12

FARM "SURPLUSES"
AND HUMAN NEED

In the early thirties the farmers of the United States faced financial ruin. Crops were sold, if at all, for prices that failed to cover bare costs of planting and harvest, to say nothing of upkeep of farm plant and machinery, the maintenance of soil fertility, or interest payments on indebtedness. Ever since the fall of 1929 land ownership had been passing from the farmers who worked the soil into the hands of banks and insurance companies. There were instances of direct action by groups of farmers. Sometimes they controlled the bids on farms put up at auction or stopped the operations of the courts where foreclosures were being prosecuted.

Meanwhile in the towns and cities—and on the land itself—people were hungry. They faced physical ruin. America's children were growing up without enough nourishment to make either strong bodies or strong minds. This hunger was due to no lack of food in the nation. On the contrary, we were told there was a surplus, that we suffered from overproduction. This was hard, of course, for hungry people to understand, but the orthodox economists assured us it was true.

The nutritive value of the foodstuffs the farmers raised was not one whit less than it had been a few years before. The need for it, the real "demand" for it in the human sense, was greater than ever. A dozen eggs, a bushel of wheat, a box of oranges contained just as many vitamins, just as many calories as before. And there were even more people who desperately wanted them. But we were told on every side that the "value" of farm commodities had dropped. We were not told, as we should have been, that the purchasing power of money had been artificially increased and that this one fact gave the appearance of a drop in the "value" of everything else.

In the face of the craziness of the general economic situation there was only one thing for American agriculture to do. If industry was going to lay off men—as it was certainly doing with a vengeance—and thus destroy the cash demand for farm products, the farmers would have to lay off pigs.

Mr. Henry Wallace will probably never live down the events of those early months of the new "farm program." It was he who presided over the reduction of the pig crop as well as other crops. Everybody woke up to the sudden realization that this was wrong. Mr. Wallace prefaced his action with the explanation that it was something like a fourth or fifth best substitute for the right thing to do. He didn't like the method any better than anyone else. But agriculture couldn't control the action of industry, much less of banking, and it had to operate in its own barnyard. The dramatic action of the farmer who killed his pigs was only a minor reflection of the preceding action of shoe manufacturers in "killing" shoes and pay checks of shoe workers, of automobile manufacturers in slaughtering production schedules and pay rolls, of bankers in destroying some eight billion dollars of America's so-called "money."

But the people who hadn't enough to eat just didn't understand. I remember how often I was asked by my friends among the unemployed and especially by members of the self-help cooperatives why they couldn't have the meat to eat. They believed —sometimes mistakenly—that food was being destroyed. Such questions I simply could not answer.

For much too long a time we struggled along, trying to reduce our real wealth enough to make it compare once again with the skyrocketing "value" of the dollar.

But Americans are an intelligent people. And, though with great travail and effort, sanity did return with the passage of time. It came back in the person of Mr. Milo Perkins, president of the Federal Surplus Commodities Corporation, an agency of the Department of Agriculture under Mr. Henry Wallace. The idea was neither complex nor original. But Mr. Perkins began, along in 1939, to make it stick. It was, briefly, that our trouble was not overproduction but underconsumption. On February 24, 1940, Mr. Perkins made a great speech to prove it. It was delivered at the Fourth Annual National Farm Institute in Des Moines, Iowa. In the course of his speech Mr. Perkins said:

"A less drastic, but similar story of underconsumption is told with regard to families who have to get along on an average income of $758 a year. Almost without exception, the percentage increase in purchases is larger as incomes increase to $1200 per year than it is when they increase above that level. The farmer's real stake is in the bottom two thirds of our city families who are fighting for an income of $100 a month on which to exist. That's his greatest potential market—and it's right here at home. The overstuffed third at the top, to which most of us in this room belong, has enough to eat anyway. . . .

"What we know is that many of our people have been underfed or badly nourished. May I repeat—if every family making less than $1200 a year had earned at least $100 a month, under 1935 conditions, this would have increased food expenditures by the groups below $100 a month by about 51 per cent. The total demand for food by families would have been increased by 14 per cent. Agricultural income probably could have been increased directly by nearly one billion dollars. No economist would want to guess how much more could have been added to that income by this increased demand. Prices certainly would have improved on the entire production of most of our crops going largely into domestic consumption."

Mr. Perkins had something concrete to talk about too. He was able to tell the Farm Institute about a new plan that had been put into effect on May 16, 1939. It was known as the Food Stamp Plan. Its purpose was twofold: (1) to make it possible for people who weren't getting enough to eat to buy a dollar and fifty cents' worth of food for only a dollar provided they bought, with the extra fifty cents, foods that were "in surplus"; and (2) thus to expand the market for those "surplus" foods. The only bad part of the plan was that only people "in receipt of public assistance"—that is, people on relief—were eligible. There were others who had managed to get along somehow without applying for relief, yet whose need was quite as great. It seemed too bad to penalize their courageous forbearance.

Mr. Perkins briefly described the plan as follows:

"Under the Stamp Plan, therefore, persons receiving public aid can get surplus foods at the corner grocery store. They have seven and one-half cents to spend for each meal rather than the five cents a meal they formerly spent. That improves farm income as well as the public health. The idea is to eat the surplus—that is, the part that can be consumed in this country."

The Stamp Plan had just begun to operate in a number of cities when the war broke out in Europe. Tragic as it is to say it, this meant war prosperity in America. Employment expanded rapidly, until there were too few people for the jobs instead of too few jobs for the people. What we could not do for the purpose of building a better, more peaceful world was quickly done under the necessity of defeating our enemies. Farm "surpluses," of course, disappeared and we learned, once again, the hard, hard, way, that food is of infinite value to the human race.

How far the Stamp Plan by itself could have gone in bringing about balance between the supply of food and the ability of people to buy it is impossible to tell. But certainly it contained a basic philosophy for the solution of our farm problem which was essentially right. It said that as long as people are hungry there can be no real surplus, nor should farmers be without a market for the food they have produced. It said that the right solution of the surplus problem is to eat it up—to increase the demand until it equals the supply instead of reducing the supply to the level of a cash "demand" which is far below the human demand.

There was one possible danger in the Stamp Plan, however. It might have accustomed people to depending on the government to meet part of their food bill. It might have been used to keep wages and other incomes depressed on the excuse that not so much was needed since part of the food bill was being taken care of by government subsidy.

But the same argument could not truthfully be made against another program begun in a small way somewhat earlier than the Stamp Plan. This was the School Lunch program. It is significant that while the Stamp Plan was discontinued early in the war, the School Lunch program, quite correctly, was allowed to go on and even the most conservative of the Congresses continued to make appropriations for it.

The introduction of the Stamp Plan seemed like a return to sanity, the beginnings of basically right policies. But, while I gave full support to the Stamp Plan, I had from the very beginning an almost religious zeal for the success of the School Lunch program. Nor do I know why I should say "almost" religious. For why indeed did God give seeds the quality of sprouting, and their fruit the quality of nourishing human bodies? Why did He give us as adults the blessed obligation of guarding and caring for children during years of helplessness unless it is our solemn duty to see that the bounty of His harvest is devoted to the nourishment of children's bodies and minds?

No doubt the School Lunch program had many more effective champions than I; but I am sure it had none more devoted.

Most of my life I had been a schoolteacher and a large part of that time had been spent working with homeless boys. I had seen boy after boy come to our school undernourished and almost sick, considered "dumb" and "lazy," lacking emotional stability. I had seen those boys grow and awaken as soon as they began to get enough to eat. I had seen boy after boy score so low on the first intelligence test which we gave him on entrance as to be classified almost subnormal, only to find that as his general health improved, largely because of proper diet, his I.Q. improved too. Psychologists were telling us that an individual's I.Q. can never be changed. They were mistaken.

In Europe, in the terrible years immediately after World War I, I had seen the results of malnutrition among the children— scrawny bodies ridden with rickets, overlarge heads that gave the appearance of being inflated with air or water, eyes whose lusterless sadness bespoke the tragedy of that generation. These were some of the reasons why I believed in the School Lunch program.

Before 1939 about all the federal government did was to buy surplus farm commodities and distribute them free and in a more or less hit-and-miss fashion to certain schools. Something less than a million children were helped in this way.

Meanwhile, however, some alarming and most revealing facts were being brought to light. A nationwide survey of the diets of American families made by the Bureau of Home Economics in 1935–1936 discovered that thirty-five per cent of American families were getting along on diets that were deficient in one or more absolutely necessary elements of minimum nutrition. This was even true of one fourth of the farm families of the country. The poorest families, of course, suffered most—especially their children. We found from another survey that children in families whose income was less than $1000 per year had less than half the milk, less than half the vegetables, less than one third the citrus fruit which children in families with incomes of more than $2,500 a year enjoyed.

Yet most of the children are in poor families. In May 1939 the *Social Security Bulletin* published a table showing how America's children are distributed relative to family incomes. It was found, for instance, that fifty-two per cent of all the children in families of six or more children were in families that were on relief. Twenty per cent of all children in non-relief families of four or more children were in families that had incomes of less than $1000. Only two and four-tenths per cent of the children in this size family were fortunate enough to share in a $3000 income or better.

The idea of America has always been that all the children of all the people shall have the opportunity for a good education. Therefore one of the strongest arguments for the School Lunch program will always be that undernourished children cannot take advantage of their school opportunities, however excellent those opportunities may be.

Each year the appropriation for the School Lunch program would come before the House. And each time there would be a fight made against it. Three principal arguments were used by the opponents: (1) that the provision of lunches at school was "undermining the American home"; (2) that "parents would cease to feel responsibility for their children's welfare"; and (3) that the program was an "unwarranted interference in local affairs by the federal government."

I remember pointing out in debate that the first two such arguments were the same ones that had been used against the establishment of public schools in the first place; that the same dire predictions made then had simply not been fulfilled; that exactly opposite results had been obtained.

I carried on a heavy correspondence relative to the School Lunch program through the years—particularly as my position on the matter became better known. Each year hundreds of letters would come in from teachers, parents, local officials, and others all over the country. From time to time I would prepare brief explanatory statements for enclosure in my replies and for circulation to other people as well. One of these answered directly the third opposition argument:

> There is no extension of federal bureaucracy, no federal control, no "regimentation" about this program. Briefly, the School Lunch program works this way: Commodities purchased by the Surplus Marketing Administration are allocated to state Departments of Welfare, who in turn allocate them to schools which certify that they have undernourished children in attendance. Whatever commodities are available are allotted to schools on the basis of the number of undernourished children, and these children are given free lunches. At the same time, every effort is made to have all children in the school served the same food, so that there is no discrimination whatever between the paying and non-paying children. Local sponsors of the program, who may be Boards of Education, Parent-Teacher Associations, or other public-spirited civic groups, furnish labor, equipment, and foods to supplement those furnished by the Surplus Marketing Administration. The children don't need to even know and in many cases, I expect, don't know that the federal government is giving them anything. There is just a lunch, that's all, where there didn't used to be any.
>
> Administration of the program is left entirely to the local sponsor.

In the beginning the only funds used to help out with the school lunches were the thirty per cent of customs receipts which Section 32 of the Agricultural Adjustment Act says are to be used by the Secretary of Agriculture to broaden the market for farm crops produced in surplus. As the program was expanded after 1939, however, we succeeded in getting through the Congress additional special appropriations for the Stamp Plan and School Lunches. In 1941, $100,000,000 of such supplementary funds were appropriated. By 1941, nearly 5,000,000 undernourished children were getting some sort of noon lunch as a result of what their local communities, assisted by the Congress and the Department of Agriculture, were doing. Sometimes it was a hot lunch, sometimes just milk or orange juice. But it was helping in more ways than one.

On April 9, 1942, I assembled the data which I had been gathering and made an exhaustive speech in the House on the School Lunch program. It was basically an argument for extending the program, wherever local sponsorship and participation opened the door, until every undernourished child in the nation was benefiting from it. I based my appeal first on the fact that such action would open, for the long run, greatly expanded markets for our farm products and, second, on the good it was doing and could do in the future for our nation's children. I pointed out that, as of that date, there were about 9,000,000 undernourished children in America who needed the school lunches, otherwise their physical and mental development alike would suffer. I presented in that speech the findings of a study made in Camden County, Missouri, of the results of two years' operation of the program. Some schools in the county were providing lunches, others were not. And it was shown that in the schools that did provide lunches there had taken place a thirteen per cent improvement in attendance and a nine per cent improvement in scholarship, while in the schools without lunches there had been no improvement at all.

I bought as many reprinted copies of my speech as I could possibly afford, spending almost half a month's salary on them. I sent them out to everyone I could think of who might be a potential supporter of school lunches or who had written me about them.

Now, every member of Congress is in a business which depends for its success upon winning support for his ideas. It is, therefore, not a desire for personal "advertising" alone that makes members hope for good publicity on the things they do. I was no exception to this rule. And one of the happy days of my life was when I picked up a copy of *Pic* magazine for July 7, 1942, and found on page 6 the following article:

THE CHILDREN'S HOUR

U.S. School Lunch Program Is Building a Healthier Nation

We've got to win this war. There is such a thing, however, as winning it and losing it at the same time. We may win it for our generation and lose it for the next. That almost happened in 1918. We can take care of the present crisis, but the future is in the hands of our children. They can take care of the future only if we take care of them now. For that and other reasons, it is appalling to learn there are nine million hungry, undernourished children in the United States.

We have this figure on the authority of Congressman Jerry Voorhis of California, who has made a special study of malnutrition among America's children.

Hungry children endanger our national security. Although there may be no more wars to fight, there will always be crises to test the nation's stamina. There will be struggles against poverty, disease and crime. To fight these evils, we shall need fit, intelligent citizens. Proper nutrition during childhood is a prerequisite of fitness. Mr. Voorhis has a plan which, if executed, would go far toward eliminating malnutrition among America's school children. He would maintain and extend the present Federal free-lunch program which, since 1941, has catered to the needs of 5,500,000 school children in 80,000 schools throughout the United States.

Mr. Voorhis wants his program not only to encompass 3,500,000 children not getting free lunches, but also to subsidize purchase of non-surplus products, so free lunches will be varied and healthful.

There is in Congress much misguided pressure against

continuance of the free-lunch program on the ground that it constitutes a "non-defense" expenditure. Such a contention is exceedingly short-sighted. General Lewis B. Hershey, national director of Selective Service, has pointed out recently that one third of the men rejected by the army for physical reasons were turned down for causes which may be traced to inadequate nutrition. This has cost the Army a quarter of a million men.

From $60,000,000 to $90,000,000 will finance Mr. Voorhis' program. The cost and effort are cheap when one considers the reward; a generation of Americans who are fit to enjoy liberty and are strong enough to protect it.

In many places in the country major emphasis has been placed on what was called the "penny milk program." Under this plan school children are enabled to buy a half pint of milk for a penny, the difference between their penny and the actual cost of the milk being made up by federal subsidy. In 1942 more than 700,000 school children in twenty-nine cities throughout the country who could not afford milk at going prices were getting their half pint a day through the penny milk program. Then the Bureau of the Budget and the House decided to "retrench" and the House followed a budget recommendation to refuse any special appropriation at all for the penny milk or School Lunch programs. Dairy farmers, school people, thoughtful citizens fought against this as hard as they knew how. So did I.

In discussing the situation, the Washington *Post* for March 29, 1942, had this, among other things, to say:

> Cognizant of the fact that all these activities must be curtailed in 1942–43 if Congress withholds a supplementary appropriation, Representative Jerry Voorhis (Democrat), of California, tried in vain to have a 40 million dollar allotment inserted in the Agriculture supply bill when it was brought out on the House floor March 12.
>
> In a five minute speech, Voorhis argued the inconsistency of cutting down on surplus food relief in this country when millions of tons are being shipped abroad under lend-lease—"this, I believe, is right"—to launch identical projects over there.

He quoted figures showing that 15 per cent of all men examined for selective service have been rejected because of nutritional deficiencies. He pleaded that "farmers who are now engaged in this food-for-freedom program have a right to expect that we will not go back on our moral obligation to see that their prices do not collapse."

The Senate fortunately restored a part of the cut that had been made.

But there was one great weakness in the position of the School Lunch program so far as Congress was concerned. All its funds except the customs receipts provided under Section 32 were subject to a point of order if even one member of the House chose to make it. (According to the rules of the House any member can make a "point of order" against any appropriation of money if it is to be used for a purpose to which Congress has not previously given its approval in a legislative act. In other words, to construct a dam, a legislative bill must have been passed saying that that dam is a project approved by Congress. If this has not been done, then any member can "kill" the appropriation by making the point of order that "the appropriation has not been authorized by law." There is a way, used occasionally, to get around this. But it depends upon the willingness of the Rules Committee to grant a rule for consideration of a bill which says that no points of order can be made at all against the bill. And the Rules Committee, especially in recent years, has been refusing to do this more and more often.) The reason for this was that the School Lunch program was in exactly the same situation as the Farm Security Administration's rehabilitation loans. It had never been authorized by act of Congress, only by executive order.

Accordingly on April 9, 1942, I introduced into the Seventy-seventh Congress "H.R. 6914, a bill to amend section 32 of Public Act numbered 320 Seventy Fourth Congress, approved August 24, 1935." The effect of my bill, had it been passed, would have been to authorize by congressional action the appropriation and expenditure of funds for the assistance of local schools in providing lunches for their children.

In each subsequent Congress I reintroduced my bill, making

minor changes and improvements as time went on. In the Seventy-ninth Congress I introduced the bill on the first day of the session and its number was H.R. 149. I spoke for my bill during each Congress a number of times and attempted to arrange for a hearing on it. But the membership preferred, apparently, to go along as we were, appropriating from year to year for school lunches but never taking the basic action which should have been taken by Congress at the very beginning.

During the Christmas recess of Congress in 1944 the subcommittee on Agriculture of the Special Committee on Postwar Economic Policy and Planning held hearings in Chicago. Mr. Zimmermann, of Missouri, was chairman of our committee. The members were Republicans Hope, of Kansas, and Fish, of New York (who had just been defeated for re-election), and Democrats Murdock, of Arizona, and myself from California. I doubt that the problems of American agriculture could have been better summarized than they were in those four days. We heard officials of the great farm organizations, eminent college professors, farm machinery manufacturers, labor leaders, managers of farm cooperatives, several of the nation's leading agricultural economists.

Through the hearings there ran one major theme: the basic difference between American agriculture and American industry is one so obvious and so essential to the very nature of farming as to have almost escaped notice. The difference is this. Agriculture produces an abundance of food and fiber in "bad" times just the same as in "good" times, whereas industry responds to every economic downturn by sharply reducing production in order to maintain price levels. Farmers are the only large group of producers who carry on their work in time of depression in the way which, if generally followed, would enable the nation to make its economic recovery quickly. As a matter of justice, it is clearly a national duty to see that the market for farm products is sustained just as the farmers keep up the supply. The "way out" of our agricultural problems is therefore to devise ways and means of preventing a slump at any time in the effective demand for farm products.

Admittedly that is far more easily said than done. But the best and most vitally interested students of the problems of American agriculture agreed during our hearings that it is the one road that can lead us to an ultimate and long-run solution.

Again and again in the course of our hearings witnesses pointed out that in the School Lunch program we had already made a very good beginning.

As I returned to Washington from those hearings for the opening of the Seventy-ninth Congress, I was determined to press the School Lunch program with all the vigor at my command. And for once the circumstances were favorable for such an effort.

Mr. John Flannagan was the new chairman of our Committee on Agriculture as the new Congress opened. It was my second term as a member of the committee. One of the things I most hoped for was that basic legislation for the School Lunch program could be taken up by our committee and passed. Much to my joy I found that Mr. Flannagan felt very much as I did on the subject and that among the many important measures which he proposed to consider in the committee was school lunch legislation. In fact he himself proposed to introduce a bill.

And he did. It was, even at the beginning when he first introduced it, a better bill than mine. Mine was a simple skeleton authorization bill, introduced in the knowledge that before such legislation could be passed hearings would have to be held and amendments added to the bill. The chairman's bill, on the other hand, contained detailed provisions for the operation of the program, as was of course necessary in any rounded piece of legislation. Naturally, from the day on which Mr. Flannagan introduced his bill, I stopped pressing my own bill and went to work for his.

People outside of Congress find it hard, apparently, to appreciate how the legislative process works. Almost every thing depends upon the committees. Except where 218 members sign a petition and except in the rarest instances when the Speaker agrees to recognize a member in the closing days of a session to bring up a bill by unanimous consent (if he can get it), no bill reaches the floor unless and until the committee to which the bill has been referred has acted favorably upon it. Since committees consist of congressmen and all congressmen are human beings, it follows that a bill which is introduced by a member of the committee to which it is referred has a much better chance than one introduced by someone who is not a member of that committee. Furthermore, committee chairmen have it in their power to call meetings of their committees to consider specific bills. If a bill is reported favorably by a committee, then normally the chairman will take the lead in securing a rule for the bill from the Rules Committee and in defending it on the floor. So it is even more likely that a bill will actually pass if a committee chairman introduces it than if some other member of the committee does so. This is the reason why a few senators and congressmen have their names connected with a number of laws whereas most of them never enjoy this distinction. The few are chairmen of important committees.

Hearings on Mr. Flannagan's School Lunch bill were held by our committee in the latter part of May 1945. The bill before us as the hearings opened was H.R. 2673. But as certain provisions were discussed by witnesses and later in executive session, the chairman introduced two revised bills, H.R. 3143 and H.R. 3370. The later was finally reported favorably to the House on June 5, 1945.

The School Lunch bill hearings will always stand out in my memory as one of the most satisfying experiences of my congressional career. So far as I can recall no witness appeared to testify against the program. However, there was criticism and opposition expressed, sometimes with what seemed to me hard bitterness, by one or two of the more conservative committee members.

Among those who came before our committee in support of the bill were Judge Marvin Jones, then War Food administrator and formerly a member of the House and chairman of the Agriculture Committee; Dr. Thomas Parran, Surgeon General of the United States; and Major General Lewis B. Hershey, director of Selective Service. The Boards of Education of New York City and Chicago sent representatives. So did some of the least populous rural counties of the nation. Mrs. Paul Leonard, chairman of the National Congress of Parents and Teachers, herself a South Carolinian, came to express the wholehearted support of that organization. She told us she believed the school lunch should be made an integral part of the educational system of America, and that a lunch should be available to every school child in the land, with all of them paying for it who possibly could but without discrimination against those who couldn't. She said she was proud of her state of South Carolina because, despite the fact that its resources are much less than those of most other states, it provides a school lunch supervisor for every county in the state.

Some members of the committee raised the question of whether or not the federal government should not leave this problem entirely to the states and localities. But this was answered by representatives of agriculture who pointed out that, under those circumstances, it would be impossible to use the program as a means of putting to good use the food crop "surpluses" which are at times so serious a problem for the nation's farmers.

To me, the high point of the hearings was the testimony of Joseph Barnard Meegan, the executive secretary of the "Back of the Yards Council" of Chicago. He explained that "the yards" were the stockyards of Chicago and that his organization consisted of representatives of 185 churches, labor unions, fraternal groups, racial groups, and schools in that area. He told how a parochial school of one of the foreign-language groups had started providing a noon lunch for its children. He told how the improvement in those children's health, scholarship, and attitude had spread the idea to other schools. He stated that in one Lutheran school the children had gained an average of fourteen pounds in the first three months after the lunch plan was started. He told how not only the children but their families had learned to use more healthful foods. He explained that, in many hard-pressed families with large numbers of children, both parents worked in the "yards," that their hours were most irregular and that only by means of the school lunches could the nutritional needs of these children be decently met at all. Then he painted a picture of how, sometimes at real sacrifice, all the schools, public and parochial, in that area had by that time started to serve noon lunches for their children. He explained that without the federal aid this would have been impossible. Then he told us what would happen if that aid were withdrawn.

One of the points at issue in the committee had been whether or not the parochial schools should be included in the federal aid program. But those of us who believed they should be had no serious difficulty in carrying our point after Mr. Meegan had testified that many of the schools in the area about which he had told his dramatic story were parochial schools.

After the hearings had been concluded the committee went into executive session to read the bill through, to discuss it and to give members their opportunity to offer amendments to it at any point. It was pretty generally agreed that the federal monies should be divided into two parts. Seventy-five per cent would go in a direct grant to the state educational agency in each state. The other twenty-five per cent would be spent directly by the Department of Agriculture for the purchase of surplus foods which would then be distributed, in accordance with the degree of need, to the schools of the various states but always under direction of the state educational authority. There was argument as to what the ratio should be between the federal grants on the one hand and expenditures for school lunches by the states and local school districts on the other. It was finally agreed that for the first two years the bill should provide one federal dollar for each local dollar spent but that for the next year the ratio should be one federal dollar for every two local dollars; for the two years next following, one federal dollar for every three local dollars and thereafter at the ratio of one to four. Some of us felt that the one-to-four ratio was too high for some of the poorer states to meet. We also felt that the increase in the requirement upon the states and localities was too rapid. But the main thing was to secure a favorable report on the bill from the committee, and a majority of the members favored these provisions. All of us agreed that the most important objective of the federal grants was to encourage the states and local districts to provide school lunches and to take as much of the responsibility, both financial and otherwise, as possible. It was a question of how best to accomplish this purpose.

The majority of the committee voted in favor of an annual limitation of $50,000,000 on the amount of money which Congress could appropriate for the program. I believed that this was like putting a child in a strait-jacket at the very period when you wanted him to grow and develop, and argued against the limitation—but to no practical avail.

A bitter fight took place over what was then "Title II" of the bill. (Bills are sometimes separated into "titles." This is done where there are clear divisions as to the type of work that will be carried on under the two or more parts of the bill, where different agencies of government will carry on the work, or where there is some other rather important difference.) The purpose of Title II was to encourage education in nutrition in the schools by a system of grants-in-aid. The idea was that, for the school lunch money to do the greatest amount of good, something about foods and their best use and their different values to the human body should be taught to the children at the same time. But some members saw in this a diabolical scheme to impose federal control upon the local schools. Another feature of Title II was that under its provisions aid could have been given to poor school districts in buying necessary equipment, such as cooking utensils, stoves, and the like for the serving of the school lunches. This seemed important because some schools had had to give up their school lunch programs due to lack of such equipment. We succeeded in holding Title II in the bill as it left the committee, but it was destined to be stricken out by an amendment before it had passed the House.

At last we came to the final question—should the bill be reported out of the committee? There was a rather acrimonious discussion, but at last on June 5, 1945, our committee voted to "report H.R. 3370 to the House of Representatives with a recommendation that bill do pass." The first big hurdle had been cleared.

By this time, however, Congress was in its "drive for adjournment" which always begins around the first of June. A number of appropriation bills still had not been acted on and these had to be passed before the close of the fiscal year on June thirtieth or the government departments affected would be without funds. As a matter of fact the Congress did not adjourn until the end of July, but the month was taken up with other pressing bills and there was no chance to get our School Lunch bill to the floor.

Then, while Congress was in recess, the first atomic bomb ever to threaten mankind's continued existence on this planet was dropped on Hiroshima, Japan, and shortly thereafter Japan surrendered and World War II came at last to an end. The special session of Congress which was speedily called was busied with matters connected with the end of the war and again the School Lunch bill was pushed aside.

In January 1946 when Congress reassembled after the Christmas recess for its new session, we were determined to press as hard as we knew how for early action on our bill. It finally reached the floor on February 19, 1946, and was passed that same day by a very comfortable majority.

In the debate the same arguments pro and con which have already been described in this chapter were used. I had with me on the floor that afternoon the material I had assembled through the years in support of the School Lunch program. In the two brief speeches I made, I could use only the tiniest part of it.

However, one or two of my notes, used during the course of the debate, may be interesting:

> If members are for a farm price support program how do they propose to carry it out without purchases of periodic "surpluses" by the U.S. Department of Agriculture? And if such purchases are made what do opponents of this bill propose to do with the food? Waste it? Dump it abroad? Use it to build roads? Or use it to give America's children, *who need it,* a healthy start in life?

> Answer to Mr. Wadsworth, of New York:
> Under this bill there cannot be one single school lunch served to a single child anywhere in the U.S.A. unless the local people—the people of that community—decide they want it done, do all the work of setting up the program, hire necessary people to carry it out, and give it their sponsorship.

> It is only proposed that in communities where this is the case the local people may apply through their state educational agency for the federal government to pay the cost of a part of the food or to supply some of it from surpluses which the Department of Agriculture will have to purchase anyway if we are to keep faith with our farmers on the price support program.

The bill was amended somewhat. Title II was stricken out. An "anti-discrimination" amendment was adopted, though this was quite unnecessary particularly from the point of view of "minority" groups since there had never been even a charge of discrimination against them in all the years of the program, and whatever "discrimination" there may have been had all been in their favor. A few other minor changes were made. And then the House passed the bill.

It was not enough of course to pass the bill in the House. The Senate still had to act and some of us very much hoped that body would enact an even better bill than we had done. That is exactly what happened. The Senate bill proved to be decidedly more liberal than the House bill. After its passage conferees were appointed from the Agriculture committees of the two houses to agree upon a final form for the bill which would compromise the differences between them. The report of that Conference Committee would then have to be passed by both houses before the bill could be sent to the President for his signature.

For months the conference dragged on. The senators refused to change certain features of their bill and some, though not all, of the House conferees refused to agree to changes in ours. Naturally I hoped the Senate position would prevail on most points, though I did not want the conference report to go so far in the Senate's direction as to endanger its passage in the House. There were long periods when the conferees simply did not meet at all. Then they would have a meeting, fail to agree, and break up again.

Finally, however, the deadlock was broken.

Late in the afternoon of May 20, 1946, almost a year to the day from the date on which our committee had begun its hearings, the conference report on the School Lunch bill was presented to the House. It was a much better measure, from my viewpoint, than I had dared to hope for. The argument over what the maximum limitation on annual appropriations should be had been resolved by providing no limitation at all. The final bill—now the law—simply says "that such sums as may be necessary" are authorized to be appropriated. The requirements for state and local expenditures are, in the final act, more reasonable than in the House bill, the federal government agreeing to match dollar for dollar until 1950. From 1951 to 1955 the localities must spend a dollar and a half before they can receive a dollar of federal assistance and thereafter three dollars for each federal dollar. There is no four-to-one matching requirement in the law. Finally, the conference agreed to annual appropriations of $10,000,000 to help needy schools obtain necessary equipment.

Within a few moments and after a very brief explanation of the final provisions, the conference report was agreed to and congressional action on the School Lunch bill was completed. It became the law of the United States as soon as the President's signature was affixed to it.

As I walked back from the Capitol to my office that evening I felt a genuine sense of uplift. I knew the Congress had been motivated, as always, by practical more than by religious considerations. Nonetheless, it had enacted into law a bill which was in accord with the injunction of our Lord, "Inasmuch as ye have done it unto one of the least of these my brethren, ye have done it unto me." The bill had come from my committee and I had helped as much as I possibly could to secure its passage. Indeed, just three bills which were passed during my ten years' service—the Wage-Hour Act, the Farmers' Home Administration Act, and the National School Lunch Act, were ample compensation for all the hard work, worrisome days, and deep disappointments that filled those years. And of these three acts, the one I care about the most is the School Lunch Act.

I believe the simple reasonableness of that act, if not its basic humanity, will prevent any Congress—even the most conservative—from repealing it.

But there is more than one way to prevent a great objective from being realized. And the objective of the School Lunch Act is nothing less than the ultimate elimination of undernourishment among the school children of the United States. Such a goal can only be reached if we constantly push toward it. The vital questions for tomorrow are, therefore, these: Will present and future Congresses attempt to "save money" at the expense of the health and vigor of the next generation? Or will they with foresight provide funds sufficient to encourage expansion of the School Lunch program in the local school districts of the country until in fact the objective of this act of the Seventy-ninth Congress is attained?

People who are concerned for the future of America will wait and watch with deep interest for the answers to those questions.

Chapter 13

MY BIG "CRUSADE"

I was a college freshman on the day in May 1920 when John Skelton Williams, President Woodrow Wilson's comptroller of the currency, talked himself hoarse and worked himself to the point of nervous exhaustion trying to persuade the Federal Reserve Board not with deliberate intent to plunge the nation into a deflation. But they did not listen. The chairman of the Board pointed out to Mr. Williams that it wasn't good for the country to be as prosperous as it was. People were getting spoiled. Besides, production and consumption couldn't go on expanding indefinitely. Both would have to "accommodate themselves to the availability of finance"! This was just another way of saying that, if the bankers had decided that it was time to deflate, the rest of the nation would have to stop producing so much—and correspondingly reduce its standard of living.

Part of what happened is fairly well-known history. The Federal Reserve Board, influenced if not completely controlled by the nation's biggest banks, suddenly raised its rediscount rate to seven per cent, an almost unheard-of figure. (The rediscount rate is the percentage by which the Federal Reserve Banks "discount" the face value of notes or mortgages or other commercial paper when they make advances to member banks on such paper. Ordinarily the rate is one per cent or less.) This had the immediate desired effect. Banks all over the nation raised interest rates, called loans wherever possible, refused to renew loans, much less to make any new ones. And since most of America's so-called "money" consisted then, as now, of credit on the books of banks, what was really happening was that a lot of the nation's "money" was being not only withdrawn from circulation but destroyed. There were a lot of bankers who knew what the consequences would be and didn't want to help bring on this deflation. But they couldn't help themselves.

As bank-credit money disappeared from circulation the purchasing power of the dollar, of course, rose. And the "value" of everything else went down—not its real value, but its "value" as measured in dollars. The worst impact was on farm commodities because their supply was so abundant and could not be cut down as could that of many industrial goods. In eight short months the selling prices of farm commodities fell, on the average, about fifty per cent. This was not due to any deterioration in the quality of farm crops, nor was it due to any reduction of the need for them. It was due solely and completely to the fact that money, which is the common denominator of all our transactions and the absolutely essential bridge that we depend on to carry goods from producer to consumer, had been deliberately made scarce in order to give it greater power over real wealth.

Most of the farmers were in debt. It was bad enough for them to receive only half as much as they had expected for their crops. But it became ruinous when it came to trying to repay their debts. The money they had borrowed when each dollar would purchase one half bushel of wheat had to be repaid in dollars that purchased one whole bushel of wheat. In other words the farmer who had borrowed the equivalent of two thousand bushels of wheat had to pay back to the bankers the equivalent of four thousand bushels plus interest. No wonder thousands of farms were foreclosed in 1920–21 as in every period of deflation in our country's history. I knew enough farmers in 1920 to understand what was happening to them.

Meanwhile, millions of workers lost their jobs. I knew a good many of them too.

And what was happening to farmers and workers was happening to little businessmen and to everyone else who didn't have either a goodly supply of the dollars which alone were being increased in value or the power to manufacture them. I began to see why the Bible condemned "usury" and why Moses had provided long ago that all debts should be wiped out every seven years.

Why didn't we do something about it? It was indefensible to allow the measure of value of everything in our national life to change as the value of the dollar was allowed to do. It would be just as reasonable, I thought, to let the people who sold cloth change the length of the yard whenever it suited them! The whole situation seemed to me as rank an injustice as anything in all the economic history of mankind, except for human chattel slavery itself.

A few years later I was to be eyewitness to another tragedy, similar in its devastating effects upon a whole society and caused again by a violent change in the value of money. I was in Germany in the winter of 1923–24. Postwar inflation was at its height. I saw people running down the streets to spend the wages they had received a few minutes before, lest those wages lose a quarter of their purchasing power before they were turned into goods. I saw the middle classes of the nation so impoverished on their "fixed incomes" that they could afford neither light nor heat in the bitterness of winter. I saw the "smart" people growing fabulously rich while the hard-working, provident people were losing their life savings. I saw the prelude to Hitler.

Long before I ever thought of running for public office I had started to study this subject of money in earnest. I had been surprised at first to read in Mr. Robert Hemphill's introduction to Professor Irving Fisher's book, 100% *Money:*

> If all bank loans were paid, no one would have a bank deposit, and there would not be a dollar of currency or coin in circulation. This is a staggering thought. We are completely dependent on the commercial banks. Someone has to borrow every dollar of cash or credit which we have in circulation. If the banks create ample synthetic money we are prosperous; if not, we starve. We are absolutely without a permanent monetary system.

I had gone on to read Professor Fisher's book and been deeply impressed with his presentation of the case for one hundred per cent dollar-for-dollar reserves to cover demand deposits. His arguments were unanswerable and his facts irrefutable. I wondered why I hadn't learned any of this at Yale where Professor Fisher used to teach.

Then I talked to a man who was himself a retired banker. He explained to me how it is that the money of America consists mostly of bank deposits subject to check, how that kind of money is created by banks with the stroke of a pen, how it can be destroyed the same way. He showed me how the fact that banks need keep on hand and in reserve only a minor fraction of the money people think they have on deposit enables banks to lend five, sometimes ten times the amount of actual money which they possess; how this is the reason they can create and destroy our money and thus determine its purchasing power and the monetary value of all goods and property and services in the nation. Once I had thought, along with most other people, that the United States Government created the money with which our country transacts its business. I now discovered that all along the private banks had been doing it. I had been thirteen when the Federal Reserve Act was passed and had believed the "Federal" Reserve Banks had something "federal" about them. I thought they belonged to all America. But now I discovered that that was not the case. My banker friend showed me where Senator Glass, author of the Federal Reserve Act in the House, had said:

"The United States Government owns not a dime of proprietary interest in the Federal Reserve Banks. They belong instead to the private banks which are members of the 'Federal Reserve System.' "

After my first election this same gentleman came to see me. We talked for one whole afternoon. He showed me bank statements, facts, and figures. He begged me to go to Washington prepared to work for the reform of the very financial system to which he had devoted his life. I went to Congress with his words ringing in my ears.

By the time I took the oath of office as a representative in the United States Congress, I had already formed certain deep convictions. The first was that, in the absence of certain changes in its monetary system, the nation faces the appalling choice between ever-mounting debt on the one hand and utter helplessness before threatened or actual economic collapse on the other. The second conviction was that, by the adoption of a few comparatively simple measures in the monetary and fiscal field, we could greatly reduce the danger of either inflation or deflation and go far toward assuring a balance between consumer buying power and our capacity for production. We would thus be holding the key to the "economy of abundance" for which all hope but in the realization of which so few believe.

I spoke about our financial system a good many times while I was a member of Congress.

The first time was on April 26, 1937.

It was a great encouragement to me to receive, in the very first few weeks of my service, a letter from some of the older congressmen inviting me to a meeting to discuss monetary legislation. I attended, of course, and found that the group really had two leaders, Congressman Charles Binderup, of Nebraska, and Congressman Wright Patman, of Texas.

A number of meetings were held, and about 130 members formed an organization to work for what we believed would be constructive legislation in the monetary field. At first there was almost complete unanimity in the group. This was when we were discussing what was wrong and the general principles of the remedy. It was agreed that someone should make a statement on the House floor in behalf of our organization and, though I was a new member, I was chosen to do this.

I worked hard on my speech and received considerable help from other members. The speech was directed primarily at problems connected with the twelve Federal Reserve Banks. It analyzed the trouble, which we sought to correct as follows: "First, it is wrong for the bank of issue of the money of the United States —the Federal Reserve Banks—to be the private property of private banking interests.

"Second, it is wrong for our government to have to pay interest on its own credit.

"Third, it is wrong for the American people to have to borrow into circulation the money they need to carry on their business.

"Fourth, it is wrong for one kind of businessmen—about seventy-five big banks and financial houses—to be able to force the government to print money for their use and back it with the government's credit when other kinds of businessmen cannot do the same thing. This leads to financial and industrial monopoly.

"Fifth, the twelve Federal Reserve Banks were created to stop booms and depressions: they were intended to pay all surplus earnings into the Treasury of the United States—see Section 7, paragraph 1, of original Federal Reserve Act; they were supposed to pay interest for the use of government-issued and government-backed money—see Section 16, paragraph 4, of original Federal Reserve Act; they were supposed to prevent the growth of a financial monopoly in this country.

"Sixth, the facts are, however, (1) that the worst depressions in our history have occurred since the passage of the Federal Reserve Act, and that it is at least an open question whether the Federal Reserve Board is at present in a position to prevent another and yet more violent cycle of boom and depression; (2) that the twelve Federal Reserve Banks have only paid about $150,000,000 into the United States Treasury in all their history, and that by the Bank Act of 1933 the franchise-tax requirement that surplus earnings be paid into the Treasury was repealed outright—see Section 7, paragraph 1, of the Federal Reserve Act as amended; (3) that the original provision empowering the Federal Reserve Board to charge interest to the private Federal Reserve Banks for the use of the government's credit has never been carried out, and through all of these years the banks have never paid any interest on the Federal Reserve notes issued for their use; (4) that whatever else may be claimed for our present financial policies, certainly they have permitted a steady growth of financial monopoly, until today seventy-five great financial houses control half the assets of all the 15,000 banks in America and are reaching out to control our industries as well. The small bank is helpless before these great aggregations of capital and is disappearing from our economic scene."

Then the speech set forth five steps to correct the situation. They were:

"First, there is only one agency in the nation which has a moral or a constitutional right to issue money, and that is the federal government. We propose, therefore, to make the bank of issue of the United States—the twelve Federal Reserve Banks—government property.

"Second, when government credit is extended it should benefit all the people equally: the consumers, farmers, wage earners, businessmen, and small bankers as well as the large bankers; and this can be brought about by stopping the process of borrowing credit from a few big banks, and, instead of that, by having the government handle its own financing through its own Federal Reserve Banks, save the interest on bond issues, permit payment of the national debt, and remove the necessity of further bond issues.

"Third, our national debt should be gradually liquidated by replacing it with government money. As this is done the legal reserve requirements against demand deposits should be raised correspondingly so that not a penny of inflation need result.

"Fourth, historically the function of the banks is not to manufacture the monetary means of payment for goods. That belongs to the government. The function of the banks is to receive money, manufactured by the government, as deposits from the people; to safeguard such deposits; to keep the accounts of their depositors; clear their checks thereon; to lend their own capital and the money of their depositors as trustees. They can make ample profits by legitimate service charges for handling accounts and serving as agent and trustee on behalf of their depositors as lenders and investors.

"Fifth, we desire to bring about a complete unification of the banking system of America by bringing all our banks into one truly national system effectively controlled by a really national Federal Reserve Board consisting of twelve members, one from each Federal Reserve district, and employing as a central bank of issue the twelve Federal Reserve Banks, which would be as much a part of the government as the Treasury itself."

My speech was well received on the whole—especially by members of our organization. And one member of the Federal Reserve Board, who for obvious reasons must be nameless, called me on the telephone the next day to say that he agreed fully with what I had said, believed my analysis of what was wrong with the system was "the best he had seen," and would be glad to help our group in any way he could. The fact that he later informed me that, while he felt as strongly as ever on the matter, "his hands were tied" as a member of the board did not greatly dampen my appreciation of what he had said.

As the work progressed a split began to develop in the ranks of our organization. Mr. Patman had introduced a bill which provided simply for the purchase by Congress of the capital stock of the twelve Federal Reserve Banks and for making of them a national central bank. Mr. Binderup had a bill which went much further than Mr. Patman's and included a far-reaching program of monetary reform. The question was, which bill would the group support. A meeting was held to decide this question. Several members including Mr. Patman and Mr. Binderup spoke. A large majority then voted to work for the passage of the Patman bill and to concentrate all effort to that end. Whereupon most of the members who had been for the Binderup bill ceased attending the meetings. I tried my best to work with both factions. We built up a list of more than 150 members, pledged to vote for the Patman bill, but never succeeded in getting it onto the floor. At no other time in my ten years were so many members of the House ready to commit themselves in support of legislation of this sort. Nineteen thirty-seven and 1938 were the years of the so-called "recession" when, as a matter of fact, there was an even sharper decline in economic activity for a period of several months than had taken place in 1929. Many people believed the Federal Reserve Board failed to do all it might have to prevent this. There was also fear that the country might slip back into the condition of 1931–32. An about-face in fiscal policy prevented this, but these were years of concern and uncertainty to say the least.

The interest of some members in the Patman bill, to say nothing of more far-reaching legislation, declined as "deficit" spending was resumed in 1938. The easy, temporary palliative was more attractive than the fight for a basic cure.

By this time, however, my own course had been pretty well charted in my mind. I was going to do the very best I could for the constructive correction of the monetary system. And I proposed to do this not only in co-operation with other members of like mind, but also on my own individual initiative. Early in 1938 I decided to bring together into one speech what I at first thought would be a brief outline of the major features of the monetary and fiscal problem and proposals for dealing with them. When it was reprinted from the *Congressional Record* it turned out to be a pamphlet of twenty-seven printed pages! I called it *Dollars and Sense.*

What I was basically trying to develop was a workable and acceptable method of overcoming the unemployment problem (we still had 8,000,000 unemployed in 1939) without the necessity of continually increasing the nation's interest-bearing debt. Since public works loomed so large as a means of combatting unemployment at that time I conceived the idea of shifting our public works program entirely away from made-work projects and depending instead on such projects as could be made wholly or almost wholly self-liquidating. I prepared and introduced a bill which I called the "Public Works Finance Act." Its principal provision was to set up a government corporation, the Public Works Finance Corporation, which would sell its bonds to the Treasury of the United States and buy the bonds of states, counties, and municipalities issued to finance public improvements. Then the bill provided for the Federal Reserve Banks to discount at zero interest the bonds of the Public Works Finance Corporation. The essential point was that the Federal Reserve Banks would create credit on their books just as before, and buy government securities with it just as before, except that they would receive no interest when they did so. This because the Reserve Banks actually employ the credit of the nation when they buy the nation's bonds or notes. Simplifying the proposal and eliminating intermediate steps, the bill aimed to enable local and state governments to borrow at nominal rates of interest from the federal government for public works construction and to enable the federal government to use the Federal Reserve Bank machinery to monetize the state and municipal bonds. The main objection raised was that the Federal Reserve Banks would receive no income to cover their expenses. My reply to this was, first, that they had a large accumulated and unobligated surplus and, second, that I would have no objection to paying them in honest fashion for the actual cost of servicing the government accounts, which cost would be nominal in any case.

During this same period I also prepared and offered an amendment to the United States Housing Act (slum clearance) whereby the interest on the obligations of the United States Housing Authority would have been turned into income to the nation's taxpayers instead of the banks.

Orthodox finance, however, remained in the congressional saddle and in that of the Executive Department, as was the case all through the New Deal period, and my proposals were not accepted. I would be a rich man if I had a hundred dollars for every official of the government who told me at that time that there was nothing wrong with my proposals but that in his position he couldn't say so out loud.

In the fall of 1938 a number of members who had been leaders for monetary change were either defeated or retired from Congress. There was, therefore, no one on the horizon who appeared inclined to put into legislative form a well-rounded sound program for a scientific monetary system. Apparently that was my job.

First of all I "organized" (in my own mind) a "brain trust" to guide the work. It was to consist of Professor Irving Fisher, America's number-one authority on money, former Senator Robert L. Owen, who still lived in Washington and who was the Senate author of the Federal Reserve Act, Mr. Robert Hemphill, former credit manager of the Federal Reserve Bank of Atlanta, and two men who must be nameless, since one was in the Treasury Department and the other on the Federal Reserve Board. I asked these five men if I might submit a rough draft of my bill to them and then have the benefit of their comments and suggestions. All of them said yes.

Then I went to work on the bill. I obtained copies from the document room of all bills in the field of money which had been introduced in recent years, especially one by the late Senator Bronson Cutting, of New Mexico. I studied all of them carefully and made a list from these bills and from my own head of the main points which seemed essential to such a measure as I was attempting to draft. Only then did I begin to write my bill. Section by section I wrote and rewrote, added to and deleted, changed phrases and whole paragraphs. Night after night I worked in this way.

At last I had a draft that suited me pretty well and I sent copies to the five men. I received from each of them his comments and suggestions. They were in substantial agreement, of course, as to objectives. They were not, however, unanimous as to the methods to be employed in reaching those objectives or, consequently, as to the language to be used in different parts of the bill.

On the basis of their criticisms and proposals I redrafted the bill, including those changes which seemed necessary or desirable. Then I resubmitted it to my authorities.

For several weeks I spent as much time as I possibly could on this job. The final result was H.R. 4931, which I introduced into the House in the spring of 1939. None of the five men with whom I had consulted would, I knew, be completely satisfied with every detail. It represented the synthesis of their ideas plus my own study of the subject, as best I could bring them together.

The main objectives of my bill were: (1) a stable dollar whose purchasing and debt-paying power would not change appreciably from year to year; (2) a means of maintaining a constant relationship between the capacity of the nation to produce and the volume of money in active circulation; and (3) an answer to the problem of ever-mounting debt and a means of cutting the knot that makes our supply of money absolutely dependent on the volume of our public and private debt.

I summarized its main provisions in a speech delivered in the House on July 5, 1939. They were:

(1) That the capital stock of the twelve Federal Reserve Banks be purchased by the government, thus making the central banks of issue of the United States the property of all the people.

(2) That a new Federal Reserve Board be appointed, and that the Board be made the direct monetary agent of Congress to

regulate the value of money, to exercise sole power to issue all lawful money of the United States, and to control the volume of demand bank deposits.

(3) That funds needed for payment of old-age pensions, wages on public works, loans to agriculture and industry, and other recovery purposes be obtained not by borrowing or increase in debt, but by direct use of the nation's credit through its own Federal Reserve Banks.

(4) That this expansion policy be continued until either full employment was restored or the dollar brought back to the value it held in 1926, and that thereafter a stable value in the dollar be maintained.

(5) That as a protection against inflation and in order to assure one hundred per cent liquidity in demand deposits, banks be required to maintain dollar-for-dollar reserves behind all demand deposits and be assisted in establishing such reserves.

(6) That existing governmental controls over banking and all monetary matters be simplified, that guaranty of deposits be extended to savings and time deposits, and that duplicate examinations of banks by several governmental agencies be eliminated.

I kept on with the work, sending out copies of speeches and copies of my bill. I was well enough satisfied with the basic provisions of H.R. 4931 so that, with minor changes to keep it in accord with altered economic conditions, I reintroduced it in every Congress in which I served.

There were weighty reasons why I continued to believe that transformation of the twelve central Federal Reserve Banks into a nationally owned central bank of issue was the first and fundamental step to be taken. I introduced in every Congress a simple bill to do nothing except this one thing. I was under no illusion about the difficulty of securing actual passage of a bill to accomplish this. When I went home during recesses of Congress people would ask me whether any of my monetary bills had passed. This was always a somewhat disheartening experience. For I knew that basic monetary reform, affecting as it inevitably must the greatest economic special privilege ever to be enjoyed by any private interests in history, would be achieved only after a political battle at least equal in intensity to those which raged over the imposition of a federal income tax, the conservation of natural resources, prohibition, or even the abolition of slavery.

One reason I believed that the purchase by Congress of the stock of the Federal Reserve Banks (the Federal Reserve Act specifically gives the government the right to purchase such stock) was so important was given in a speech delivered in the House on April 19, 1940, in which I said:

"Right now it is a function of the Federal Reserve Board to expand the monetary supply when the needs of business and industry require it. This it does primarily by using a device known as 'open-market' operations, whereby government bonds outstanding in the hands of banks are purchased by the Federal Reserve Board with credit on their books. The credit on the books of the Federal Reserve Banks is the credit of the American people and their government. There is no question about that. Furthermore these transactions take place because the inventors of America, the executives of America, the workers and farmers of America have increased production and exchange of real goods and services. Nevertheless, the purchase of those bonds by the Board does not result in a decrease in the public debt.

"On the contrary, the public debt remains right where it was. All that happens is a transfer of bonds from the portfolio of a member bank to the portfolio of the central Federal Reserve Banks. I believe that is wrong. If these Federal Reserve Banks belonged to the people of the United States, as they ought to, and as they could with the expenditure of some $132,000,000 for the purchase of their capital stock, then every time the people of America expanded their production of wealth and there was need and justification for expansion of money in circulation the national debt would be reduced. The Board would then buy bonds with national credit exactly as it does now. The transaction would not need to be changed a single bit. But when government bonds were bought by the Board of a central bank belonging to the people, which the Federal Reserve central banks would then be, then those bonds would belong to a government agency and the public debt would be decreased, the bonds retired, and the interest on them saved to the taxpayers."

In a speech made on January 30, 1940, and repeated with

additional facts and material on May 16, 1944, I argued this question about the Federal Reserve Banks. With more prophecy than I knew I quoted a statement the great English economist, David Ricardo, made in 1824 about the Bank of England. He said:

> If the view which I have taken of this subject be a correct one, it appears that the commerce of the country would not be in the least impeded by depriving the Bank of England of the power of issuing paper money, provided an amount of such money, equal to the bank circulation, was issued by government, and that the sole effect of depriving the bank of this privilege would be to transfer the profit which accrues from the interest of the money so issued from the bank to government.

The Bank of England is now the property of the British people and Ricardo has been proved correct.

Then I went on to point out that in 1928 only twenty per cent of the earning assets of the twelve Federal Reserve Banks consisted of United States Government securities. Eleven years later over ninety-nine per cent of their earning assets were United States Government securities. The business of the Federal Reserve Banks today consists almost entirely of creating money and lending it at interest to the United States Government. When the Federal Reserve Banks buy government bonds, they buy them with credit created for the purpose—with entries on their books. But the people of America pay interest on those bonds from that time on. This sovereign nation has given to these privately owned banks the power to create its medium of exchange. But on the other hand, the Treasury of the United States must raise by means of taxes the money to pay the interest on or to retire the bonds which were purchased with costless credit by these private banks.

As I have said, there was more sentiment in Washington for the measures I was working for than appeared on the surface. Having talked about them to many other people in the Administration, I decided to go to the President himself. I managed to secure an appointment without the customary requirement of stating beforehand what I wanted to discuss. Now the occasions were legion when members of Congress had gone to see the President about some difficult matter, had been ushered into his office, but had barely got started with presenting their problem when Mr. Roosevelt began to talk to them about one of the many things weighing heavily on his mind. So interesting would his discussion prove that the member of Congress would suddenly find himself being told that his time was up and would see the next appointment of the President standing at his side. Frequently the member, so intrigued by what the President had told him, would get clear back to Capitol Hill before he suddenly realized that he never had got around to telling the President about the matter on which he had asked the appointment. Much less had he secured any commitment as to what Mr. Roosevelt would do about it.

I resolved on my way to the White House not to let this happen to me, as, I confess, it had happened on at least one previous occasion.

So when I was admitted to the oval office I said in as loud and clear a voice as I possessed—and before I had fairly crossed the threshold: "Mr. President, I believe the time has come when the Congress should pass a bill for the purchase of the capital stock of the twelve central Federal Reserve Banks."

The President reared back in his swivel chair, took a draught of his cigarette, opened his eyes as wide as they could possibly have been opened, waited just a moment before replying, and said: "Well, why don't you do it?" It was my turn to rear back—at least mentally. I replied that it was hardly within my power, that I had come to see him in the hope of enlisting his support. I recited one or two of the main arguments. Then the President said: "I think we probably should do it. I think the time has come to buy that stock."

"But, Mr. President," I said, "can I tell anyone on the Hill that you said that?"

He hesitated, I thought, just a moment. Then: "Surely, you can. Tell Henry Steagall and Bob Wagner if you want to." (The chairmen respectively of the House and Senate Banking and Currency committees.)

"Can I tell them you hope their committees will take action on a bill?" I asked.

"There wouldn't be much of any other way to do anything, would there?" he laughed.

"No, of course not," I said, "but I want to be sure it's all right for me to quote you to this effect."

He rang for General Watson, his secretary. When he came in the President said: "Call Eccles on the phone and tell him I believe it's time for the government to buy the stock of the Federal Reserve Banks. Ask him to call me back." It was time for me to go. The President smilingly bade me good-by as if this talk were just part of the day's routine.

It certainly was far from that to me. I had got from my talk with the President so much more than I had imagined possible that I could scarcely contain myself.

Back on Capitol Hill a few minutes later I began calling on members of the Banking and Currency Committee, telling them that the bill for the purchase of the Reserve Banks' stock by Congress had the support of the President of the United States. This, I was certain, would be enough impetus to at least get hearings on the bill and perhaps to bring it to the floor.

I was still seeking out committee members when I was called to the telephone in the cloakroom off the House floor. It was General Watson at the White House. "Please don't say anything about what the President told you for a little while. Eccles and he are talking it over. I'll call you in an hour or two." I told the general what I had already done. He seemed a little disturbed but said for me just not to do any more.

I had been afraid this would happen. I was afraid something more was going to happen. It did. About two hours later General Watson called again. This time it was to tell me that the President had decided he had better not do anything about the matter I had discussed with him just now. Mr. Eccles wanted to talk it over with Mr. Currie, a member of the White House staff who had formerly been with the Federal Reserve Board. But Mr. Currie was in China! After he got back and they had a chance to talk it over, the general would call me. I understood.

Just what took place after I left the White House I will, of course, never know. I wonder, however, what might have happened had Franklin D. Roosevelt been left to his own counsels about the question. In the course of time he might, I think, have publicly advocated passage of the bill to make the Federal Reserve Banks a national institution. Or maybe he spoke to me in too great haste.

Needless to say, General Watson never called me again about the Federal Reserve Banks.

With the outbreak of the war the immediate monetary problem became a different one, though the basic principles remained unaltered. Whereas we had been trying to overcome deflation, we now faced grave danger from runaway inflation. The degree to which we failed to pay for military expenses by means of taxation would roughly measure the inflationary pressure. For all the production for war is economic waste, however necessary it may be from the standpoint of national survival. The goods produced in war plants aren't for sale to the people. Therefore the profits and wages which people receive for war production cannot be matched by a corresponding flow of goods to be bought with the money. Furthermore, civilian production in other plants must be artificially restricted to keep it from using up material needed for the war. So, unless we had the courage to levy taxes equal to the cost of the war in terms of consumption of men and materials by the war, we'd get an inflation. We didn't tax that much. We did get an inflation, though some aspects of it were temporarily concealed by price control.

When we failed to tax we had to get the money another way. Very briefly, we got the money to finance the war by adding over $200,000,000,000 to the national debt of the United States. We got part of this money by borrowing from the people. We made up the difference by borrowing from the banks. The difference was very great. Borrowing from the people reduced the danger of inflation because the people gave up some money they had earned or saved when they bought the bonds. That is the only way an ordinary citizen can buy a bond.

But with the banks it was different. More than $100,000,000,-000 of bonds of the United States, mortgages against all the property of all the people of America, were sold to commercial banks and Federal Reserve Banks to finance the greatest war our nation ever fought. They were "sold" in all practical effect for nothing. That is to say, all the banks did was to establish book-keeping credits in their War Loan Deposit accounts in favor of the Secretary of the Treasury. They needed no money to buy the bonds. All that was necessary was that they be banks. They were not even required to have a cent of cash reserves to secure the deposits created in the government's name. The bonds were the only security for the very same bookkeeping entries with which the bonds themselves were bought!

A banker friend of mine explained it to me once this way: "You see, we wanted four per cent instead of two per cent interest. So we just bought twice as many two per cent bonds as we would have bought if they had carried a four per cent rate." What he was saying was that, since he could create as much money as he liked, there was no limit except his own desires to the amount of certificates of the people's debt which he could acquire.

The reader need not take my word for it. Mr. Lewis W. Douglas, ambassador to Great Britain and former director of the Bureau of the Budget, who left that job because the New Deal was, in his opinion, "too radical," wrote in the *Atlantic Monthly* in 1935:

> Banks, when they buy government bonds, rarely pay for them with cash that someone has deposited in the bank. Instead, they create a bookkeeping credit, against which the government is entitled to draw. . . . In a country in which more than ninety per cent of all business is done by the use of checks there is no essential difference between the creation of bank deposits by fiat and the creation of printing press money. Bank deposits, not currency, constitute our chief circulation medium.

Thus, over $100,000,000,000 of brand-new bank-credit, bank-created dollars, sometimes called "invisible greenbacks," were put into circulation during the war. They were inflationary money, too, for the most part, although increased production of civilian goods and the increase in capital plant in the country would have justified some expansion of money in circulation.

It was bad enough to permit so great an inflation. It was worse to saddle soldiers coming back from the war with $100,000,000,-000 of debt which ought never to have been debt at all. If any agency was going to create money to save America it should certainly have been a public agency—an agency of the United States Government—that did it. This would not have been one whit more inflationary than what we did. And it would have left us with $100,000,000,000 less national debt than that from which we now suffer.

I tried my best. I drew two bills with some expert assistance and introduced them. Briefly, they would have prevented the sale of bonds to banks for bookkeeping entries and required that in place of such borrowing the Treasury should issue its own notes in such amounts as might in addition to the tax revenues be necessary to pay for the war. But the bills also declared it to be the policy of Congress to provide for a sufficient increase in taxation to pay currently for the cost of the war as measured in the wastage and destruction of life and wealth. Had such a policy been resolutely followed, no Treasury notes would have had to be issued.

When a bill was presented to the House providing for direct borrowing by the Treasury from the Federal Reserve Banks I offered an amendment which would have required that any such loans be at a zero interest rate. Since the Federal Reserve Banks would use the people's credit to loan to the people, it seemed to me a little stiff to make the people pay interest on it!

My amendment was not adopted. And the Federal Reserve Banks, with a total capitalization of only $156,000,000, "bought" from the United States Treasury some $20,000,000,000 of interest-bearing certificates of the people's debt during the war. How could they? Simply because Congress had given to the Federal Reserve Banks the power to create money. When an institution exercises that power, it can buy a lot of almost anything including government bonds.

The war was costing America the lives of thousands of its finest and noblest young men—and young women too. Beside that cost nothing else mattered so very much. But some of those other costs would have tremendous effect on the hopes of the men who did come back and who would deserve to live in a better world than the one they were being called upon to save.

And among those other costs was this one: a burden of national debt which had started at $42,000,000,000 in 1940 and which was destined to exceed $260,000,000,000 at war's end. Worst of all, we had demonstrated that as a nation we had as yet no clear idea of what to do to meet the great and perilous problem with which a debt of that magnitude would confront us.

In the spring of 1945 Professor Irving Fisher was in Washington and I had opportunity to see and talk to him. He was more deeply concerned than ever about the future of our country, a feeling I earnestly shared. The upshot of our conversation was a decision to draft a new bill aimed immediately at reducing the debt burden and preventing a serious inflation and, over the long run, at monetary stability. After some correspondence we were both reasonably satisfied with the draft and the bill was introduced by me on July 2, 1945. In many respects it was similar to H.R. 4931 but it contained more detailed provision for the separation of the demand-deposit business of banks from their savings and loan business. In describing these features of the bill to the House I said:

"The demand-deposit departments of banks would no longer create money nor would their depositors or the banks ever again run the risk of bank failure; for each demand-deposit department would be required to keep in ready cash the full amount of its demand deposits, on hand or in safekeeping with Federal Reserve Banks held in trust for its demand depositors. Under the terms of the bill banks would be paid honestly for the services which they render. They would be paid service charges for the warehousing of the people's money and for the accommodation they afford for its transfer by means of checks. At present we do not, by and large, pay banks for such services.

"Under the terms of the bill the other department of the banks would be the saving and investment department, the true field of banking anyway. From such departments loans and investment of pre-existing money would be made. The bill provides against the possibility of savings depositors withdrawing their funds without due notice and the lapse of a reasonable period of time.

"Never was the time more opportune for the passage of such a bill. The total amount of demand deposits held by all member banks of the Federal Reserve System as of March 20, 1945, was $61,175,000,000. The total amount of reserves carried by these banks against those demand deposits was $14,605,000,000 on the same date. But these same banks held $67,915,000,000 of United States securities. Thus the reserves held by such banks and the government bonds in their possession exceeded by $21,-345,000,000 the total amount of their demand deposits."

It will be seen from the above figures that some $46,570,000,000 of government securities held by the banks would have had to be used as part of the demand-deposit reserves of the banking system as of March 1945. As the bonds matured they would have been paid off by the government with new money created for that purpose. Every dollar of that new money would have gone into the bank's reserves to replace the bonds. Thus $46,570,000,000 of the nation's debt to the banks would have been paid off in the same manner in which the banks bought the bonds originally— namely with newly created money. In this manner, without a cent of inflation or the necessity of levying a cent of taxes, the national debt would have been reduced by $46,570,000,000 as an incident in the establishment of a sound banking system.

Professor Fisher mailed copies of the bill to a large number of prominent people throughout the nation and received from a very substantial majority of them authorization to use their names in support of the measure. Not at all discouraged by some of the results of the recent elections, he organized a National Anti-inflation and Anti-deflation Committee and came to Washington in the spring of 1947 to arrange for the reintroduction of our bill. In the midst of these efforts, however, his strength failed and after a brief illness he died. In his passing America lost one of her great intellects and one of her most devoted citizens.

A brief three months later Robert L. Owen followed him to the grave.

None of my monetary legislation was passed while I was in Congress. Neither was any other legislation affecting the basic faults and wrongs inherent in the present system. This was not surprising to me, for this is an issue too deep to be lightly carried. It is also too fundamental, too vital, to be forgotten. Furthermore, I know that progress in this direction is constantly being made. There are businessmen in ever-increasing numbers who see its significance. One of them of my acquaintance is ready to spend some of his own money on an educational program if he can find the man to prepare the material in clear enough form to be effective with large numbers of readers. Among the farmers of the nation there is, and always has been, more support for monetary reform than in any other population group. For example the California State Grange is officially on record in support of all the basic principles set forth in this chapter. Industrial workers are showing a growing interest such as never has existed before. The Oil Workers International Union has repeatedly passed resolutions endorsing my monetary legislation. The Minnesota Federation of Labor has taken similar action.

Most encouraging of all was a request I received early in 1946 from Mr. John Connors, director of the Workers Education Bureau of the American Federation of Labor. I was asked to write a series of articles on money for the news service bulletin of the Bureau. Not only did I work hard on these articles but I succeeded in keeping all but one of them within the six hundred words which Mr. Connors told me was the "limit." The articles were syndicated through the Bureau to most of the labor and many of the farm and weekly papers of the country. The reaction to them was heartening and the Workers Education Bureau has reprinted them in pamphlet form.

America needs a monetary system that will provide a dependable "measure of value" instead of a corrupted and variable one, a scientific system that will keep the supply of money in balance with the need for it, a system that will end the usurpation by special interests of the money-creating power which the Constitution vests in the Congress. In or out of Congress the task is for the time being one of education and the awakening of the people. Once challenged by that task, no man can lay it down.

Chapter 14

EQUAL OPPORTUNITY FOR ALL,
SPECIAL PRIVILEGE TO NONE

In governmental circles it has not been the weather about which everybody talked but did nothing. It has been monopoly. Practically everyone has said he was against it on principle. But when it came to a specific problem there was always a tremendous gap between profession and practice. The Anti-trust Division of the Department of Justice and some other people have done their best.

But in the very nature of the case it couldn't be enough. The American people have been steadily losing ground to the forces of monopoly ever since the Civil War. They are still losing ground.

This is one of the central dangers of our time. If the present trend is not reversed, it will cost America the basic qualities in her national life that made her a great nation.

America was first settled by people who came to this new continent to escape the tyrannies of an old one. Her great men have been those who fought for the freedom of the people. That freedom has been denied or threatened at various times and places all through our country's history. Even today millions of our people are not yet completely free. In every age and time the menace to freedom has been concentrated in a few hands of some kind of power—political, religious, cultural, or economic power, power over men's bodies, minds, or souls.

The golden thread that runs through the best traditions of our nation is the struggle to realize the title of this chapter: "Equal Opportunity for All, Special Privilege to None." Every great political movement in American history has been based on that principle. If progressives and liberals of today would regain the strength they ought to have, they must once again make this principle the cardinal purpose of their action and their philosophy.

Life is not divided into watertight compartments. Concentrated power in one field begets the same condition in others. Those who inveigh against the powers of government are all too often the same people who expect for themselves inordinate control over other people's economic lives. Concentrated industrial power brings on corresponding concentration of power in labor unions. Wherever special privilege exists, it is afraid and tries to control the molding of the opinions of the people and the influences that form the "public mind." Moreover, political dictatorships are a result of totalitarianism in the economic life of men. Where monopoly power exploits a nation over the years, one of two things will eventually take place: either the people will rebel and set up a totalitarian government of the left, or else the monopolists, fearful of that result, will create a fascist state to guard their privileges. This is not prophecy alone. It is history as well.

A good many years ago I met a courageous woman who came to our house to visit my mother. Her husband had been stricken with an incurable ailment a few years before. She had had to find a way to support the family. So she mustered all the family capital and embarked on the venture of manufacturing electric-light bulbs. She made a success of her enterprise. So far the story was in the best American tradition. But one day a very polite gentleman came to "offer" to buy her out. She told him she didn't want to sell. He informed her she was making a great mistake since he represented the dominant corporation in this particular field. A few days later he returned. But this time he was not so polite. Had she changed her mind? No, she hadn't. Then it was his painful duty to inform her that unless she did so his company proposed to undersell her until she was forced to give up. It would be better for her to surrender before her resources were all gone. The lady sold her factory.

I also remember the days when sign painters came to the towns and cities of California and other Western states and painted out "First National Bank of Centerville" and then lettered in the words "Bank of America." The people of those towns didn't have any banks of their own any more. They were but subjects of the greatest financial empire America has ever known.

These were homely instances of the most powerful trend in American economic life. *"Big* Steel," and *General* Motors, and *General* Foods, and *General* Mills, and *General* Electric, and a lot of other generals were part of it. So was *International* Harvester Company. Few people seemed to know it but the Du Ponts who ruled the chemical industry controlled General Motors too. And many of these industrial giants were only façades for the real control which rested in the hands of finance: J. P. Morgan and Co., Chase National, National City, Guaranty Trust, Bank of America.

And this was before the war. The war made the situation vastly worse. It is getting worse today.

A few people were concerned. Among them was the Temporary National Economic Committee. It was a joint committee including senators, congressmen, and people from some of the executive departments. Senator O'Mahoney, of Wyoming, was chairman. Great effort has been expended in attempts to minimize the importance of the work of the TNEC. But the only trouble with it was that, from the monopolist's point of view, it was altogether too effective and too penetrating. During my first months as a congressman I used to sit in on as many TNEC hearings as I could. It seemed to me they were getting pretty close to the cancer itself. Some of the committee's findings, after months of the most careful and exhaustive work, were:

"The monopolist limits output."

"Monopoly affords the consumer no protection against extortion."

"Monopoly is not conducive to economic progress."

"Monopoly prevents the full utilization of productive capacity."

"Monopoly impedes the raising of the general plane of living."
And finally the committee said:

"Monopoly threatens the existence of free enterprise and representative government."

That was strong language. But it was true. It had happened in Germany. The monopolies and cartels of that country had given Hitler his chance—on his promise to protect them, in their positions of power, from the wrath of the people. Russian Communism was, at least in part, a reaction from the monopolization of the land of Russia by a few people.

And now America was at war. Her guard was down at home. Probably it had to be. Concentration of economic power was going forward as never before. One reason for this was that it took "big men" to run a war. At least so we were told. Unfortunately we were also told that the only "big men" in the country were in the big corporations. So they came to Washington. They came for a dollar a year salary—and a fifty-dollar-a-day expense allowance. They and their corporate employers were donating their time and efforts.

But in so doing they made all the decisions of the United States Government concerning the war-production program. And a lot of those decisions affected very vitally the future pattern of America's life. It would have been better, it seemed, if the government had hired the very best men it could find—even if they came from little companies—and paid them what they were worth. It was bad practice, surely, to have men on private pay rolls—very big private pay rolls in most cases—making public policy.

The trouble wasn't with the men. It was with a point of view which they couldn't get rid of however hard they tried.

One day I read that one of the senators had introduced a bill to prohibit the hiring of "dollar-a-year men." The bill required that anyone working for the government and fixing public policy must be paid a proper salary by the government and must not receive a salary from any other source. I called the senator and asked if it would be all right with him if I introduced a companion bill in the House. He said it would.

That little bill might have made a lot of difference. There can be no doubt that the "arsenal of democracy" was crippled and delayed by men who were almost as worried about "surplus capacity" after the war as they were about supplying the war at the critical moment. Incredibly optimistic reports about steel, the light metals, and many other vital items were made to the War Production Board. Plant expansion was delayed. It took more than three years for one West Coast company to get permission to construct, out of materials already in its possession, a pipe and wire plant. It was an independent company. Before aluminum plants were built, the overall program was examined by the Aluminum Corporation of America. For months the high-cost, independent copper mines remained idle, because there was opposition to the payment of a subsidy to hold down the price. Three companies control eighty-five per cent of America's copper supply. For months the wrangle over rubber went on. But at last the major oil companies won out over those who wanted to produce from farm products. And then the rubber program went ahead. Most of the plant was built for the use of major oil companies. By that time there was, perhaps, nothing else to do.

Everyone wanted to win the war. The dollar-a-year men, some of them working very hard and very long hours, wanted to win the war. But they didn't want the winning of the war to destroy the system of controlled production which made the monopolistic power of their great corporations possible. And it didn't. The lion's share of the new plant was so built that none but the very biggest companies could ever hope to buy it. And all through the war it was in most cases men on the pay rolls of the industrial giants of America who made the decisions about who should get the contracts, where expansion should take place, who should receive the material.

Not that all the decisions were biased nor more than a few of them dishonest. But these men had been tutored in the school of monopoly. They could not, even to win the war, change the thought habits of a lifetime. The main idea in industry, they will always believe, is to keep supply from getting ahead of demand, to prevent expansion from "going too far."

That monopolistic idea, however, is the very opposite of free enterprise. It is exactly the opposite of what the nation and its people need if they are to escape economic disaster in this atomic age. From the people's point of view, from the point of view of freedom, the object of all commerce and industry is to supply the community with an abundance of what it needs, and then to see that demand remains in balance with supply.

The big corporation men wanted to tap the Elk Hills oil field. At least Standard Oil of California wanted to, and arranged a contract with the Navy whereby it would have been possible to draw heavily on the field. It was the last important oil reserve the Navy had. The only other possible reserve lay in the tidelands around the coasts. The point was that Elk Hills oil was mostly Navy-owned oil. And big business doesn't like publicly owned resources—even for national defense. So if the people's oil could be used up instead of the privately owned oil—so much the better for the major oil companies.

One day in May 1943 a friend from California, Mr. John C. Packard, came into my office. He asked me if I had seen the contract already entered into between the Navy and Standard Oil Company of California. I told him I knew nothing of it. He said he had succeeded in getting hold of a copy of the contract and would let me read it. When I had read it my hair stood on end. The contract had been in effect for six months and its provisions were almost unbelievable. As soon as I could get prepared, I made a speech on the House floor about it. This was on May 21, 1943. I said:

"One of the greatest dangers to true freedom in America is monopoly control of national resources. It is, therefore, nothing short of alarming to discover that last November an agreement was entered into between the Navy and the Standard Oil Company whereby the Standard Oil Company was given the exclusive right and privilege of developing the Elk Hills Navy oil reserve in California.

"Approximately one third of the lands in the Elk Hills field belonged to the Standard Oil Company prior to the signing of this contract and those lands are deeded to the government under its terms. In return for this, however, the Standard Oil Company receives a monopoly of the right to develop and market all the oil in this whole great reserve. . . .

"The Standard Oil Company is to receive for a period of five years the entire production, with no obligation to pay the Navy anything whatsoever during that period. . . .

"This will constitute giving to the Standard Oil Company about 18,000,000 barrels of Navy oil, worth approximately $20,000,000 at present prices and will amount to providing the Standard Oil Company with approximately $20,000,000 of capital at no interest whatsoever. . . .

"Not only for five years but as to the future life of this oil field this contract provides as follows:

" 'Disposal of products: That Standard will buy and Navy will sell Navy's share of production . . . at the average posted market price offered and paid by the major oil-purchasing companies for crude oil and natural gasoline of similar grade and quality in Kern County, California.' . . .

"This provision means that the Navy itself can get no oil from its own reserve except by selling it to Standard and then repurchasing it. Standard will have complete control of the marketing and disposal of all this oil. . . .

"The all-important paragraph in this contract, however, is the following one:

" 'Navy hereby grants to Standard the exclusive right and privilege, subject to the conditions hereinafter provided: (1) To drill for, mine, extract, remove, and dispose of the oil, gas, and other hydrocarbon deposits in or under said lands, together with the right to redrill and repair any wells thereon and to use all property thereon belonging to the Navy.' . . .

"Every competitor of Standard is shut out from any opportunity of having a part in the development of this great field.

"It is quite impossible for me to believe that we could not have obtained such production from this oil reserve as is required by the war without increasing the strangle hold of the oil monopoly upon the nation. And I rise at this time to protest with all the force at my command against this contract."

My speech was the first public discussion of that contract that had taken place, though needless to say many other people were deeply concerned about it and knew far more than I concerning details of the situation.

Shortly after I had finished my speech I was called on the telephone by Assistant Attorney General Norman Littell, then in charge of the Lands Division of the Justice Department. He informed me that he had been working on this same matter and had a great many additional facts which I did not know about. He also told me he would present all those facts as soon as the opportunity offered.

The Committee on Public Lands scheduled hearings. But before the hearings had fairly started it was announced by the Navy and the Standard Oil Company that the contract had been canceled. It wasn't the sort of thing that mixed well with daylight. The Public Lands Committee proceeded with its hearings. A number of witnesses were heard, including Mr. Littell and me. The high point was the testimony of Mr. Littell, who presented detailed facts and figures covering the whole question of the Elk Hills reserve.

The general principles which should govern public policy became more and more clear as the hearings proceeded. And the main one was that the two thirds of the Elk Hills field which belonged to the Navy must not be used as a means of further building up the major oil company monopoly. Instead, it should to the maximum possible extent be reserved for emergency future use in the interest of the entire nation. The best way—indeed, the only sure way—to accomplish this was, it seemed to me, for the Navy to buy from Standard Oil its interest in the field—amounting to about one third of it. I am still of that opinion.

Another solution, however, was finally arrived at. The Naval Affairs Committee held its own hearings and a great deal of public interest developed. A second contract was worked out by the Navy and Standard, in some respects worse than the first one, and a bill was introduced to authorize this contract. The chairman of the Naval Affairs Committee, Mr. Carl Vinson, refused, however, to support this bill and it never cleared his committee. Instead, on June 2, 1944, more than a year after my first speech had been made, the Naval Affairs Committee brought a bill onto the House floor setting forth in legislation the standards that must govern any present or future Elk Hills contract. They were not all I might have desired. But the committee bill was certainly a great deal better than any previous proposal.

Whereas the earlier contracts had provided for joint decisions on all matters, the Naval Committee bill vested absolute final authority in the Secretary of the Navy. Standard could no longer veto a decision about the people's oil. There was to be no advance to Standard of oil for five years or any other period. And neither was the Navy bound to sell its oil only to Standard. It was to be sold by competitive bidding. Finally, and probably most important, much tighter safeguards were provided against the draining of the naval reserve by the Standard Oil Company, a process that had been going on for many, many years. (Petroleum experts— some of them retired naval officers—to whom I have talked point out that every barrel of oil taken by Standard from Elk Hills depletes the underground pressure and will make it more difficult and expensive for the Navy in future to get its oil out of the ground. They believe the field should be closed down completely except for exploratory drilling until national necessity requires it to be opened up.)

The Naval Committee's bill passed, and during the period of the war such oil was produced from Elk Hills as the Navy believed essential to its operations. But the scheme that would have given this richest of all remaining oil reserves on the North American continent over to exclusive control of one major oil company had been thwarted.

The Los Angeles *Times* devoted a whole editorial to paying its dubious respects to me on the Elk Hills proposition. I had, according to the *Times,* deprived the people of California of gasoline, and this was very bad for the "war effort." I had delayed the signing of a contract between Navy and Standard Oil and prevented Elk Hills oil from being used to relieve the shortage.

I was ready to admit most freely that I had played some part in blocking the contract. And further than that, I thought Elk Hills oil ought not to be used at all if it could possibly be avoided —certainly not for ordinary uses such as civilian gasoline consumption.

It is seldom a man has a chance to quote something of which he is genuinely proud and were I to neglect this opportunity I'm afraid I'd not forgive myself. So for the sake of the grandchildren, I hope I'll be excused for including, along with what the Los Angeles *Times* said, the remarks of the Hon. Carl Vinson, chairman of the House Naval Affairs Committee, concerning my Elk Hills work.

> The Committee on Naval Affairs knew nothing about the first contract. The distinguished gentleman from California [Mr. Voorhis] knew of it because the field being located in the West naturally the people of the West would talk about it. He went before the Committee on Public Lands which was holding a hearing in regard to expanding the domain and he called the attention of this committee to what was going on. The distinguished gentleman from California [Mr. Voorhis] in making this exposure rendered to the country the greatest kind of service, because if that contract had gone through the Elk Hills reserve could have been completely dissipated and we would have had no oil in future years.
>
> Speech by Carl Vinson
> *Congressional Record,* June 2, 1944, p. 5290

It is to be observed that even the Naval Affairs Committee of the House of Representatives "knew nothing" of that first indefensible contract.

The fight against the major oil company monopoly was a lot bigger than Elk Hills. I fought the scheme to have the government build an oil pipe line clear across the Arabian Peninsula from the Persian Gulf to the Mediterranean. While the pipe line would have belonged, at first at least, to the government, there would have been but six great private oil companies that could possibly have used it. And these companies had steadfastly refused to share, by sale or in any other way, any interest in or control over their Arabian oil concessions with the government and people of the United States.

We had just learned about the Canol project where the United States taxpayers' money had been spent by hundreds of millions in opening up a great area where all the oil was controlled—and continued to be controlled—by a Standard Oil Company of New Jersey subsidiary. If the people of America were to run the tremendous risks involved in the trans-Arabian pipe-line project, I wanted the people to get something for their money—as had not been the case at Canol. One of the companies that stood to benefit most by the Arabian pipe line was the same Standard of California which had almost gotten away with Elk Hills. It was the same Standard of California which had its vice-president, Mr. Ralph Davies, sitting at the very top of the Petroleum Administration for War in Washington and making decisions affecting the entire oil industry.

I had several things to say about that situation too. I said them largely because of conversations I had with independent oil men whose very existence in business was threatened by the control of governmental decisions by the major companies.

For example, I spoke in the House on October 28, 1943, about Directive No. 70, issued a month before by Mr. Davies, deputy administrator of the Petroleum Administration for War. Directive No. 70 created the "Foreign Operations Committee." It was composed of thirteen members and was given power, as I stated in my speech, "to determine how much oil each country will get and through what companies it will receive it. It was also empowered to determine just how much oil this country is to import and through what companies we can import it." And yet, despite the sweeping nature of the powers granted this group of private citizens, drawing salaries from oil company pay rolls, Directive No. 70 provided that the anti-trust laws should not apply to any action taken by this Foreign Operations Committee.

Who were the thirteen members? I said: "With one exception there is not a man on this committee who can by any stretch of the imagination be considered to represent any other interest than the major oil companies."

That was the story. It still is. America's petroleum business is controlled by the major oil companies. The wartime decisions of the American government were made by those companies. So are the peacetime decisions. My protests got exactly nowhere.

In May 1944 I gathered all my oil material together into one major speech. I gave figures to show that the Petroleum Industry War Council, which was determining absolutely all governmental policy regarding oil included only fourteen members who could be regarded as independent producers or refiners. All the rest were either major oil company, major gas company, or trade association executives. I pointed out that, largely because of special tax privileges enjoyed by oil companies, Standard of New Jersey and its direct subsidiaries had made profits *after taxes* of $121,000,000 in 1943 on total sales of $1,302,000,000. A table was inserted showing the profits of other major oil companies to have been comparable.

The major portion of the speech was devoted to showing how monopolistic control operates in the petroleum industry of the United States and how the oil "shortage" was largely traceable to this monopoly. The major "integrated" companies not only produce crude oil but refine it, distribute it, and sell its products both at wholesale and retail. This is reason number one for their power, for it means that the independent producers have no way of getting their crude oil into marketable form except by selling it to the majors. This is why the majors let the independents take the bulk of the risks of exploration, and why they were not interested in getting an increased price for crude during the war unless the price of refined products was correspondingly increased, as it did not need to be. There are a few independent refineries. Some of the co-operatives are making a courageous start toward breaking the major companies' strangle hold in this field. But this basic factor in major company control still prevails.

Secondly, I pointed out that the major companies own the pipe lines. They have, historically, kept the charges so high that small companies could pay them only with difficulty. Enormous profits have been made; in fact the pipe lines have made more money in proportion to investment than any other branch of the oil industry. Independent producers, to get their oil to market, must use the pipe lines belonging to their major company competitors. To protect this monopolistic position a terrific battle was put on by the major oil companies to induce the government to forget its $150,000,000 investment in the Big Inch and Little Inch pipe lines and seal them up to deteriorate.

On September 30, 1940, the Department of Justice instituted in the district courts of the United States three test suits against the Standard Oil Company of Indiana, the Philips Pipeline Company, the the Great Lakes Pipeline Company. These were to determine whether or not the huge dividends paid to the major oil company owners of the pipe lines were not in fact rebates disguised as dividends and, therefore, violations of the Elkins Act, which forbids the "giving, granting, accepting, or receiving of rebates by any means or device whatsoever" in connection with the operation of petroleum pipe lines.

The government stood, according to Senator Gillette, of Iowa, to recover penalties amounting to some $1,500,000,000 from the major companies. For a while it looked as if major oil company pressure would cause the suits to be dropped completely. But speeches in the House and Senate by Senator Gillette, Congressman Coffee, and me, as well as other publicity, brought the matter to public attention. The suit was not dropped but what did happen was that the government agreed to enter into a consent decree with the companies and allowed eighteen other major oil companies to become parties to the suit and to enter into the consent decree on the day before it was handed down. No wonder they wanted to do so. The consent decree imposed no fines or punishment. It provided only that any pipe-line earnings of the major oil companies which in future exceeded seven per cent on invested capital should be used by the owning companies for "expansion"! The government thus stayed its hand from the collection of any fines, then or in future, though it had what Senator Gillette described as "an open-and-shut case." Why this was done I simply cannot understand. But the judge who read the consent decree remarked that no doubt the government's action was prompted by a superabundance of "the Christmas spirit," since it was near that season of the year.

The third monopolistic control lies in ownership of reserves. At the time of my speech (May 1944) we were being told that America was about to run out of oil. We were being told this, mostly, by the major companies which only a few years before had been insisting on federal and state laws to prevent "too much" oil being produced. It was not the independents who have made seventy-five per cent of the important oil discoveries in American history who told us this, but the majors who at that very moment held 48,920,000 acres of undeveloped potential oil lands either in fee-simple ownership or under lease. This contrasted with the 3,763,000 acres which they had developed. And no one but the major companies knew—or knows today—what underlies those acres. They are held, by and large, by the major companies not so much in order that they may develop them as to prevent anyone else from doing so.

Toward the end of my speech I made five recommendations for action.

"First," I said, "we have inadequate knowledge of the real situation with regard to oil reserves in the United States. We ought to be finding out what underlies the 48,000,000 acres of undeveloped land now held in fee or under lease by the major oil companies. We ought to be finding out these facts through a government agency completely divorced from these huge corporations and serving exclusively the public's interest.

"Second. The basic reason for the oil shortage in the United States is the policy pursued by the major oil companies of discouraging independent investment or exploration, at the same time doing everything possible to control and reduce production in order to be able to maintain artificially high prices and to increase monopolistic control.

"Third. The shackles of monopoly must be removed from the independent companies and especially the independent geologists and engineers. True facts will help and so will a change in the whole situation with regard to pipe lines, so that every one of them will be made, by public ownership if necessary, a common carrier in order to put all companies and all crude-oil producers on an equitable basis.

"Fourth. The determination of government policy must be carried on by people who are government officials and government officials alone. As of June 1943 there were over a hundred men in the Petroleum Administration for War who were on the pay rolls of one or another of the major oil companies.

"Fifth. Independent oil companies should have far more representation in the Petroleum Administration for War than they

have at present. The consumer, the farmer, laborer, and the
great mass of the public should be represented."

Most of all, I wanted to see all the facts brought out where
the people could pass their own judgment. I introduced a resolution for a complete investigation of the petroleum industry.
But it never received even serious consideration. Neither were any
of my other recommendations acted on. How could they be with
the major companies in complete control of governmental policy
and able to come pretty close at times to dictating the action
of Congress itself?

Nonetheless, in concluding my speech I expressed the hope
"that we can restore conditions of healthy competition. Whether
this can be done in the oil industry, I do not know. It may be
that the oil monopoly has grown so powerful that no agency,
except the United States Government itself, can cope with it,
and if this is true, then the time has passed when talk about the
oil business as an essentially private business can have any real
meaning. Private monopoly and democracy cannot live together.
Either the monopoly must be broken so that the people generally can engage freely in the business, or else government will have
to enter the field, not only to take the risk and pay the bills, but
also to participate in the financial gain thereof, even in ownership,
particularly where an exhaustible natural resource is involved."

A year later my hope certainly had not been realized. On the
contrary we were apparently getting ready to continue the sort
of dictation of governmental policy by the oil monopoly that
had gone on during the war.

In July 1946 I read the press accounts of the new "National
Petroleum Council" formed to carry on in peacetime where the
Petroleum Industry War Council had left off. I read the names
of the men appointed by the Interior Department to this council.
A few were independents. Some others, though associated with
major companies, had, at least, clean records so far as law
violations were concerned. But as for the rest, far less could be
said. I wrote the Attorney General asking for the facts and received in reply a summary of Department of Justice records.

What these records showed was briefly this. Of the 85 members
of the National Petroleum Council set up to advise the govern-

ment on oil policy no less than 37 had been indicted at least once and some of them a number of times for violation of the anti-trust laws. And a majority of the 37 had been convicted at least once.

Oil is no more than an outstanding example. There are a good many other lines of business wherein the whole trend of the past few years has been toward greater and greater monopolistic control, less and less of what may properly be termed the "American system."

In the summer of 1943 the fire insurance companies suddenly decided, after losing a lawsuit to the government, that they wanted to be exempted from all the anti-trust laws. They wanted it quickly, too, before the Supreme Court had a chance to confirm the decision of a lower court. Bills were promptly introduced to give insurance this exemption. A California woman wrote me in opposition to the bill as follows:

> It is high time that the practices of various insurance companies and their boards were investigated and brought before the public's attention. Their attempts to dominate and control the insurance business have worked a decided unfairness on the insuring public.
>
> My husband, who is now overseas serving his country, has worked for 17 years in this city as an insurance broker. He realized many years ago the injustice of a few large insurance companies controlling the business, and laying down rules and charging rates which were to their own advantage and no one else's.
>
> All the so-called board companies are banded together by membership in the Board of Fire Underwriters of the Pacific. This board promulgates rates and rules which remove any possibility of honest competition between these board companies at the expense of the insurance purchaser.
>
> These facts you may already have, but I wanted to put in my bit in behalf of my husband who is doing his bit to make the world a better place to live in.

And the venerable Josephus Daniels wrote in his Raleigh *News and Observer:*

The attempt of the fire-insurance companies to be exempt from the antitrust law can be understood from the statements made in the indictment by the Department of Justice. They allege that fire-insurance companies charged $52,000,000 to policy-holders and only returned $18,000,000 in losses in the States of Florida, Georgia, South Carolina, North Carolina, and Virginia. It also says that in the years 1931 to 1940, inclusive, the companies received $436,000,000 and paid out only $197,000,000 for losses.

I spoke and voted against exemption of insurance companies from the anti-trust laws. There were insurance company executives who told me they "could understand my point of view." They knew, while they lobbied in Washington against the anti-trust laws and for "state control" of insurance, that in most states there just wasn't any effective state control. Had there been, I might have felt differently.

They had to compromise somewhat. But in the end the insurance companies got most of what they asked for.

As I studied and worked at this monopoly problem, it became more and more clear that it is largely out of concentration of financial power that concentration of industrial power grows. A few brief sentences in a speech I delivered in April 1944 put another nice wide board in my 1946 political coffin. For they concerned the most sacrosanct of all California business institutions, the Bank of America. I said:

"In my own state of California the Bank of America and its holding company, Transamerica Corporation, already control almost fifty per cent of the financial business of the state. At this moment it is seeking to enlarge that control by buying up the stock of the Citizens Bank in southern California, one of the few remaining strong competitors."

It might not have been so bad if I hadn't advocated on several occasions that Congress should pass legislation giving the Comptroller of the Currency and the Federal Reserve Board powers over bank holding companies corresponding to those already possessed with regard to branch banking. Before a bank can open a branch of its own institution it must secure the permission of these agencies and a finding that such action will not promote banking monopoly. But a bank holding company can go on buying out independent banking institutions to its heart's content and there is no law giving any public agency any power to do anything about it until after such an extension of the bank holding company's power has become an accomplished fact.

Since Bank of America, through Transamerica Corporation, is the greatest bank holding company in the nation and probably in the world, officials of that institution didn't like what I had to say about the need for legislation to protect little banks from being swallowed up. They no doubt liked much better the fact that Congress did exactly nothing about the matter.

It alarmed me to have to say in my speech of April 25, 1944, that "there are only six states in the union which have assessed valuation greater than the assets of the Metropolitan Life Insurance Company." Several other corporations, including Bank of America, are almost as big. It alarmed me quite as much to point out that one man was at that time president of the Anaconda Copper Company, the Diamond Coal and Coke Company, the Butte Water Company, the Andes Copper Mining Company, the Chili Copper Company, and the Chile Exploration Company. This same man was a director of the National City Bank of New York, of the Mining Investment Company, of the American Brass Company, of the Mining Investment Corporation, and of the International Smelting and Refining Company. His case is no more than typical of some two hundred "industrial leaders" in the United States.

But it alarms me much more to be compelled to state that in my opinion the outstanding failure of all the Congresses in which I served was their refusal to do anything effective to break the strangle hold of monopoly on the economy of the United States. Instead, various Congresses took action to actually strengthen monopoly. Dollar-a-year men were permitted to run the war program. The Petroleum Administration for War was left in the hands of major oil company executives. Bills that might have helped were left in pigeonholes. Among these were a number of my authorship—one of which would have prevented the sale of surplus war plants to any corporation where a monopolistic control by that corporation would thereby be increased. The huge Geneva steel plant at Provo, Utah, would have been sold to an independent producer rather than to Big Steel had this bill passed. But it wasn't. And Big Steel got Geneva. Another bill introduced by Senator O'Mahoney and me would have required the registration for public inspection of all cartel agreements entered into by American corporations. Had such a bill been in effect in the years before the war the American people would at least have known *why* they lacked magnesium and synthetic rubber and a number of other vital items.

A third bill embodied a positive effort to encourage small business. It would have made the Smaller War Plants Corporation a regular agency of government under a new name and given it power to guarantee private bank loans to small business under a plan similar to the Federal Housing system. Thus some progress might have been made toward equalizing the credit opportunities of small and large business. Instead of passing a bill like this, Congress permitted the Smaller War Plants Corporation to be abolished. In the midst of all the talk past and present about "tax relief" there has been no serious consideration by the Congress of the proposal for a specific exemption from business taxes of the first $20,000 or $25,000 of earnings. Such an exemption would really help small established business. It would also enable new small enterprises to build up reserves more easily and enjoy a better start. But "tax relief" has generally been provided in very different directions.

While the Congress was failing to take any effective action to protect the American system of economic freedom, there was but one thin line of defense in the whole country against the onrushing legions of monopoly. That was the Anti-trust Division of the Department of Justice. Year after year it was given inadequate appropriations and thus denied enough personnel to do its job effectively. No move was made to bring the Sherman Anti-Trust Law up to date or to implement good enforcement of the law as it stands. It would have been a small investment in freedom indeed to have devoted $10,000,000 a year to anti-trust enforcement, especially in view of the fact that that amount and more too would probably have been recovered in fines, at least in the early stages of genuine enforcement. But Congress regularly allowed only a fifth or a sixth of that amount. When the Justice Department appropriation bill came before the house in 1946 I offered an amendment on the Anti-trust Division item. In appealing for its adoption I said:

"The Anti-Trust Division of the Department of Justice is the one agency of government upon which we depend to defend the American theory and, we hope, the American practice of a free economic system. We propose to appropriate in this bill $1,700,000 for that great purpose.

"Mr. Chairman, I would not offer this amendment had the committee not seen fit to cut the budget recommendation by $200,000. The effect of the committee's action is to give the Anti-Trust Division exactly the same amount of money it had last year, but since then Congress has authorized certain increases in salary, so the net effect of this action is to say to the Anti-Trust Division: 'You have got to fire thirty-five professional employees.'

"Such cases as those having to do with the price of farm machinery, plumbing supplies, the small-loan monopoly, the matter of fluorescent lamps, and a lot of other cases are going to have to be let go by the board unless we give this agency at least the number of people they have now.

"Mr. Chairman, it might be different if we had, as we ought to have, a true national policy of an anti-monopoly nature. But instead of that we let the matter drift, depending entirely upon the action of the Anti-Trust Division to try to protect this nation against the hold of monopoly upon it."

Needless to say, my amendment was defeated.

The vote was interesting. About half the Democrats present voted for the amendment. Another quarter didn't vote at all. The rest of the Democrats, all the Republicans except six courageous souls, and every one of the extreme left-wing (united front) members voted against the amendment.

If the Congresses in which I served permitted and even encouraged the growth of monopoly power in the United States, what will far more conservative Congresses like the one elected in 1946 do? I shudder to think. I imagine the Anti-Trust Division appropriations will be cut still further, that there will be even less concern about the growth of corporate power, that however much "small business" is talked about nothing whatever will be done to give it practical help or protection. At the moment of writing, some of its most capable men are leaving the Anti-Trust Division, despite reports from the division itself that conditions of monopoly are the most dangerous and widespread in all the nation's history.

Meanwhile there is talk in congressional corridors about "tax equality." But this does not refer to correcting, for example, the injustice to all other taxpayers which is inherent in the fantastic "depletion allowances" permitted to oil companies which go on and on after all "development costs" have been fully compensated for. No. It refers to efforts now under way to strike a blow at the co-operatives, the institutions which have demonstrated the greatest ability to stand up to a monopoly and break its power in the name of the people—and freedom.

No true co-operator wants any tax advantages from the government. Nor do co-operatives generally enjoy a single such advantage. All urban consumer co-operatives and more than half the farmer co-operatives pay every tax that any other business pays. And any other business willing to bind itself to refund earnings to its patrons in proportion to their patronage would place itself in exactly the same tax position as the co-operatives. There is a statutory federal corporation income tax exemption granted under severe restrictions to some agricultural co-operatives as an encouragement to farmers to solve their marketing problems and protect themselves against speculative practices by their own efforts. Some farm co-operative leaders believe that repeal of that exemption would actually strengthen the "co-ops'" position, in the eyes of a largely misinformed public. And since true co-operatives have little or no taxable income, it would make little difference in the amount of taxes paid. But it is no such reasonable change that the big business enemies of co-operatives are after. Their objective is to destroy their sucessful co-operative competitors—nothing less. And if Congress should lend itself to such an enterprise it would strike the most telling blow for monopoly in its history.

There is a better way to meet the dangers of monopoly than

the ones discussed so far in this chapter. That is to go into competition with it. True, by definition a monopoly has succeeded in killing off all effective competition in its chosen field. But there is one type of competition which, in some lines of business at least, just can't be killed. That is the competition of a business organization that belongs to its customers.

Now if you are the customer of a business and if the business belongs to you, you are likely to patronize it pretty well through thick and thin. And especially is this true if, along with a considerable number of others like yourself who also own small shares in the business, you have a strong *esprit de corps* about the matter. These are characteristics of co-operative businesses. There are a good many instances in recent history both in this country and abroad where the spirit and organization of a co-operative have proved strong enough to break the control of a monopolistic combination and then to open the way for healthy competition in a certain line of business. Among the classic cases are the ones where the Swedish co-operatives broke the electric-light bulb and the galosh monopolies. (What could be more important in Scandinavia than electric bulbs and galoshes!)

Here in our own country the major oil companies tried for years to prevent the co-operatives (who sell hundreds of millions of gallons of refined petroleum products each year to their members) from getting into the production and refining end of the business. Every sort of device was used. And with good reason. For in the Consumers Cooperative Association region west of Kansas City, in Indiana and Ohio, where the Farm Bureau co-operatives are strong, in Minnesota where Midland Cooperative Wholesale operates, and in some other states the co-operatives now produce, refine, and distribute—all three. The results have been: (1) that the capital costs of the new plants have been paid off out of savings in such unbelievably short periods of time as a year, eighteen months, two years; (2) that a yardstick is thus established to indicate to everyone—not just co-op members—how wide a margin exists between actual costs and market prices for refined oil products; and (3) that healthy competition has at last been introduced into the petroleum industry of America, a competition from businesses belonging to their customers, a competition that cannot be eliminated and behind whose "interference," therefore, other non-co-operative small oil businesses can continue in existence and expand.

The fertilizer trust a few years ago was in a position to charge whatever the traffic would bear. Formulas were kept locked in the inner sanctums of the few companies that controlled the trade. Prices were held at unjustifiably and artifically high levels. Some of the farmers, notably Farm Bureau members in Ohio and Indiana, became angry and decided to do something about it. But instead of going to Washington they first pooled their purchasing power for fertilizer by forming consumer co-ops to act as their agents in purchasing fertilizer. The trust refused to sell to them. They found their own sources of independent supply in the South. But the product was not altogether satisfactory. And so, having already assured themselves of their market—themselves—these farmer co-operatives proceeded to build their own fertilizer plants. By 1940 the Farm Bureau co-operatives were handling fifteen per cent of the fertilizer sold in Indiana and Ohio. Today it is a larger percentage. The Co-ops survived a price war, initiated by the trust, for the simple reason that sensible men don't doom their own enterprises to destruction by refusing to buy from them—even when there are temporary advantages in buying elsewhere.

But the most interesting feature of this story is that, after the co-operating farmers had made and won their fight for a free fertilizer industry in the United States, the Department of Justice won a suit against the fertilizer trust as a "combination in restraint of trade." Important as this was, the Ohio and Indiana farmers had taken a better way, a way which the people themselves could use.

There are voices in the land today which tell us monopoly doesn't matter, that Theodore Roosevelt's "trust busting" was actually a great mistake, and Woodrow Wilson's "New Freedom" only a pious hope. They say that bigness is here to stay, that competition is wasteful, that the people who now control the economic life of the nation "must be" the most capable or else they would never have got where they are. They even oppose such farsighted businessmen as Eric Johnston and Paul G. Hoffman and say they are "too liberal" to speak for American industry. But most of all these voices tell us to surrender. They say that foreign nations are committed to monopolies and cartels, whether state owned or privately owned, and that America must, therefore, adopt the same structure of economic organization. They want the anti-trust laws repealed or at least forgotten. They want us to surrender America's faith in economic freedom. Yet unless we believe in economic freedom for the people we cannot indefinitely protect their political freedom, for freedom is not divisible. It is one sacred principle. Whether or not our nation will continue to seek to establish that principle is the underlying question of our times. Upon its answer will depend the pattern of the future.

Chapter 15

INVESTIGATION OF "UN-AMERICAN ACTIVITIES"— THE DIES COMMITTEE

A monopoly of economic power in a few hands imperils the liberties of the people; a monopoly of political power in a few hands means that those liberties have been destroyed already.

The stock in trade of the demogogic politician is the dire prediction that if his opponent is elected the Constitution will totter and perhaps fall. The danger of totalitarian revolution in the United States is undoubtedly exaggerated.

But it is a danger that no free people can afford to completely discount. Some of them have tried—and suffered terrible consequences.

Every democracy in the world faces a constant dilemma. For in a true democracy all the people of every sort, kind, and shade of opinion are free—even the people who don't believe in freedom. In recent years particularly, such people have taken to forming organizations with the avowed purpose of seizing supreme power, eliminating the freedom of everyone except themselves, and destroying the very democracy that makes it possible for them to form such organizations. To add to the seriousness of the problem, these organizations have been largely guided in their actions by the dictates of foreign governments.

None of the "simple" solutions of this problem will work. No democracy can safely embark on a course of "trying to put ideas in jail." Suppression by law is dangerous business and violates fundamental democratic principles. Furthermore, it only drives the movement underground. On the other hand, those who advise that nothing need be done fail to reckon with the relentless effort, the clever tactics, and the absolute discipline which characterize these totalitarian movements. Cases of outright treasonable acts can, of course, be dealt with under the law. But such cases are rare.

The one thing, therefore, which a democracy can do to protect itself is to put its trust in its own people's good judgment. The American people, for example, will not deliberately choose either a fascist or a communist dictatorship for their country. Not, at least, if they know what they are doing. Democracy's best defense, therefore, lies in exposing all the facts about totalitarian movements and thus enabling its own people to pass intelligent judgment upon them. To accomplish this requires, from time to time, an "investigation of un-American activities."

But if such an investigation is to be effective it must create in the public mind the clearest possible distinction between fascists and communists on the one hand and all loyal citizens, however radical or conservative their views, upon the other.

Such an investigation can become a political instrument pure and simple. It can readily be used to discredit perfectly legitimate minority opinion and thus undermine democracy itself. The whole affair must be conducted with scrupulous care, fairness, and adherence to demonstrable fact.

The line that marks off un-American activities must divide people on the basis of their loyalty. If a man's loyalty is to the United States, its Constitution, and basic institutions, he is not un-American whatever may be his ideas about labor unions or capitalism or the National City Bank or the Wierton Steel Company or the *New Republic* or the Washington *Times-Herald*. If a man's loyalty is to some other country and some other government, or if he is fundamentally disloyal to human freedom and wants to destroy it, then he is un-American even if he is a member of a Chamber of Commerce or of the Congress of the United States.

My account of the work of the Dies Committee cannot, I know, be a wholly objective one. What I write about it will necessarily reflect the part I played and the positions I took. On each issue there were other sides. There was the side of those who sincerely believed the whole business a "witch hunt" and a danger to all the liberties Americans hold dear. Then there was the side of those who believed, with equal sincerity, that the danger to human freedom from totalitarian movements was so great that it mattered very little if the Dies Committee or its members made a "few" mistakes or wrong accusations. There were those who believed the menace of communism so great that corresponding danger from the fascist right should be disregarded. And there were those who believed just the opposite—that fascism was so great a danger that the communists should be forgotten.

I was in the midst of all this. I still am. So are all of us. For these problems will not be solved nor these dangers wholly averted until we have built a society in which men can be both free and reasonably secure at the same time.

The Dies Committee, in my opinion, got off to a bad start. It began on May 26, 1938, when the House passed a resolution, "To Create a Special Committee to Investigate Un-American Propaganda Activities in the United States." As the author of the resolution, Representative Martin Dies, of Texas, became chairman of the committee.

The original resolution could authorize the committee's existence only for the remainder of the Seventy-fifth Congress—a period of about seven months. During that time its work consisted of hearing a heterogeneous series of witnesses, releasing all their testimony without any serious question as to its validity, and writing a rather voluminous report. Some of the witnesses were competent, many of them were not. Some of them were little more than hired purveyors of sensational exaggeration, if not of outright untruth. Some outrageous accusations were made by one witness against certain Californians whom I knew to be as loyal to the United States as any member of the Dies Committee, let alone their accuser. Nor was theirs an isolated case. A congressional committee fails in its duty if it does not see that testimony which will go out over every press wire in the nation is true and can be substantiated.

So, when I returned to Congress after the 1938 election, my mind was made up to oppose continuation of the Dies Committee.

I was not against an effective and proper investigation. In my speech I told the House that "were this committee not continued I should certainly favor the setting up of another committee to carry on that work.

"My vote against continuation of this committee is a vote of protest against its methods. I imagine the resolution will be adopted. If it is, I can only hope that the investigation will be effective in bringing to light facts regarding movements seeking to overthrow our constitutional democracy and substitute any sort of dictatorship for it; and I can only also hope that the mistakes of the past will be avoided."

A few days later Speaker Bankhead called me into his office. He wanted to know if I would be willing to have him appoint me a member of the Dies Committee. One of the former committeemen had been defeated and he wanted me to fill the place. I replied that a number of members of whom I was one hoped he would appoint a certain new congressman from Tennessee. This proposal the Speaker flatly rejected. I then pointed out that I had spoken and voted against the continuance of the committee. But the Speaker said that he had made up his mind to appoint someone who had done exactly that. He said he liked the reasons I had given for my opposition. Would I take the appointment?

It was a hard decision and I shall probably never be sure that I made it correctly. But I had a deep personal affection for Speaker Bankhead and, when he put the matter to me as a thing he would appreciate my doing, I couldn't and didn't refuse.

So I became a member of the Dies Committee on Un-American Activities.

There were some who were at first very pleased with the appointment of this little-known Californian to the Dies Committee, who expected me to play a role of consistent obstructionist to everything the committee might attempt to do. There were others who seemed to take my acceptance of the appointment as evidence that I thought I had been mistaken in opposing the committee and that I would "go along" with almost anything the majority proposed. That both these groups were deeply disappointed in my work on the Dies Committee has been one of my reasons for feeling fairly well satisfied with the job I did.

The hearings during the year 1939 were, to say the least, dramatic. Almost every important leader of the Communist party and the German-American Bund was called before the committee. William Z. Foster, long-time Communist leader, was on the stand when the news of the Hitler-Stalin non-aggression pact came over the wires. A wide assortment of would-be fascist "Fuehrers" stormed across the stage. Leaders of "front" organizations of both the Communist party and the Bund testified. Testimony was taken from disillusioned former members of some of these organizations. The pattern of an attempt to form a united fascist movement in America was revealed. The American League for Peace and Democracy was quite clearly shown to be a "front" organization, substantially controlled by the Communist party. Considerable testimony was taken on Communist efforts, sometimes temporarily successful, to infiltrate and gain control of American labor unions, especially in the CIO.

If, as stated in its annual report for 1939, the "purpose of this committee [was] the task of protecting our constitutional democracy by turning the light of pitiless publicity on the activities of organizations seeking to work the will of foreign dictators in the United States, or to destroy our constitutional democracy and set up a totalitarian regime of some sort in its place," then that work was genuinely advanced by these hearings. The case against the Communist party and the German-American Bund as organizations fitting that definition was copper-riveted.

But on December 11, 1939, there took place an occurrence which, in my opinion, not only violated fundamental principles of decent committee procedure but which would be interpreted as a deliberate attempt to protect a vested interest against legitimate criticism. When I read the newspapers that day I found that the "Committee on Un-American Activities" had charged in a report that "a great part of the current popular and official attack upon advertising is the direct result of Communist propaganda in the field of consumer organizations." The report was played up in the newspapers in such manner as to leave the impression that attempts on the part of consumer organizations or government agencies to insist upon honesty in advertising was part and parcel of a communist program. A number of individuals and organizations of consumers were accused of being communist or "communist-dominated" in the committee report, according to the press accounts. I managed to secure a copy of the press release made available under date of Monday, December 11, 1939, by a "Subcommittee of the Special Committee to Investigate Un-American Activities." From it, I discovered that the "subcommittee" consisted only of Mr. Dies and that the entire "evidence" was a statement by J. B. Matthews, who up until a short time before he had been hired by the Dies Committee had been associated with a consumers' organization which was not accused or mentioned in the report.

I knew nothing of the background of this action. No discussion had ever taken place in the committee with regard to consumers' organizations, advertising, or anything else dealt with in the report. And I was certain that if procedure of this kind were continued it would destroy any effectiveness the committee might hope to have. Therefore I wrote and released to the press the following statement:

> I have defended and will continue to defend the work of the Dies Committee insofar as it has presented substantial facts regarding communist, Nazi, or fascist activities in America on the basis of full and open hearings and competent evidence.
>
> But the circumstances surrounding the release of this so-called report on consumers' organizations leave me only one course of action. That is to disavow and disclaim any responsibility whatsoever for the report and to state publicly that it was released to the press by a suddenly appointed one-man subcommittee before other members even knew such a report was in process of preparation, that not a single hearing has been held on any of the matters contained in the report, that none of the persons men-

tioned has ever been called to the stand, that committee members have done no work at all in this field, and that the entire report is purely and simply the opinion of Mr. J. B. Matthews, who in spite of his past connections with a consumers' organization other than those attacked in the report sits as sole investigator, judge, and juror on the whole consumers' protective and co-operative movement in America.

If anything is undemocratic in the world certainly this procedure is. The only decent thing for the committee to do now is to hold full and complete hearings on this matter and let facts developed in such hearings speak for themselves, whatever they may be. The organizations and persons attacked in this report are entitled to this. So are the millions of people who know that consumers' organizations are the very antithesis of the whole philosophy of communism and fascism. They have been the foundation of the successful democracies of Finland, Sweden, Norway, and Denmark, the very nations now under attack or threat of attack by Red Russia.

To this day, I do not know why the Matthews report on consumers' organizations should have been issued in the clandestine manner in which it was. My concern was hardly alleviated by the fact that the hearings I proposed were never held. Why they were not held I cannot explain—especially since on the basis of what I have later learned I believe some of the charges made by Mr. Matthews against certain individuals were probably valid. However, his general conclusions, in my opinion, were neither valid nor defensible.

I never could forget this incident. And I never felt any assurance as to "what might happen next," after that.

In January 1940 the committee issued its annual report for the year 1939. That document and the annual report for the year 1940 are, in my opinion, factual, fair, and able papers. And they contain information which the American nation very much needs to have. To me, those reports are worth the effort, the worry, the criticism from both "right" and "left" that were part and parcel of my work on the Dies Committee. Taken together with a voluminous document popularly called the "Red Book" and containing a mass of documentary material regarding the aims, purposes, tactics, and methods of operation of the Communist party and a similar document, the "White Book" on the German-American Bund, these reports will for a long time serve very well the legitimate and necessary purpose of an investigation of un-American activities. They can guide Americans working for progress along genuinely democratic lines and can help us to avoid falling into either communist or fascist traps. These reports resulted from true committee action. They were prepared by the committee acting as a whole. Needless to say, I signed both of them.

In its issue of January 15, 1940, *Time* magazine summarized the report for 1939 in part as follows:

> Evenly divided between discussion of Fascists and Communists, made up of 15,000 well-chosen words, the report had not a line to justify the hell and damnation that preceded it. It began: "Every modern democratic nation is confronted by two pressing problems. The first is the preservation of the constitutional liberties which their people have gained through the years of struggle, the second is the problem of adjusting their economic life to the difficulties of the machine age. . . ." Although rival groups seek power and influence by exploiting economic distress, attempting to undermine democracy, main problem in combating them is to avoid taking action "which would undermine the fundamental structure of constitutional liberty itself."
>
> Report high lights:
>
> The German-Russian pact crippled U.S. Communist and Nazi groups, just as the Communist Party was gaining its greatest influence as an anti-Fascist force, the Fascists as an anti-Communist force.
>
> Not more than 1,000,000 U. S. citizens have been seriously affected by essentially foreign or un-American activities.
>
> The Communist Party is a "border patrol" of Russia, led, financed, dominated and directed by Russia for the benefit of Russia. U.S. workmen "have borne the brunt of the Communist efforts" and suffer most from them, but

have resisted so successfully that only ten or twelve of some 48 C. I. O. unions are "more than tinged" with Communism.

We believe that the committee would render a disservice to the Nation if it left the impression in its report that there is anything in the present situation to cause anyone to lose faith in the American people as a whole or their devotion to their basic institution.

There were others who thought considerably less well of the 1939 report than did *Time*. The *People's World*, West Coast Communist party organ, was downright angry about it and centered its attack upon me. Its editorial of January 23, 1940, was written during the period of the Russo-German non-aggression pact, when World War II was still a war of "capitalist imperialism" against Germany, according to the Communist "line" of the hour. And what this Communist organ had to say about the report is, I believe, proof of the correctness of my belief that what communists on one hand and fascists on the other fear most is their isolation in the public mind from all sincerely democratic and non-totalitarian groups in the population. For note the feverish effort in the editorial to persuade all progressives and liberals that if anything is done against communists it will also be done against American liberals and that, therefore, they should make "common cause." Here is what the *People's World* had to say:

> The "liberals" are waking up, perhaps too late, to the scurvy trick played upon them by their fellow "liberal" on the Dies Committee, Jerry Voorhis. Waking at the eleventh hour, they are attempting to lay the blame on Martin Dies, though the plain fact is that if Voorhis had not voluntarily helped, there could be no trick.
>
> It all originated in the pleasant but false idea of the "liberals," including Voorhis, that the Communist Party can be outlawed "without interfering with democracy" (meaning liberals and liberalism and social reformists of the kind once called "New Dealers").
>
> All agreed that the Communist Party ought to be outlawed, because it opposes America entering the imperial-

ist war, which the "liberals" insist is a war for democracy. The pretext could be that Communists are "foreign agents" —a theory invented by Dies, but adopted by the liberals.

Martin Dies, of course, has different ideas. A majority of his committee, and Dies, himself, are aiming at outlawing not only Communists, but everything and everyone democratic, progressive or "liberal." But, since the committee is asking for more money and new authority from Congress, the way to get it is not to reveal its real aims, but, as one liberal reports in alarm, "to create the wholly false impression that Dies and his majority have changed."

So Jerry Voorhis was "allowed" to re-write the committee report to Congress because Dies wants to keep the committee going, and when a new appropriation is granted, Dies can step in and run the committee in the same old way. The report as re-written by Voorhis was gladly hailed by the "liberals" as fine stuff.

It denounced Communists even harder than the original report, written by Dies but suppressed. And it rejected the idea that "liberalism and communism differ only in degree." It spoke highly of civil liberties which it proposed to take away from Communists, but not from liberals and progressive Democrats. It tipped its hat in passing to unemployment which it said, without proposing any, should have "solution." And—it asked Congress for more money for Martin Dies.

The work of the committee for the year 1940 attracted less public attention than that of 1939, probably because most of the "main attractions" in the way of witnesses had been heard in the previous year. It was during 1940, however, that a bill of my authorship was enacted into law. So far as I am aware, this bill is the only measure ever to be considered by the Congress which was opposed by both the Fuehrer of the German-American Bund and the secretary general of the Communist party. The committee's annual report for the year 1940 stated:

> One of our members introduced legislation which will require such foreign-controlled agencies as the Communist Party and the German-American Bund to make a public

record of all pertinent facts concerning themselves. This bill was passed unanimously by both Houses of Congress. In its effort to evade the provisions of the Voorhis Act, The Communist Party has now made the gesture of "severing its connections with Moscow."

Some of my liberal friends criticized me severely for introducing this legislation. But the Washington *Post,* itself a liberal newspaper, summarized the argument for the bill editorially on April 8, 1940, as follows:

Undercover political organizations have no place in a democracy. Government by the people is predicated upon the assumption that all groups will seek their objectives through persuasion, open discussion and the ballot box. When any faction resorts to secret devices and intrigue it takes an unfair advantage of the system under which it is permitted to operate. Particularly is that true when elusive political organizations are affiliated with foreign governments which free people have good reason to distrust.

One charge frequently made against the Dies Committee was that it "failed to investigate fascists and Nazis." And it was true that the committee never had on its staff anyone who had had intimate connection with fascist or Nazis organizations, whereas in J.B. Matthews it did have a staff member who knew the communist movement intimately. I also believe that a far more thorough job was done in exposing communist "fringe" or "front" movements than was done with regard to corresponding co-operators with the Nazis or fascists. But when I re-examine the report for the year 1940 and recall the work that was done in that year, I find it hard to agree with those who say that the committee did not try, during that period at least, to uncover all the evidence it could on all types of totalitarian movements in the United States. Indeed, this report for 1940 featured the findings of the committee on the German-American Bund and allied organizations.

Just where such an organization as the Ku Klux Klan is to be catalogued is a question arousing violent debate. For even as it wraps the flag about itself and vows to combat all the nation's enemies, it will undermine the basic institutions of democracy by taking the law into its own hands, employing intimidation, and spreading religious or racial prejudice.

During this period the committee did observe in practically all its official action the definitions of un-American activities which it had itself laid down. In the annual report issued January 3, 1941, the committee said:

> The committee's view is that a great gulf lies between those who, because of attachments to foreign powers and dictators, are basically disloyal to America and those who simply hold unorthodox economic views and, hence, advocate changes in the status quo which they sincerely believe would benefit the majority of the American people.

What that language clearly meant was that the mere holding of minority views on economic or social questions was not an un-American activity. It meant that so long as an individual or group was committed to seeking its ends within the framework of the American Constitution and in a spirit of loyalty to our country, the committee would leave them alone. For a considerable period of time the committee did. It centered its work, as it should have done, on those seeking to overthrow our institutions by force, and especially those guided in such efforts by foreign powers. One of the clearest examples of this was when a Washington policeman breathlessly brought to the committee rooms the brief case of the secretary of the Socialist party organization in Washington, D.C. He thought surely he would receive profuse thanks for having brought to light such "subversive" material. He had "lifted" it out of the man's stranded automobile—rather questionable action from a civil liberties point of view. But Chairman Dies merely said: "No, we're not concerned about the Socialists. Send the secretary back his brief case."

Whatever opinion may be regarding their economic views, the fact is that socialists are among the bitterest opponents of the communists. Postwar Europe has demonstrated that fact repeatedly. Socialists believe in and adhere to constitional processes, personal liberty, and peaceful change. Moreover, American socialists hold their convictions and decide their course as free people and are in no respect subject to foreign control as are the communists. The chairman's action was, I took it, a forthright holding to the principles of the 1940 report.

But if the committee as a whole was doing its job well, a good deal less could be said of related happenings. Speeches and pronouncements by individual committee members, based on investigators' preliminary reports or "something in the files," were an all too frequent occurrence. House members who were not even Dies Committee members somehow obtained speech material from the committee files. Without any findings or action by the committee and without notice to other committee members, someone would make a speech saying that "the committee had evidence to indicate" that such and such a person, organization, or group was engaged in un-American activities. Lists of persons in some government department, labor union, or other organization were released to the nation in this manner with an "un-American" brand on them. The press, naturally enough, I suppose, ate such matters up. Then protests would begin to come in from persons named, almost always with the result that at least some of them would be found on more careful examination to have been falsely accused. It is quite true that some of those who cried the loudest were not falsely accused at all. But the entire work of the committee was severly damaged by such mistakes, to say nothing of the effect on the injured people.

It was the contention of myself and some other members that the observance of a few simple rules of procedure would avoid all this and keep the committee on the track. I tried each time the committee was renewed by the House to get that body to impose such rules on our committee. The House never did so. Neither would a majority of the committee vote to impose the rules upon itself. The proposed rules were described editorially by the San Francisco *Chronicle* on January 24, 1940:

> What Messrs. Casey and Voorhis proposed was that the committee should be told to hold executive sessions at least once a week; to issue no statements and press releases until

they had been submitted to the entire committee and approved by a majority; to attempt to call as witnesses all persons accused in testimony by others of un-American activity, and to bind members not to make unauthorized charges or predictions as to future revelations. . . .

These proposals seem mild, perhaps too mild. How they they could "hamstring" any proper efforts is beyond our understanding.

No rules of procedure were adopted, however, and from time to time I was compelled to publicly state my protests and disagreements to "unilateral action" by other members which I believed mistaken or wrong or unfair. Furthermore, toward the close of 1941 the whole tenor of the committee began to shift. More and more it veered away from the policy laid down in the report of January 1941. "Attacks on the capitalist system," or even the painting of dark pictures regarding living conditions of tenant farmers or some other group began to be filed by the committee as evidence of an un-American point of view.

One day in June 1942 I was called on the telephone and told there would be a committee meeting that same afternoon to consider a report. When I got there I found it to be a report on "Subversive Activities Aimed at Destroying Our Representative Form of Government." As I have explained, the committee had for some time been meeting to discuss reports with opportunity for members to at least present their point of view and suggest changes.

But this time—and indeed from that day on—it was different. Exactly what had taken place I don't know, but I have had the feeling that a decision was taken somewhere about this time that the majority "just wasn't going to bother with Jerry" anymore. I could either take the reports or leave them alone.

Four members of the committee attended this meeting. Mr. Dies himself was not present. I suggested that we read the report, paragraph by paragraph, as we had done on previous occasions. This was promptly voted down. A series of motions was then made to approve various portions of the report. All the motions carried 3 to 1. The statement was approved and went to the press that afternoon.

The report purported to be a defense of Congress as an institution against attempts to destroy it. It began by showing that it was an aim of communist tactics to discredit and attempt to destroy parliamentary bodies everywhere. No one, of course, would disagree with that. But then it attempted to make the case that criticisms of Congress and attacks upon its members, then current, were part and parcel of a communist scheme. This was nothing short of ridiculous. Even such organs as *Life* and *Time* were, the report said, somehow involved. The main attack, however, centered on the Union for Democratic Action, an avowed anti-communist organization from its very inception and one which at the very time of Hitler's attack on Russia had warned American "liberals" in an official statement that "the foreign policy which the new situation requires must not persuade us to relax our vigilance against Communist penetration into the liberal and labor movement."

Why, then, this report? Because the Union for Democratic Action had just issued a report urging the defeat of certain congressmen and senators. I now know that great pressure was put upon the committee to "do something" to counteract this. And the committee had responded, in direct violation of its own statements of its own principles.

As soon as I could I prepared a minority report. The majority report was released to the press June 25, 1942. My minority report, signed only by myself, was not filed until July 7. Some of its paragraphs will make clear the point of view I was trying to express:

> This minority report is not prompted by any desire to defend the recent publication by the Union for Democratic Action of an analysis of Congress' voting record and a list of people it recommends for defeat. . . .
>
> The minority of this committee has learned to hold in sincere respect many members of Congress with whose views on certain matters he does not agree, but whose personal integrity he never would question. . . .
>
> To give so fragmentary an interpretation of the attack on Congress as this comes perilously close to outright deception, and to imply that the Communist party is the

source of attacks on Congress is to run the risk of stifling all such criticism and, as stated above, depriving democracy of its basic element.

Furthermore, this criticism of Congress has reached into most smaller newspapers in the whole country and practically every metropolitan daily as well.

It has been heard night after night over the radio. It is a sort of national pastime.

To criticize and attack the publications of the Union for Democratic Action is the obvious right of every member of Congress. To do a constructive job of protecting the independence, power, and position of the national legislature is the clear duty of every earnest American and particularly every member of Congress. But for the majority of this Committee on Un-American Activities to say that the Union for Democratic Action is responsible for the nationwide attack that has been made upon Congress in recent months is, in the opinion of the minority, ridiculous. To imply that this organization is in any way dominated by or a front for the Communist party is contrary to the facts of public record. And for the majority of the committee to say in effect that, although the Union for Democratic Action is neither communist nor communist-dominated, nevertheless it is un-American because some of its members are radicals, is to put the Committee on Un-American Activities in the position of judging people not on the basis of their fundamental loyalty to the United States and its constitutional form of government, but on the basis of the particular economic beliefs which they may hold and which are not in accord with those of the committee.

All the minority is contending for is the right of loyal American citizens to disagree politically with a majority of the Dies Committee without being branded as subversive and un-American.

It is at least interesting to observe that the Union for Democratic Action so roundly attacked by the Dies Committee is the same organization which on January 4, 1947, called a meeting in Washington, D.C., which resulted in the formation of Americans for Democratic Action, an organization of liberals and progressives, from which communists and their fellow travelers have from the beginning been absolutely barred. In its first official statement, the A.D.A., child of the U.D.A., said:

> We reject any association with Communists or sympathizers with communism in the United States, as we reject any association with Fascists or their sympathizers. Both are hostile to the principles of freedom and democracy on which this Republic has grown great.

As I sat with those members of the A.D.A. and voted to issue that statement, I could not help remembering what had happened when I was a member of the Dies Committee. I was, to say the least, glad I had issued my minority report.

But there was one more minority report to come.

On December 29, 1942, I received a letter from the secretary of the Committee on Un-American Activities, enclosing a draft of the committee's annual report to the House for the years 1941 and 1942. (No such report was issued for 1941.) The letter stated that "due to the fact that it will not be possible for a majority of the committee to meet prior to the expiration of the present Congress I respectfully suggest that after you have gone over the report you notify me as soon as possible of your approval or disapproval, or of any changes you wish made in the report."

In other words, there was to be no committee meeting at all on the annual report. Members had all of four days to read and digest it and to either approve or disapprove! It was a foregone conclusion that a majority of the committee would approve the report without change. I did not believe it a good report, but there was no opportunity to go to work to improve it, or to secure agreement from the other members to a fair compromise between our respective views. Any proposed changes would have had to be mailed to other members at their home addresses in their districts, since most of them were not in Washington at this time. It would have been utterly impossible to receive replies before the January third deadline. So I informed the committee I could not sign the annual report for 1942. I went to work on a minority report.

It was a year since Pearl Harbor had brought America into active participation in the war. Our country was fighting the most powerful enemies it had ever faced. I believed the report of the committee should have been written with but one idea in mind—that of helping to win the war—and that it should therefore have been powerfully focused on forces, people, and influences which were giving aid or comfort of any kind to the enemies of our country. It did, of course, contain material of this sort. But its major emphasis was criticism of our own government for failure to act more drastically on recommendations made to it by the Dies Committee.

Surely there was nothing any more serious than for totalitarian agents to gain positions in the government of the United States. Certainly if any such had done so they should be rooted out. But it was elementary that, whoever the real Nazi, Japanese, fascist, or communist agents were, they would not be people whose names were publicly listed as members of controversial organizations. Finding them was a job for the FBI, not for the Committee on Un-American Activities. The committee was not a secret service agency and could only do its work by means of publicity and exposure, devices hardly calculated to promote the apprehension of persons guilty of espionage or treason. The committe, not the FBI, had to tell the country the story of Un-American activities. But the FBI, not the committee, had to discover the basic facts on which the story could be built. Hence, when this annual report complained that more action had not been taken against "eleven hundred and twenty-four Federal government employees who were members of organizations which this committee has found to be subversive" (to quote the language of the annual report for 1942) I could not help pointing out in my minority report just how those 1124 names had been compiled.

The committee had obtained lists of four organizations: the Washington Committee to Aid China, the Washington Bookshop, the Washington Committee for Democratic Action, and the Washington branch of the League for Peace and Democracy. It had sent to the Justice Department every name that appeared on any one of those lists. In at least one case, I was certain that the list was only a mailing list.

I said in my minority report:

> The fact that a person's name was carried on its list by one of these organizations seems to me to constitute no substantial evidence of "subversive" activity, especially since in many instances the person's name was included without any action on his part or even his knowledge. For these reasons, it is not surprising to me that investigation by the Department of Justice failed to disclose that there was any evidence of "subversive" activity or point of view in the case of more than a very small fraction of the people contained on these lists.

To find out that these organizations with the innocent names were, at times, influenced, if not controlled, by certain communists had taken the Dies Committee a long, long time. How then could the committee expect a clerk in the Department of Agriculture who gave three dollars to the Washington Committee to Aid China to know she was "contributing to the coffers of Moscow"?

If there were any communists in the government, I wanted them out as much as I wanted the fascists out. But I thought it outrageous to state that 1124 employees of the government were "subversive" when in all but a handful of cases the only evidence in the committee's possession were the lists of four "front" organizations, as to three of which these had been, up until very recently, no reason for the ordinary uninformed citizen to be even suspicious. The committee failed also to take account of when these 1124 people's names had been placed on the organizations' lists, or what they had done when they first heard of the charges of communist infiltration into it. Somewhere along the line they had gotten on the list of either the Washington Committee for Democratic Action or the Washington Committee to Aid China, or the Bookshop or the League for Peace and Democracy. That was all. It certainly wasn't enough to base a charge of subversion.

So I dissented from the committee's annual report for 1942. It was the first time since I had become a member of the committee that I had been unable to sign an *annual* report.

I was heartened to find my action approved by the New York

Herald Tribune, which printed the following editorial on January 5, 1943:

> Representative Voorhis, of California, has long been an extremely valuable member of the Dies Committee. . . . When, therefore, he comes out in sharp dissent from the committee's latest report he should and will be listened to. His objections are on three main grounds: first, that the report was prepared without consulting individual committee members and was presented to them on a "take it or leave it" basis; secondly, that it offers no guide by which the American people might identify enemy agents and resist their propaganda, and, thirdly, that it is "inaccurate" in its charges respecting the retention of "subversive" Federal employees.
>
> We have heard relatively little from the committee or Chairman Dies since September, 1941, when the latter wrote a letter to the President accusing Leon Henderson, Price Administrator, and more than fifty of his aids of communist affiliation and demanding their removal from the Federal pay roll. The evidence he produced was flimsy in the extreme, consisting merely of what he considered displays of sympathy with communism through writings or membership at one time or another in so-called Communist front organizations. That he picked on Henderson himself was proof enough of the extravagance of his blast, and we said so at the time.
>
> It is, unfortunately, easy to agree with Mr. Voorhis that the same hand is responsible for the present report. It berates Henderson, already a victim of the Dies imagination, for the failure to dismiss one of his aids charged with "communist affiliation and background." It damns Attorney General Biddle because the Federal Bureau of Investigation "actually investigated" only 601 of the 1124 Federal employees on the committee's roster of subversive suspects. The Voorhis commentary on this phase of the report is simply that the membership lists of alleged subversive groups had not always been obtained, as stated, by subpoena and identified by their officers, and that in one instance the list was "nothing more nor less than a mailing list."

Mr. Voorhis is right, we believe, in deploring this type of document, as compared with one dedicated not to loose indictment and vituperative faultfinding but to "the stiffening of the resistance of the American people to open or covert pro-Axis propaganda and to the building of a vigorous and unified democratic sentiment in the United States.

The circumstances that made it impossible to sign the annual report led me to believe that I ought to resign and even to oppose the continuance of the committee.

Then, shortly before the continuing resolution was to come before the House, something happened which completely sealed my decision. Mr. Dies offered an amendment to an appropriation bill, the effect of which was to arbitrarily cut from the government pay roll some thirty-nine persons. His evidence against eight of them was sufficient to warrant investigation and probably action by the committee. But no such action had been taken. As to the other thirty-one persons, the "evidence" was little better than supposition.

In any case, the method was completely wrong. To strike individuals from the federal pay roll by naming them—offhand—in congressional bills is certainly contrary to basic principles of the Constitution. The Supreme Court has so held more than once. Moreover, such a practice by the Congress would force every employee of the executive department to fear for his job unless he curried congressional favor. Efficient operation of the government would become impossible. There was a right way to "purge" the federal service of people hostile to democracy. It was the careful, orderly way proposed by President Truman in his directive to executive agencies in March 1947.

Once again those of us who opposed this amendment had the support of the New York *Herald Tribune*, which paper had consistently supported, though not uncritically, the work of the Dies Committee. In an editorial on February 10, 1943, the *Herald Tribune* said in part:

Here is a witch hunt sure to play into Hitler's hands. That this is not too strong a designation of the "purge" which **Mr.** Dies has just proposed and to which the House appears committed may be gathered from the report that Representative Voorhis, of California, contemplates re-signing from the Dies committee and working against the resolution to continue it. Mr. Voorhis, who in the past has signed more than one of the committee's reports, has always seemed to us a conspicuously level-headed member, but in his devotion to Congress, he has explained, he is "at all times concerned that its work be dignified and effective, and I do not want anything done by us here to be recorded in the chronicles of the future as narrow minded, bigoted, foolish or unfair." That statement has eloquence.

The *Herald Tribune* was correct about my decision to resign. I submitted my resignation to the Speaker of the House, and when the resolution for continuance of the committee came on the floor a few weeks later, I spoke against it.

As a member of the Dies Committee, my work never pleased any group wholly. From both the right and the left it was criticized and attacked. Neither was I satisfied myself. There were the fears that I was wrong in opposing the action of the committee because perhaps there was evidence of which I had no knowledge. And there was the fear that I was wrong in not opposing it more vigorously and resigning outright because its impact might create unnecessary bitterness among the people. I did the best I knew how. That is about all that can be said.

However, both the value and the dangers in investigation of un-American activities were later illustrated by events of 1946–47. Every American got mad clear through when it was revealed that Russian spies in Canada and the United States had been trying to find out about the atomic bomb.

That everyone was angry over these discoveries was only natural. But that so many expressed shocked surprise was evidence of serious lack of thought and information. Of course the Russians —and the Germans before them—were carrying on espionage. So, no doubt, was every other country in the world, including our own. Perhaps ours was better conducted. At least none of our people had been caught.

Apparently many Americans missed the point. But there was a

point—and a vital one. It concerned the fact that the first loyalty of every Communist party member in the United States or Canada or any other country lies with the Soviet Union, just as the first loyalty of every member of a half-dozen Nazi organizations around the world was owed to Germany while Hitler ruled that unhappy nation. This means that every Communist party member is, potentially at least, an agent of the Russian government. Some of them, no doubt, are not fully conscious of this—especially the newest ones. But if the American Communist talks at all in party meetings, he is already a "passive" agent, since everything he says will be transmitted to Moscow by the first convenient means. The difference between a Communist and all other American radicals is very simple. A Communist is, to use a badly overworked phase, an "agent of Moscow." Nobody else is, however radical his views. It is the primary duty of a committee on un-American activities to make all these facts clear.

The worst of the entire situation was that the communists had two groups of very useful helpers. The first of these groups was pretty obvious. It consisted of people like the non-communist members of the Progressive Citizens of America who still tried to insist that communists are simply "extreme left-wingers" and that a united front is possible between people who believe in freedom and people who don't believe in it.

But the other helpers were far more beneficial to the communist cause. When President Truman proposed, by investigation, hearing, and judgment, to remove from federal office all sympathizers with totalitarianism, some members of Congress seized upon his statement as an excuse for attacking their political enemies and people they "just didn't like." One member of the House declared that in line with what the President had said he would attempt to strike from appropriation bills any money to pay David Lilienthal's salary! Before long a large number of the remaining liberals in government service were similarly designated for congressional slaughter by at least one congressman or senator. The only people who could find any real comfort in this sort of thing were the communists themselves—or the fascists who saw in it the beginning of the same series of events that led to the growth of the Nazi movement in Germany. If Mr. Lilienthal was a communist, so were a majority of American citizens, who were almost surely as far "left" as Mr. Lilienthal. If the TVA was "communism," then perhaps it "wasn't so bad." All the private businesses and all the farmers and all the other people in the Tennessee Valley area had benefited from it. Here was being proved again that the best friends the communists have are the reactionaries who insist upon labeling as a "Red" everyone with whom they disagree. This sort of propaganda gives to the real Communist the very kind of smoke screen behind which he can operate best. The one thing communists fear most is that they will be isolated from the sincere liberals and will have to fight their own battles. As long as reactionary propaganda helps them to avoid this, they are relatively safe and, whether the Communist party is "outlawed" or not, can go merrily on in one guise or another playing "hob" with every decent move for a better nation that may arise in these United States.

With new personnel and leadership, the Committee on Un-American Activities still goes on. What its future course will be I do not know. Some apparently important revelations about key communist figures were brought out in early 1947. If the committee hewed to this line and did not forget that communists beget fascists and vice versa, it could serve well the cause of our democracy.

But it could also do great harm.

As I reread what I have written and ponder our country's future, I see the possibility of divisions among our people growing deeper and ever deeper until at last there is no crossing over of understanding. Such a result will be made more likely if the work of such a committee degenerates into a castigation of any loyal American simply because he seeks to make progress faster than the majority is willing to go. These are the free souls who have built every great nation and every great age, especially in America. If America tries to become a reactionary or even a conservative nation, she will lose her soul as certainly as she found it as a young struggling people. If, through the action of such a committee or from any other cause, we become a people afraid to venture, we shall never build that better world without whose building there is only death ahead.

All men who have ever lived have tried to find an answer to their problems. If they could not find it one way, they have sought another. And as long as mankind lives upon this earth it will be so. Nor can one group of men with one set of beliefs sit in judgment, ultimately, upon any other group. Fascism, communism, capitalism, all these and many other "isms" will with time pass and be forgotten. But there is one thing that will remain —the mind and soul of a free man.

It is when powerful, highly disciplined forces presume to fetter the human mind, to condition it to cruelty, to make it afraid of new clear thoughts that we must rise with all our strength and say no. This is why believers in liberty must oppose and expose and weaken, if we can, every totalitarian movement in the world. They are bad because, under their heels, people are not free. I happen to believe that if democracy in America should ever be destroyed it is more likely to be fascism, better masked, better financed, and wrapped in more familiar trappings, that will perpetrate that crime, although communism at present makes the greater noise. But I believe with even greater earnestness that the only course for the man who would defend freedom is to defend it on all fronts and against all enemies at once. His methods of defense must be such as do no violence to the principle which he seeks to save. And he will be stronger for his work if he remembers that there are always some who shout the loudest for systems of enslavement who would like to be free also if only they thought they dared.

Chapter 16

"WHEN IN DOUBT,
DO RIGHT"

"When in doubt, do right." This sage advice to young congressmen is credited to the late Claude A. Swanson, senator from Virginia and the first of President Roosevelt's many Secretaries of the Navy.

The congressman who faithfully follows that rule will practically always do what he believes to be right for the simple reason that he is practically always in doubt.

Before I was elected to Congress I had the idea that from day to day members would face clear-cut issues between right and wrong and that as the roll was called the membership would divide itself between white-plumed knights and doers of evil. I had not served more than a week of my first term before I discovered how inaccurate a conception I had.

I should have known that the business of Congress, like the business of every democratically elected legislative body, is the business of compromise. All the people of America cannot possibly be in agreement on any issue. The action their Congress takes, therefore, is bound to be the result of conflicting forces and varying ideas. And only the sort of congressman who can make up his mind once and for all on a question and then close it to all opposing argument—a practice which generally makes for very bad legislation—can be free of severe conflict within his own mind as he attempts to decide whether, when his name is called, he will answer aye or no.

It would be a great deal easier if only one could answer, "Fifty-five per cent aye," or "seventy per cent no," or "I vote aye but with the reservation that I do not like Section 3 of the bill," or "I vote no but God have mercy on my soul if I am wrong, as I may very well be."

Time and again, as the debate proceeded on a bill it would become all too evident that there was right on both sides and wrong on both sides, with the choice not between black and white but rather between a light and dark shade of gray. At such times I envied those members whose minds were, apparently, completely made up about the question. There was no use for this "perpetually worried" congressman to talk the bill over with them. But there were always other members who, like myself, were deeply disturbed. We would talk with one another behind the rail or in the seats, each of us hoping that the other would bring up some point that would seem conclusive and resolve our doubts. We knew that it was only a matter of time before the debate would end, the reading of the bill for amendment would be completed, and the clerk would begin to call the roll. Then it would be too late for "on the one hand—but on the other hand" discussions. It would be either aye or no—one hundred per cent one or the other.

And after the vote was cast all the arguments on the side on which I had not cast my vote would keep dinning in my ears and would attain a persuasiveness greater than they had had before. I remember the night after we voted on the Hatch "clean politics" Act. I had voted for the bill, primarily because I believe it wrong for people doing faithful work in the federal service to be *required* to contribute to political campaign funds. But all that night I kept hearing Speaker Bankhead saying that the rights of citizenship are sacred and that the bill would take some of those rights away from federal officials. As time passed my concern became less, my reasoning before the vote was cast became clear again, and I would not have changed my vote even if I could have done so. In fact, if I could do my ten years over again there are no more than three or four votes that I would change. But right after the casting of each vote I always experienced the thoughts and feelings I have described.

No congressman will ever get to heaven—at least not the traditional kind of heaven—except by the path of repentance, confession, and forgiveness. Even then purgatory may be about as much as can reasonably be expected, for every congressman violates his convictions to some degree every time he votes. He has to. It is his business. Except for a few supremely happy exceptions, every time a conscientious congressman votes he feels he is doing wrong. The more conscientious he is the more poignantly does he feel this. It isn't that he is one hundred per cent wrong. It's the ten per cent of right on "the other side" which he necessarily has disregarded. He may be ten per cent wrong, or twenty per cent, or even forty-nine per cent. Up to the point of being forty-nine per cent wrong and fifty-one per cent right he is "doing the best he can." But if he casts a vote where he believes in his own mind that he is fifty-one per cent wrong, then he ought to be kicked out of Congress. In such a case his motives themselves can hardly be worthy ones.

Votes on domestic bills are hard enough. But the ones where this feeling of guilt and wrong becomes almost oppressive are those where the issues of war and peace are involved.

All through the 1920s and 1930s there was agitation throughout the United States for the passage of a "neutrality law" by Congress. The proponents of such legislation argued that World War I had accomplished little, that peace had not been established by that war. They said, therefore, that while the United States should strive for world peace we should at the same time determine that if war came elsewhere in the world we would stay out of it. Furthermore, it was contended that if this country could avoid war it would be in a better position to induce belligerents to make peace and to bind up the world's wounds afterward.

By the middle 1930s this point of view was held by many people. Each day it became clearer that peace in Europe hung by a very slender thread. Japan had taken over Manchuria by force and no one had heeded Secretary of State Stimson's warnings that if Japan were allowed to succeed in her enterprise her course would be copied by other nations and ultimately war would become inevitable. Mussolini attacked and conquered Ethiopia. Although an effective embargo of oil and gasoline alone might have stopped him, nothing was done. Hitler built up the armed power of Germany, marched into the Rhineland, took over Austria. France, the only nation with a will to stop him, hardly dared attempt it since she had no assurance that Britain or America would back her in case of war.

And so over against the "neutrality" school of thought there grew an opposite opinion among many people in America. That opinion held that since the German, Japanese, and Italian dictators had been so successful with their course of aggression there would be no stopping them except by war. It held that in such a war America could not remain neutral but would find her very existence dependent on the defeat of these dictatorships. These people believed neutrality legislation was a positive danger to peace and should be opposed. They also were convinced that America should at once begin to arm. It is my opinion that long before 1939 President Roosevelt had come to this point of view.

What was the right thing to do?

Nothing could be so contrary to Christian principles or precepts as war. Nothing indeed could be so contrary to any decent human principles of any sort. Moreover, we had been pretty thoroughly "debunked" about the wars of the past. We had read for two decades how economic causes of wars lay behind whatever façade of moral issues might be erected to conceal them. Wouldn't this be the case again? Were there really evil forces and good forces in the world or were there only conflicts of interest? And if the latter were the case, then should not a United States congressman concentrate on doing what he could to keep his own country at peace—whatever might come elsewhere in the world? Otherwise, if one didn't do all he could to that end there would thousands, maybe millions, of young men killed, to mention only the greatest of the losses. These were the thoughts that led me to vote for the Neutrality Act of 1939. That act provided, among other things, that either the President or Congress could "find a state of war to be existing" and that thereafter (1) no arms or ammunition could be shipped to any belligerent, nor (2) could loans or credits be extended to them, nor (3) could goods of any sort be shipped to them unless title first passed to the foreign purchaser, nor (4) could funds for the benefit of any belligerent be collected in the United States except under strict regulation."

Would such an act keep America out of war? Certainly not by itself. I voted for it in the hope that it might help. I couldn't conscientiously have voted against it—not at the time it was passed. It would have meant refusal even to try to protect our country from war.

But suppose nothing could keep America out of war? Suppose Hitler couldn't be stopped by any force in all Europe? And how long could Japanese bombings in China go on without some retribution from somewhere? But where? What if I were wrong about the Neutrality Act? It had been one of those "fifty-five per cent" aye votes anyway. I told the House, "I am quite ready to say that these considerations are not to me absolutely conclusive as to whether my vote to embargo arms and ammunition to belligerents was right or whether my vote for passage of the Neutrality Act of 1939, as amended by the House, was right. Were I to have to cast these votes again, I know I should have to go through the same inward struggles all over again. All I do know is that there is nothing I seek so much as a clear and certain answer to the question: What ought a member of the House of Representatives to do to protect the peace of his own country and to promote the peace of the world? May a guidance wiser than any human mind give us courage, wisdom, and vision in these difficult days."

The people, I am convinced, favored the Neutrality Act. I sent several thousand questionnaires out to the Twelfth California District and asked some of my friends to circulate them. They came back to me showing a very large majority of the people saying yes to the question, "Do you favor an all-time embargo on munitions of war?" Some people qualified their answers by saying "To aggressor nations only," but not very many. Almost everyone favored a prohibition on war loans to foreign countries.

That was how the people were feeling. So was I. Events alone were to teach us that we were reaching for a peace that was, under the circumstances then existing, unattainable.

A year before I had faced another vote on a related issue and I had done what some of my best friends regarded as an act inconsistent with my general point of view. I do not believe they were right. I had voted in 1938 for the Naval Expansion bill. I had even voted for the three new battleships that were included in the bill. Some of the liberal congressmen had nicknamed me "Three Battleships Voorhis." Liberals weren't supposed to vote for such things. Moreover, for years I had been talking against war, pointing out the danger in great national armament, urging that our nation take the lead in working for peace. And now here I was voting for the biggest naval expansion bill in the nation's history. I felt I was doing wrong—but that I would, in all the circumstances, be doing something even more wrong if I opposed the bill.

It certainly was true that I wanted our country's influence to be used for peace. But I could see no reason why the passage of the bill should interfere with efforts to bring about world economic adjustments which seemed then the best hope for peace. It was clear that the world was coming to be dominated more and more by force. In Europe tensions were rising, the hope of peace was growing dimmer. It was hard to see how America's influence for peace could be effective unless the nation was strong. Furthermore, we were doing a lot of talking about "the protection of the Western World."

This navy might under the circumstances be used as an instrument for peace—not war. In a world where dictators responsible to no one but themselves were pushing their power further and further it might be an absolute necessity to the keeping of peace.

So I voted for the Naval Expansion bill. And I voted for the Neutrality Act. Maybe I was inconsistent. I was doing the best I could. My first objective was to keep America out of war. But I had a feeling of terrible responsibility for what might happen in case full-scale war did break out.

In September 1939 Hitler's legions crossed the Polish border. We heard the President and others on the radio saying America was resolved to stay out. Could we? We tried to think so. Yet then and there began the "steps toward war." Repeal of the arms embargo, arming of merchantmen, fifty destroyers traded to

Britain, Lend-Lease, the cutting off at the eleventh hour of war supplies from Japan. Could we have done differently? And what would the consequences have been if we had?

As the days passed it became clearer that America couldn't afford to let Hitler and his Japanese allies win. Once France had fallen, a lot of people saw that it was only a matter of time. Pearl Harbor was to decide when the time would be.

But, however inexorable the course our country followed from peace to war, not one decision on a single bill was, at the time, clear. Hindsight is easy; foresight is the awful responsibility of every member of Congress. And all the while there was on the one hand a world in flames and on the other the young, fine, ofttimes gentle American boys who bore not one shred of the blame for bringing on the war.

What *was* right? Was there any right? Or was it a choice between wrongs? Certainly that was the case, for me at least, when the Conscription bill came before the House in the summer of 1940. I voted for the bill because, with war already raging in Europe and Asia and with the Germans and the Japanese winning on all fronts, it was obviously impossible to have any assurance that America could remain at peace. And, if she did not remain at peace, then she would call on her young men to defend her. Under these circumstances the argument was unanswerable that it would be a tragic and irresponsible betrayal of the very men who would be drafted then to deny them previous training.

But, however unanswerable the arguments for the bill, I could not as I voted aye escape the feeling that I was doing a morally wrong act. What right had I to require young men and even older boys to leave their homes and go off to learn to kill and be killed? Looked at from that point of view, it was as impossible for me to justify my action as to argue successfully against the national need for the legislation.

Perhaps these thoughts were in my mind so much that they influenced my vote on the bill which followed a year later. This was the Draft Extension Act of 1941. When the original Conscription bill had been enacted, a great deal had been made of its provision that no man would be held in service for more than one year. It was represented to the country as a "training" bill rather than as a war service bill, though actually both words had been used in the title. Most of the drafted men had made their plans on the basis of a year's training—and no more. And while it may have been—probably was—true that the men at the top of our government had believed in 1940 that war was inescapable, certainly they had not told the country or the drafted men that.

For these reasons I resolved my doubts on the Draft Extension bill in favor of a no vote. I was one of 200 members of the House who voted against the bill. Only 201 voted for it and I know personally of several men who changed their votes from no to aye at the last minute. This time the arguments about "keeping faith," doing the thing that seemed right in principle, were on the side of my negative vote. But unquestionably in the light of history my vote was wrong. It is one of the few which, in the hindsight now permitted us, I would change if I could. For that roll call was one of the times when members of Congress were called upon to "rise above principle," as a common saying among senators and representatives runs. With the change of but one vote the bill would have been lost in the House. And while I believe ways would have been devised to prevent "the breakup of the armed forces" which those who voted as I did were accused of encouraging, nonetheless, as events turned out, we were placing our moral scruples ahead of the safety of the democratic nations of the earth. There are times when congressmen are called upon to sacrifice some principles if great causes are not to be lost.

Pearl Harbor came and America, not by her choice but by the action of another nation, was at war. Thereafter bill after bill was passed to mobilize the strength of the nation for the greatest test our country had ever faced. Most of them passed by overwhelming majorities, if not unanimously. But since we were at war and war itself is as wrong as anything can be, there was hardly a bill among them which did not raise qualms of conscience when I voted for it.

One of the hardest decisions of all on the war measures came on the Manpower Mobilization bill which was passed by the House in early February 1945, right at the time of the Nazis' last great drive into the Belgian Bulge. We were told by the heads of the War and Navy departments that unless this bill was passed, giving the government power to require people to work in war industries, the armed forces could not be adequately supplied. The vote came at a time when the outlook in Belgium was about as dark as it ever became. I had my serious doubts that the bill was necessary or that it would do much good even if it were, theoretically, needed. But I could not prove any of this. Presumably the War Department had the facts. Congress did not, could not, have them. Neither was I able to justify voting against the bill right at that time, since I knew if the measure were defeated every man in the armed forces would be told, justifiably or not, that Congress had "let him down." Therefore I voted for the bill.

It never became law, however, due primarily to the work of one man, Senator O'Mahoney, of Wyoming. What he actually did was simply to delay action in the Senate until it had become perfectly clear that the tide of the war had turned and that, contrary to what Congress had been told, the bill was not and never had been necessary to bring about an adequate supplying of the armed forces. But I confess that if, with the same terrible experiences confronting American soldiers overseas, I had my vote to cast over again I would not change it. I voted in the light of what I believed would be the effect on morale of our Army of passage or defeat of the bill at the time it was voted upon. I voted not as I wanted to do but as I believed I ought to do if my single vote were to decide the issue.

Had this bill been a thoroughgoing measure—a draft of capital and property and manpower, all three—to help win the war, I would have had no doubts. We had talked a lot, in the years before the war, about how we were going to do just that, how we were going to prevent anyone from profiting from another war. A lot of congressmen, myself included, had introduced bills to "take the profit out of war." But when the time came no such bills were even reported from committee.

Less than three months after the vote on the manpower draft bill Germany surrendered. Under the impact of the atomic bomb Japan gave up in August 1945 and the world turned to the task of binding wounds, rebuilding cities, and trying to make peace. It soon became clear that it was a far more difficult and complex job than most Americans had expected. Some of them grew impatient. And the same propaganda that had led our country to make her fatal isolationist mistakes after World War I began to appear.

It was subtle and altogether negative at first. And the most serious aspect of it was that it appealed to natural and deep-seated desires in us all. Certainly it was a natural desire for everyone, including the men themselves, to demand a too rapid demobilization of our armed forces. Practically everyone in the nation must bear some share of the responsibility for this. It resulted no doubt in some weakening of our bargaining position relative to Russia. It may well have been responsible in part for the loss of self-determination by the smaller nations of eastern Europe and their absorption into the system of the Soviet Union.

In Japan the United States had a free hand and from the start the American occupation appeared likely to become an event unique in history. The power of the Japanese military caste was, of course, destroyed. So, apparently, was the power of the few mighty families whose cartel empires had controlled the whole island economy. As rapidly as possible the life of the average Japanese was brought back to normal. Democratic political activity was fostered. Local self-government was gradually restored. There was evident concern on the part of General Mac-Arthur and his staff for the people's welfare. Revival of their co-operatives and the growth and expansion of these institutions was encouraged. A remarkably good relationship, under all the circumstances, developed between the American occupation forces and the Japanese people. It appeared possible at least that a firm international friendship might develop between victor and vanquished. Only Congress failed. It "saved" money at the expense of some of the funds requested by the Army for the provision of food for Japan during the rehabilitation period.

The Seventy-ninth Congress did enact the British loan bill. But it was approved only after the most bitter debate and, probably, in the teeth of a generally hostile public opinion. A good many Americans apparently expected the impossible—that Britain could recover and be the all-important rallying point for western Europe without some help from America in the early years.

The fundamental weakness of America's postwar policy was lack of vision. If America was being compelled to accept world leadership, as was certainly the case, and if our purpose was to save and encourage free institutions and prevent the spread of totalitarian ones, then we were called upon to do much more than "support governments." We had to do something for peoples. And above all it was important that every American action be freed from any suggestion of commercial imperialism. Our failure in China was illustrative of this lack of vision.

In China finance capitalism has proven not only a failure but a curse to the Chinese people. It has meant graft and corruption, interest rates of 120 per cent per year, shameless profiteering by foreign purveyors of gadgets which the Chinese neither need nor want. American aid to China should have been completely divorced from any attempted preservation of a foreign economic system which, however well it may have worked at times elsewhere, has never benefited the people of China. The alternative certainly need not be communism. American support of the central Chinese government could have been conditional upon the introduction of salutary reforms, the very nature of which could have been proof that we were not trying to gain for ourselves.

These reforms should have included requirement of simple honesty of government officials, Chinese ownership of Chinese industry, development of China's natural resources—perhaps under direction of the World Bank to make sure the benefits actually reached the people, removal of the burden of extortionate rentals from the backs of the peasants, reduction of the unbelievable interest rates. Had America talked in these terms in China, the story might have been different. It is still not too late. But as matters stand, the condition of the long-suffering and highly deserving Chinese people appears to be going from bad to worse. And Soviet Russia stands almost certainly to be the only beneficiary of conditions so desperate for the Chinese people as to provide opportunity for the propaganda of communists and Russian agents. Military victory for the Nationalist government will not remove the causes of discontent against which the United States should have been the first to speak.

From the day of Hitler's surrender little vision was used, even by the heads of our government, in determining what was to be done with Germany. There was surface agreement at least that her war potential should be destroyed, though if this involved the breakup of cartels there were those even in the occupation authorities who offered opposition. As to the constructive work of building a new Germany, there was failure to call promptly upon democratic, political, religious, and economic forces such as the old Social Democrats, the Church, and the co-operatives and to use them as the bases for this monumental task.

Admittedly, the task was rendered supremely difficult so long as agreement among all four occupying powers was required before action could be taken. But again the basic trouble was lack of vision. Only a few people seem clearly to have understood that the problem of Germany is part and parcel of a larger problem—that of the rehabilitation of all western Europe. Such proposals as the co-operative international ownership and control of Ruhr industries by western European countries received at first little genuine support in high places. Yet in no other way could the people of that area be put to work and the key production in all western Europe revived without raising fears in all other nations of a resurgence of German warmaking powers. Ruhr production might have been—might still be—made the core of an economic union that could become a political union of noncommunist western Europe. Ruhr production might even be used as a means of parting the "Iron Curtain" and opening up two-way trade with eastern Europe. There has been desperate need of some great forward-looking project such as a "Rhine Valley Authority," to become the joint effort of several nations and to be aimed at nothing less than a higher standard of production and of living than the people of western Europe have ever known. It is not yet too late for such constructive measures.

We could help to work out regional customs unions as a first step toward regional political federations—in western Europe for example. We could help with programs of river valley developments; we could make loans for industrial expansion in the free nations or use our influence with the World Bank to do so; we could encourage the growth and development of co-operatives in countries where people in the past have depended so largely upon them. We have been slow indeed in learning that every move America makes—or fails to make—will have deep political consequences for good or ill, and that it is better to make them as constructive as possible.

But even had our Executive, our occupation authorities, and our State Department vigorously proposed such measures of genuine rehabilitation in China or in Europe, it is unlikely that the Seventy-ninth Congress would have supported them—at least not with any financial assistance. For with the end of the war our vision seems to have grown markedly dimmer. One fundamental reason for this failure has been the slowness of Congress and the nation generally to understand thoroughly world needs and world problems.

It is true that hundreds of millions of dollars were appropriated for UNRRA relief. But this was not done ungrudgingly nor was there evidence of any clear conception of the opportunity that existed to go beyond "relief" to the task of restoring genuine health to war-torn nations. Instead the Congress carefully wrote into all UNRRA bills provision against any of the money being used for "rehabilitation." We were willing to send Europe some bread and dried eggs but not to help them rebuild bridges, refertilize their land, or reconstruct their homes. I never could understand this action. If it was prompted by fear of Russia, then why was nothing done to prevent the very largest of American corporations from feverishly shipping electric locomotives, machinery, parts for chemical plants, tractors, and power equipment to the Soviet Union for handsome gold payments cleared through that great capitalistic institution, the Chase National Bank?

Meanwhile opposition mounted against the reciprocal trade agreement program which, in the absence of multilateral pacts for broader trade, stood as the one clear evidence of America's readiness to open her markets to the goods of war-stricken nations in return for corresponding action on their part toward us. The Seventy-ninth Congress amended the legislation extending the agreements to reduce the period of its validity. And the likelihood increased that the even more conservative Congresses to follow would kill the program altogether and attempt, even in the world of 1948 or 1950, to return to a policy of high tariff and American economic nationalism.

Such action cannot be taken by one nation without its being regarded by other nations as notice that they must do likewise. There is added impetus to every tendency within each country to make its economy as nearly self-sufficient as possible. Formerly free nations are driven to make such deals as they can with nations having controlled economies—for example, the Soviet Union. It is altogether possible that the very men who shouted "Communist" most loudly and most falsely at their political opponents in 1946 will themselves play directly into the hands of the world forces of actual communism.

The "economy" ax hovered most menacingly over such instruments of an improved foreign policy as the State Department's short-wave broadcasts carrying America's story to other nations. The Republican majority in the Eightieth Congress, with a keen eye to the elections of 1948 and no eye at all to world conditions in 1958 or the staggering responsibilities of our country, plunged ahead with a drastic program of tax reduction. It was even proposed to reduce sharply national defense expenditures which, while normally dangerous to peace, had become by 1947 the main hope of free nations of escaping the expanding and stifling embrace of the Russian bear.

As the months passed it became increasingly clear that the future of mankind would depend principally on relations between America and Russia and between those two nations and the rest of the world. Unprejudiced Americans understand some things about Russia. We know the Russians are afraid, and we know why. At times other countries have dealt no more honestly with Russia than Russia has seemed to be dealing with us. More than 20,000,000 Soviet citizens lost their lives defending their country against the Germans. Countless Russian factories, dams, and other installations were destroyed. Her insistence upon security is understandable to say the least.

We know also of Russia's economic needs and, if only the process of "taking over" neighboring countries could be stopped, we would favor a mutually advantageous commercial treaty—especially if it provided rights of entry into Russia for Americans equal to those granted by us to Russians. Not only toward other countries but toward Russia, too, America's economic co-operation should be held out as something to be gained by any nation demonstrating its readiness to work for world stabilization and peace. Acceptance of the American plan for world control of atomic energy or something similar to it should be made the test.

But the fact remains that the continuance, unchecked, of the general course pursued by Russia since the surrender of Germany constitutes a menace to both peace and freedom. That course cannot give security to Russia herself—much less to the world. The pall of government by decree and, sometimes, by terror has fallen over nation after nation that lies along her borders. Nor has any evidence been given that limits would be set by the Soviet Union beyond which she would not seek the establishment of communist regimes—except only the limits fixed by effective American opposition. It would be different if the Russians by their actions had won the voluntary allegiance of the peoples of these nations to the Russian system. But no such evidence exists. Economic change the peoples have naturally welcomed, but that would have come inevitably out of the conditions produced by the war. And every reliable report we have indicates that a majority of the people of Bulgaria and Yugoslavia and Rumania and Hungary and Poland and northern Korea and Finland and Czechoslovakia still want to be free. And they are not free—not by any standard—today.

Moreover, it is Russia alone which, officially at least, stands in the way of world control of the atomic bomb. It is Russia alone whose vetoes have cast doubt on the ability of the United Nations to contribute to peace. And it is the secrecy that surrounds Russia which constitutes the major obstacle to understanding among the nations and to disarmament agreements in which the nations can all have confidence.

Therefore, when President Truman asked for the big loans to Greece and Turkey in March 1947, for the purpose of preventing those two nations from falling under the Russian control which had proved so absolute in other nations, a sudden change took place in the attitude of Congress. If we were afraid of an immediate plunge into communism by these countries—then "that was different." Though they carried no "relief" limitations and could be used for all sorts of purposes—"rehabilitation" certainly among them—Congress made comparatively little protest against these loans.

The Greek and Turkish loans served to emphasize again the tremendous importance, from the viewpoint of world opinion, of ridding our action of any taint of selfish interest. In the Middle East this could be done only by a bold proposal that international trade in oil and the development of oil resources be put on some sort of international co-operative basis.

But the most disheartening aspect of the discussion of the Greek and Turkish loans was the fact that the debate did not focus on the one reason why the United Nations could not effectively handle the problem. That reason was the veto power of the "Big Five" nations. Once again the trouble was lack of foresight on the part of the United States. Long since, America should have moved for abolition of the veto power through amendment of the charter of the United Nations. So long as the big-power veto remains, the United Nations is crippled in its major task of maintaining peace at the very points where that peace is likely to be most seriously threatened. Yet those of us who belong to organizations which have been working ceaselessly for modification or abolition of the veto have found both Britain and America so far opposed. Admittedly, the American loans to Greece and Turkey constituted a blow at the prestige of the United Nations. But it was unfortunately true that both the veto power and the certainty of long delay before the United Nations could act left no other practical course open. America had to act alone if any action at all was to be taken; but the reason for this was that America herself shared the blame for failure to make the international peace enforcement machinery effective. There was criticism of the loans to Greece and Turkey, and it was contended by some that the whole matter should have been referred to the United Nations. But tragically little was said about what would have to be done before such referral of a really important international problem could result in definite and salutary action by that international body.

No doubt the President was right and the position of Greece

and Turkey *was* most critical. But those who insisted that a genuine improvement in the conditions of the masses of people—particularly in Greece—be a requisite part of the program were right too. Not only in Greece but in many another country the answer to the communist threat had to be something better than mere support of non-communist and sometimes reactionary governments. The proposal of Secretary of State Marshall, in the summer of 1947 for a master plan of European reconstruction and American aid in that reconstruction marked a hopeful if belated recognition of the magnitude of the problem. America's burden, America's responsibility, America's opportunity became clearer as the days passed.

More and more Americans are beginning, I believe, to appreciate the almost appalling magnitude of the task of building peace. We are beginning to realize that it is a task which may never end—at least not until this generation has passed into history. We are coming to understand that new methods are required by brand-new circumstances and that only by the creation of a world authority or world government which will be supreme over all individual nations—at least in certain fields—can peace be made secure. We are willing to face the fact that this will involve the sacrifice by all nations of a certain portion of what is called "sovereignty." The United States, with a foresight and statesmanship heretofore unknown, proposed that precisely these things be done with regard to atomic energy. Having advanced the proposal, its full realization should have become the cardinal purpose of every American thought and action. Tragically, this has not been the case.

There was little difficulty in securing Senate approval of United States adherence to the United Nations. Why should there have been when by the charter this nation and four others were made, in effect, immune to the law that was to govern all the rest of the world and were given the power individually to veto any action of all the rest of humankind? Likewise Congress approved without much hesitation American membership in the United Nations Educational, Scientific and Cultural Organization and in the Food and Agriculture Organization. But no mandatory powers reside in either of these bodies.

No good will come of shrugging our shoulders and saying that the great obstacles to peace have been the actions and attitudes of Soviet Russia—however much we may believe that to be true.

The question remains as to what the action of the United States and its Senate will be if and when the future peace of the world depends upon our ratification of a covenant such as we ourselves have proposed for world control of atomic energy. For under such a covenant there could be no veto and a sacrifice of sovereignty by the large nations would be involved for the first time in human history. Unless when that opportunity comes—if indeed it ever does—we Americans are willing to make the great adventure for peace, we shall condemn future generations to a war more terrible and a death more certain than our minds can conceive. If we leave our children no real law of peace to live by but only a stock pile of atomic bombs, we may be sure the people of other nations will provide likewise for their children. American bombs may blast the lives of millions on another side of the world. But there will be other bombs passing them, going in an opposite direction. Some of them, if they are loosed at all upon the earth, will find their mark in the homes of the America we have loved—but loved less well and with less courage and intelligence than the times required.

Chapter 17

POSTWAR PLANNING

The main bastion of free government will always be the faith of the people in a better tomorrow. They must believe their problems can be solved, observe the process of their solution, and feel themselves an integral part of that work. To give substance to this faith they must now, and in the future, be able to make a worthwhile economic contribution to the welfare of their nation. They must, in other words, be assured employment and the ground for hope that their children can face a brighter world than was theirs.

During the course of World War II it became increasingly evident that these hopes of the people would be directly dependent upon whether the Congress would develop a legislative program capable of meeting the nation's long-run problems. They would depend on the answer to the question: "Would Congress do its share of postwar planning?"

In the late fall of 1940 leaders of the Catholic, Protestant, and Jewish churches met in Washington in an Inter-Faith Conference. The principal recommendation of this conference was that a national commission be established to consider and make proposals for solving the future problem of employment in the United States and that there be included on such a commission representatives of the three great religious groups.

This was the inspiration from which House Joint Resolution 59 grew. I introduced the bill on January 10, 1941, "To Create a National Commission on Post-War Reconstruction." The commission was not to be limited to members of Congress but to include farmers, workers, businessmen, bankers, co-operators, educators, as well, of course, as the representatives of the churches.

Through 1941 and 1942 one of my major "projects" was to build support for H.J.R. 59. And the support of individual citizens, private organizations, and the newspapers certainly was forthcoming.

There were opportunities for speaking before various types of meetings and over the radio—of all of which I eagerly took advantage. There were conferences held with representatives of important organizations in the hope of enlisting their support. And of course there was always the day-to-day work of talking wherever possible with other members of the House about the bill.

In June 1941 the Labor Committee started its hearings. They were conducted by a subcommittee headed by Robert Ramspeck of Georgia, one of the oldest and best-liked members of the House. Since I was the author of the measure under consideration, it was up to me to submit each day a list of the witnesses to be heard, to make certain that they arrived on schedule in the committee room, and to be prepared to substitute someone else if they didn't. And since most of my witnesses were very busy people with other weighty responsibilities, all this was rather a nerve-racking task.

I am sure, however, that the hearings were good. Indeed, among the organizations which sent representatives to testify for the resolution were all of the following:

American Federation of Labor
General Federation of Women's Clubs
National Association of Manufacturers
American Farm Bureau Federation
National Grange
National Farmers Union
National Catholic Welfare Conference
Federal Council of Churches
Central Conference of American Rabbis

Congress of Industrial Organizations
Railroad Labor Organizations
Cooperative League of the United States of America
National Child Labor Committee
American Association of University Women
American Association for Economic Freedom

A number of members of the House also testified.

There were others, notably the American Legion and some of the other veterans' organizations, who later showed sincere interest in the measure and proposed some amendments to it.

A number of suggestions for amendment of the resolution— most of them of a comparatively minor nature—were made by witnesses who testified at the hearings. For their consideration as well as for the determination of committee action, it was necessary that a number of executive sessions of the Labor Committee be held. Meanwhile, other business, of course, had to be attended to by the committee. Consequently it was not until March 1942 that final action came.

It was proposed by the committee that I introduce what is commonly called a "clean bill," incorporating those amendments which the committee believed should be made. Otherwise, all these amendments would have to be offered from the floor of the House, which not only delays action but is likely to invite other amendments, some of which might prove damaging to the bill.

So on March twelfth I introduced my resolution in the amended form worked out by the Committee on Labor. It was given the number H.J.R. 291.

The resolution proposed to establish "a National Commission for Post-War Reconstruction, to be composed of (1) five Members of the Senate, to be appointed by the President of the Senate; (2) five Members of the House of Representatives, to be appointed by the Speaker of the House of Representatives; and (3) twenty-four members to be appointed by the President as follows: Three from the executive branch of the Government, three from organizations of farmers, three from organizations of labor, three from organizations of business and industry, one from organizations of banks and financial institutions, three from Church organizations, two from educational associations, three from organizations of consumers, at least two of whom shall be from associations of consumer cooperatives, one from public health and welfare associations, one outstanding economist, and one outstanding industrial engineer."

The objective of the commission's work was described as "the development of a practical plan and program for the continuous full employment of all Americans able and willing to work, and for the achievement and maintenance of a just and equitable relationship as to wages between agriculture and industry, to the end that free enterprise may be preserved."

In an attempt to bring the work as close to the people as possible the commission was instructed "to secure the greatest possible degree of participation and interest in the work of the Commission on the part of the groups from which such members shall have been chosen. Members shall constantly bring before such groups problems, findings, and proposals of the Commission and shall encourage discussion, analysis, recommendations, and criticisms from such groups." I hoped this part of the bill would give the whole nation a feeling of responsibility for finding the answer to national problems and promote a better understanding between representatives of different economic groups.

On March twenty-seventh the Committee on Labor voted to report the bill favorably and to try to secure a rule for its consideration. Whenever a committee takes action of this kind on a bill, a report must be written, filed, printed, and made available at the "document room" so that any member of the House can find out what prompted the committee's approval. The report on H.J.R. 291, which I helped to prepare, gave the main arguments for the bill in the following single paragraph:

> It is our manifest duty to do all things necessary to assure the men in our armed forces that when they return from this conflict they will find here good jobs awaiting them and substantial solid hope for a better future than they have ever known before. Nor can America expect to assume the world leadership for lasting peace, which must be hers, unless her own economic system is functioning well and her people and industries are fully employed at the time the peace is made. These are the reasons why, next

only to the provisions of the sinews of the war itself, the first duty of the Congress is to initiate now the work of preparing to meet the problems which will confront us when peace returns. There is not the slightest doubt but that those problems can be met if we have the courage and the vision and understanding to meet them. But it is not only Congress that must take responsibility for this matter. So must every important economic group in our whole country. The solution of this problem is the responsibility of our churches, of labor, of industry, of agriculture, of our schools and colleges and of our people who have found a way to do business on cooperative principles. There must be a spirit spread throughout the length and breadth of this country which will be a spirit not of demanding for one's self or one's own group, but of a willingness to give and take until a definite and specific answer to the economic problem of America, in peacetime, has been found.

Action by the Labor Committee was, of course, only the first step. It was still necessary to obtain a rule from the Rules Committee and to bring the measure to the floor. There was plenty of support and evidence of it was increasing all the time. In July the churches put on another major effort to bring about action on the bill. I called attention to this in the House, had brief editorials from the Catholic *America,* the Methodist *Christian Advocate,* the *Christian Century,* the *Christian Herald* reprinted in the appendix of the *Congressional Record.* Another interfaith statement was signed by more than five hundred priests, clergymen, and rabbis in support of the bill.

But the support was too much outside of Congress, not enough inside it. And only the people inside Congress could pass the bill. Some members of the House, including, unfortunately, "the leadership," thought it was "too soon" to do anything about postwar problems. ("The leadership" is a term constantly used in conversations among House members. It can mean the Speaker alone or the Speaker and the majority leader, or these two gentlemen plus their unofficial advisers among the older members. No one ever knows, without asking, just what "the leadership" does mean.) Other members were fearful that creating the commission might divert attention from matters bearing directly upon the war. I argued that it would help to win the war if everyone, including the men fighting it, knew someone was at work preparing against the future. I also tried to point out that if so big a job were to be done right it would require many months if not two or three years to do it. But it was still deemed "too early" by most of the House membership—at least the more influential segment of it—when the Seventy-seventh Congress adjourned.

I reintroduced the resolution of the first day of the Seventy-eighth Congress and continued to work for its passage. As the year 1943 wore on, however, and the military outlook brightened, resolutions for postwar planning began to spring up like mushrooms all over Congress. The question was which one? The authors were running to the Speaker almost daily, trying to convince him of the superiority of their particular version. I am frank to confess I contacted not only the Speaker but many another influential House member on behalf of mine. And I found, much to my surprise and disappointment, that there was something else "wrong" with my bill beside its premature birth. There was considerable opposition to what I considered the strongest point about my resolution—namely, the inclusion on the commission of anyone outside of Congress itself.

The Speaker asked one of the top leaders of the House to get all the resolutions and their authors together and try to work out a mutually satisfactory compromise that would nevertheless get the main job done. But for some reason—certainly not because of any disapproval on the part of the authors—this assignment was never carried out. We were always about to be called together, but we never were. At least not until Mr. Colmer, of Mississippi, a member of the Rules Committee, announced one day that he was going to ask the Rules Committee to report out his resolution for creation of a House committee on postwar planning. He did so and the Rules Committee did so.

It was time action was taken in some direction and Mr. Colmer's resolution was as good as any of them if the House wanted a committee of the customary type consisting only of members of the House to do this all-important job. And apparently that was what the majority of the membership did want.

The Colmer Resolution came up in the House on January 26, 1944. I, of course, voted for it and spoke in its favor, though this seemed a bit superfluous when it was passed after brief debate and without a dissenting vote.

My disappointment at not having secured passage of my Resolution 291 was markedly lessened when, a few days later, the clerk read the names of the eighteen members of the new Special Committee on Post-War Economic Policy and Planning and mine was one of them.

I served on this committee, generally known as the Colmer Committee, during all the rest of my time as a congressman. It wasn't so grueling a job by any means as the Dies Committee work. But it should have been more so. Here, after all, was a chance to hammer out before a congressional committee the answers to problems which everyone knew our country would one day have to face—such things as inflation and deflation, unemployment, farm "surpluses," labor-management relationships, and monopoly, to mention some of the toughest ones. For their solution "within the framework of liberty," courageous, bold thinking will be required of someone. Some of it, at least, ought to be done by members of the Congress. That is their job before anything else. I hoped the Special Committee on Post-War Economic Policy and Planning might begin it.

To be perfectly fair, I should say that our committee did scratch the surface. Its work in the fields of foreign trade, of public works and construction, and of agriculture was fundamental, long-range work. Otherwise, the committee's efforts and attention were bent upon the immediate problems of the reconversion from war to peace.

Perhaps this was inevitable. Perhaps those people were right who interpreted the Colmer Resolution as limiting the committee's work to getting America over the single hump of readjustment from war to peace. This was the most urgent job, of course, and what has been done about it will have considerable bearing on the future's more basic problems. Moreover, as I looked around me in one of the early committee meetings, I suddenly realized that most of the members, both Republican and Democratic, were good solid conservatives. And it isn't reasonable to expect a conservative to suddenly become a progressive just because he is appointed to a committee on "policy and planning" for the future.

The staff of the committee leaned also to the conservative side. Far too much of it, in my opinion, was "borrowed" from big business organizations. But it consisted of conscientious men who did a very able and efficient job of organizing the work of the committee, outlining reports, and arranging hearings.

By the time our committee was ready to begin its work, it was certainly not "too soon." With the war entering its later phases, the problems of economic readjustment were upon the nation before Congress had the ink dry on some of the most necessary laws to meet the situation. At first, therefore, the Post-War Committee worked pretty feverishly on such matters as contract termination (Report No. 1), disposal of surplus property (Report No. 2), and establishment of the Office of War Mobilization and Reconversion in the government (Report No. 3).

So far as surplus property disposal is concerned, there is, I am afraid, little for anyone to be particularly proud of. The thing that should have been done, as I look back, was to have put some first-class merchandiser (certainly not an army officer) in charge of the gigantic business; to have instructed him to sell either at wholesale or at retail and to establish such direct outlets for these purposes as might be necessary; to have directed him to sell in the smallest practicable quantities at all times; but above all to have commissioned him to get government surpluses into the hands of people who could use them just as fast and just as fairly and with as few middlemen along the line as humanly possible. Donald Nelson might have done it.

The committee delved into such problems as "accumulated savings," credit policies and monetary controls, taxes, unemployment compensation, the shifting of workers from war jobs to peacetime jobs—all from the short-range point of view. A report was issued on these subjects entitled "Economic Problems of the Reconversion Period."

Witnesses before the committee were the "big names" of the country—in government, business, labor, and agriculture. The refrain that ran through all the testimony—and indeed all the economic reports of the committee—was that "a high level" of production and employment, of investment and consumption must be maintained. As to how this was to be done there were, of course, differences of opinion. But that the consequence of our failing to achieve the objective would be something like disaster was agreed to by all. In the report for December 1946, written by the committee staff while most of the members were engaged in their political campaigns, there was a note of buoyant optimism. Unemployment, the report pointed out, had been much less than was feared—millions less, in fact—and even the tremendous decline in government expenditures following the victory had been almost compensated for by the very great demand for consumer goods.

All this was true, but I could not forget the word "maintain" which most witnesses had used. They had said, "We must *maintain* a high level of national income and production and employment." The question, obviously, was how to do it. Most of our committee work should have consisted in developing an answer to that question. A few measures were proposed which could supply part of that answer: expansion of mutually advantageous foreign trade through multilateral trade agreements, extending the coverage of the Social Security Act, a restudy of the whole scheme of financing the Social Security program, the stabilization of employment in the construction industry by timing public works to periods of slack private construction activity.

But generally speaking, the Post-War Committee's reports went along with the spirit of the times in which they were written— times when it was unpopular to recall the events of 1918–29, or to suggest that something more than orthodox economics and an optimistic attitude would be needed to continuously maintain that much-desired high level of economic activity.

This was evident, for example, in the overly cautious manner with which the committee dealt with the problem of a nation-wide housing shortage. Its report commended the FHA program of guaranteed loans for home construction, but failed to recommend a reduction in interest rates on such loans as a means of bringing the cost of home ownership more nearly within the reach of veterans and others of modest income. The proposal was made that state laws be amended to permit insurance companies and other fiduciary corporations to construct rental housing. But the crying need was (and is) for *low-rent* housing. To obtain any great expansion in the field something must clearly be done to attract investment into it. And, since necessarily both profit and rent margins must be lower than for high-rent properties, the only way to accomplish this lay in affording greater security to such investment. This the Wagner-Ellender-Taft bill would have done by providing for governmental guarantees of the yield from low-rent construction. But, perhaps because of the fact that that bill was "controversial," the committee neglected to recommend its passage.

The report failed to mention the opportunity for actual home ownership available to this very group of middle- and lower-income families by the proved method of mutual home-ownership associations.

The committee did, however, speak out courageously regarding slum clearance. It said that "there is an area of housing at the lowest rent levels which private industry cannot afford to serve, and which local government is not fully capable of serving." It said further that "the area of low-rental housing represents a field that is non-competitive with private construction." Thus the committee went squarely on record as saying that, if the slums are ever to be cleared at all and their children moved into decent American surroundings, the communities and the nation will have to help.

The Committee on Post-War Economic Policy and Planning was divided into subcommittees and I was assigned to the subcommittee on Agriculture. Except for the Foreign Trade subcommittee, ours was the only one that attempted the sort of work which I had conceived to be the main job of a postwar planning group. Our subcommittee on Agriculture determined at the outset to concentrate our work on basic problems and their long-run solution.

Witnesses included the nation's farm organization heads and leading agricultural economists. They told us that, while total agricultural production in the United States has been remarkably constant through the years, prices of agricultural products have fluctuated more severely than any other prices. They pointed out that co-operatives have enabled farmers to reduce distribution costs of crops they sell and supplies they buy, to keep the farmer's dollar circulating in his own community, and to reduce price instability through mutual farmer ownership of storage and marketing facilities.

To further reduce the instability of the farmers' incomes, witnesses proposed monetary and credit controls to prevent inflation and deflation, and the maintenance of a high level of demand for the farmers' products by "low-cost systems of food distribution," expansion of school lunch programs, and the promotion of improved nutritional standards for the whole nation.

Our subcommittee worked for considerably more than a year in preparing its report, which was approved by the full committee and submitted to the House as Report No. 10 of the Post-War Committee. Our report does not recommend rigid maintenance of farm prices at artificially high levels. It does, however, propose reasonable price floors to prevent sudden, serious, or speculative declines in farm prices. It opposes production controls except where they can be temporary means of "encouragement to farmers to shift into production of commodities where opportunity for higher returns is greatest." The report points out the necessity of "a program to improve the efficiency of the marketing process both as respects the farmers' procurement and the distribution of their products with recognition of the important contribution which cooperatives can make in assuring competitive conditions."

Recognizing America's dependence on her farmers for all supplies of food and fiber, our report calls for "a program to improve nutrition in periods of economic stress to assure proper diets to low-income consumers" and "an educational and assistance program to improve the nutritional standards and food consumption of the American people."

Agriculture is more than an industry or a business. It is a manner of living and should be made a brighter and more interesting one—for the sake of our national future. Therefore our report calls for better health services, for more telephones and more electric light and power, and above all for markedly improved educational opportunities for rural children.

The Colmer Committee issued two reports on postwar Europe. The first of these followed a trip to that stricken continent made in the summer of 1945 by several members of the committee (the author *not* included) and the staff. It was, I believe, a realistic and able report. It pointed out the danger in allowing conditions of misery and dependence to continue in Germany; it recommended passage of the British Loan bill and the extension of necessary financial and other help to the nations of western Europe; and it called a spade a spade with regard to the United States and Russia. The report did not shut the door to improvement in Soviet-American relationships or even to the making of a loan to Russia which was under active discussion at the time. But it did lay down conditions which the committee said should be fulfilled before such a loan or other economic aid to Russia were extended. One of these was the granting of freer trade in Soviet-dominated countries. Another was that the United States receive assurances that Americans having legitimate business there should have the same opportunity to enter and leave Russia as Soviet citizens enjoy in the United States. The whole idea of the loan was later dropped but had it been made on the conditions suggested by our committee I believe the result would have been salutary. This report, issued on November 12, 1945, was the work of the whole committee. Not all of us had gone to Europe, but there was long discussion of the report, paragraph by paragraph, numerous changes were made in it, and in final form it was a composite of the members' views.

As much cannot be said of a "summary report" on European conditions prepared by the committee staff and circulated by mail to committee members as a "résumé" of former work, on the very eve of the demise of the Seventy-ninth Congress in late December 1946. This was more than a résumé. It was a projection to advanced points of the lines of policy proposed in the report of November 1945. It caused a storm of protest on the left—and at least a flurry on the right. Briefly what was proposed was full and frank use of American economic resources, loans, and influence to bolster resistance to further extension of the Soviet sphere of control in Europe. The attitude and actions of the Soviet Union since the close of the war had led most people to believe it necessary to continue the firm policy pursued by Secretary Byrnes. But the committee staff had written "too much too soon." It had anticipated by some two and a half months the proposal of President Truman to Congress for the loans to Greece and Turkey. It sounded alarming. It involved America's taking up a burden of world responsibility which she did not want.

Future events would be shaped for good or ill depending upon whether, along with her "firmness," the United States would (1) push constructive and dynamic plans for improving the economic and social conditions of the people in the areas of decision; (2) make it clear again and again that this government is always ready to discuss legitimate problems and national needs—even national ambitions—with the Soviet Union or anyone else so long as the sacrifice of basic freedom on the part of smaller nations is not involved; and (3) use the United Nations machinery to the greatest possible extent but recognize the necessity of elimination of the veto and work sincerely to that end.

Thus some small part of the work of charting America's future course was accomplished. It still remains for every thoughtful citizen to carry that work forward. Our chance of meeting future difficulties with hopefulness and with success is solely dependent upon the foresight with which we prepare against them.

Chapter 18

ATOMIC ENERGY—
CURSE OR BLESSING?

From the moment when I walked onto the porch of a California home and its owner showed me the headlines telling of the atomic bombing of Hiroshima, this so-called triumph of modern science has had, for me, an aspect of almost mystical foreboding.

The people of the United States accepted with profound seriousness the fact of the atomic age when it first burst upon the world. But like other peoples we tend to become absorbed in our day-to-day tasks and troubles and to forget the larger ones upon whose accomplishment everything may depend.

These are times when we can afford no such retreat, when each American must either share in acts of national greatness which move the world to peace or else bear his share of the blame for tragic failure of the greatest promise of true peace which man has ever known.

We talk as if atomic energy were something new. Actually it is as old as the universe which contains our tiny solar system and the infinitesimal speck of our world. It is as old as matter, as old as creation. It was an integral part of the act of creation itself.

To anyone with so much as a spark of religious sense, therefore, the harnessing of atomic energy by man to his purposes has an appalling and awful meaning. Unlocking the atom is taking to ourselves the basic energy of the universe and presuming to steer its course by conscious human decision instead of allowing it to follow in the natural path of the countless millenniums of time. We, this generation, have snatched from the womb of matter what may be the greatest gift and secret of nature's God.

If such an energy is to be controlled by deliberate human decisions, then those decisions will either be correct ones or a terrible retribution will visit the earth. In the years that lie immediately ahead we have no business as important as·that of so governing our own action and guiding that of others as to make the fundamental energy that lies latent in all things a blessing rather than a curse to humanity.

At the forefront of sane, farsighted statesmanship in the field of atomic energy has stood Senator Brien McMahon, of Connecticut. Had he not secured passage of his resolution creating the special Senate Committee on Atomic Energy, the Congress might well have gone the way of the May-Johnson bill—attempted with childlike naïveté to lock atomic energy in a vault in the Pentagon Building and serve notice on the world that it would "perpetually" remain an American secret military weapon. The mere fact that such action would have had no effect on other countries except to induce them to redouble their bomb-making efforts seems not to have occurred to the advocates of this type of legislation.

But freshman Senator McMahon had taken a courageous position from the start. He introduced in the Senate the first bills looking toward world control immediately after Congress reassembled in September 1945, just after V-J Day. With his concurrence I introduced similar bills in the House. And Senator McMahon did get his committee. More than that, he successfully insisted that, according to precedent, he be named its chairman. When membership of the committee was first announced everyone said Senator McMahon had won a hollow victory. He was chairman, but his committee was composed of the most venerable, the most conservative, and the most military-minded of senators. What could he do?

Just one thing—expose them to the facts. And expose them he did, with the result that after months of the most carefully arranged hearings in which every possible point of view was fully presented the committee report was unanimous. Not only that but the bill, which Senator McMahon introduced as the best interim measure possible to present at that point of knowledge and world relationship, was also unanimously passed by the Senate.

The bill provided for an Atomic Energy Commission of five members, none of whom could hold any other position during their term of service on this body. The commission was "authorized and directed to purchase, take, requisition, condemn, or otherwise acquire supplies of source material (uranium and thorium) or any interest in real property containing deposits of source material. . . ." In other words the commission was to hold and control for the United States all materials capable of producing atomic energy. But the bill also charged the commission with carrying on and encouraging research and development in atomics both for peacetime and for military purposes. And, to the extent consistent with national safety, the bill also directed the commission to license the use of atomic energy for industrial, scientific, or health purposes. But, if any such licenses were granted, then the commission must grant them equitably so as to prevent monopoly. Thus the bill sought to promote American progress in atomic energy in the only way in which at the existing stage of knowledge it could be safely done.

But in the House there was no Senator McMahon. Some of us were doing our best. But the House, because of its larger membership, operates differently from the Senate. In the Senate if a single senator is absolutely determined on a given objective, the courtesies of that body, if not its convictions, pretty well assure him of at least a hearing. But in the House no one member or even informal group of members can have any such assurance. There the committees govern almost completely what is or is not to be done. Fortunate it is, therefore, that the more thoughtful members of the Military Affairs Committee had begun to assert themselves and that with Senate passage of the McMahon bill a new climate was apparent in that committee's councils. In my judgment five members of the committee were primarily responsible for this constructive change. They were the ranking member, Ewing Thomason, of Texas, Carl Durham, of North Carolina,

Melvin Price, of Illinois, and Chet Holifield, of California, all Democrats, and J. Leroy Johnson, of California, a Republican.

The efforts of every member of the House, however, were, for the most obvious of reasons, hampered by lack of knowledge. We simply could not know in any detail the facts of atomic energy. But we received invaluable aid from people who did know. Framed on the basis of the most painstaking study and the best and most comprehensive of scientific counsel, the Acheson-Lilienthal Report was released by the State Department on March 26, 1946. This report emphasized once again the peril with which the release of atomic energy confronted the world. It considered and rejected every means of protection of mankind, every method of "control" short of the type of outright world governmental agency which to some of us had, after our first talks with the scientists, seemed the only answer. It pointed out that mere treaty agreements among the nations to "outlaw" the use of atomic bombs would almost certainly be broken and could not possibly give adequate security. It analyzed the feasibility of various means of international policing of atomic energy production, and found that some of these which had been most widely discussed would almost certainly be ineffective. The entire approach of the report was constructive: how to make the potential benefits of atomic energy available to mankind without at the same time exposing all the peoples of the earth to ever-increasing danger of atomic attack.

The Acheson-Lilienthal Report presented a new point of view in two important respects. It offered hope—for the first time so far as I was concerned—that peacetime benefits of atomic energy could be had by the peoples of the world without the terrible dangers we had learned to associate with this great force. If the report was correct about the possibility of "denaturing" fissionable materials, it might not be necessary, as some of us had almost come to believe it was, to forgo all peacetime uses of atomic energy until such time as mankind had "grown up" socially and politically. In the second place, considerable doubt had been cast upon the effectiveness of systems of inspection as a means of assuring the people of one nation that no other nation was manufacturing atomic weapons. A good many scientists had expressed doubt about the possibility of making any such inspections absolutely evasion-proof. But the proposal of the State Department's board went at the problem from another angle—at once more thoroughgoing, more scientific, and more constructive. Instead of proposing negative powers of control for the "internationally controlled World Atomic Authority" it proposed the positive powers of development, production, and even ownership of all the dangerous materials and activities connected with atomic energy. It proposed that all the mining of uranium, thorium, or other minerals capable of maintaining chain reactions, all the refining of these minerals, and all production of fissionable materials should be carried on by the world authority and by no other agency. Only "denatured" fissionable material could be legally in the possession of anyone else in the world. Such a control would, it appeared, almost certainly be effective.

The members of the Board of Consultants which prepared the Acheson-Lilienthal Report for the State Department were the vice-president of the General Electric Company, the vice-president of the Monsanto Chemical Co., the president of the New Jersey Bell Telephone Co., and Dr. J. Robert Oppenheimer, of California Institute of Technology. The chairman was Mr. David E. Lilienthal, of the Tennessee Valley Authority.

Coming from a group like this, the report had at least to be taken seriously by anyone who gave heed to it at all. And to many people, among whom I certainly was numbered, the Acheson-Lilienthal Report brought more true hope for the future of our children than we had known since Hiroshima. Resolutions were introduced in both houses of Congress—one of them by me—urging the President to make the proposals of the report the official policy of the United States and the basis for negotiations looking toward international action.

In the course of time this was precisely what took place. On June 14, 1946, Mr. Bernard Baruch, speaking for the United States as chairman of the American delegates on the Atomic Energy Commission of the United Nations, presented to the world this country's proposal for the control of atomic energy and the prevention of atomic war. It was the United States of America speaking.

The issue was placed squarely before a listening world:

"Behind the black portent of the new atomic age lies a hope which, seized upon with faith, can work our salvation. If we fail, then we have damned every man to be the slave of fear. Let us not deceive ourselves: We must elect world peace or world destruction."

The proposal of the United States was summarized in one paragraph:

"The United States proposes the creation of an international atomic development authority, to which should be entrusted all phases of the development and use of atomic energy, starting with the raw material and including:

1.   Managerial control or ownership of all atomic energy activities potentially dangerous to world security.

2.   Power to control, inspect, and license all other atomic activities.

3.   The duty of fostering the beneficial uses of atomic energy.

4.   Research and development responsibilities of an affirmative character intended to put the authority in the forefront of atomic knowledge and thus to enable it to comprehend, and therefore to detect, misuse of atomic energy."

And then came words previously unheard in international councils. A great nation offered to lay her unquestioned military supremacy upon the altar of peace. In these words, more than in any others in the address, were contained the "statesmanship worthy of the times" about which I had spoken so often in the House.

"When an adequate system of atomic energy controls, including the renunciation of the bomb as a weapon, has been agreed upon and put into effective operation and condign punishments set up for violations of the rules of control which are to be stigmatized as international crimes, we propose that:

1.   Manufacture of atomic bombs shall stop;

2.   Existing bombs shall be disposed of pursuant to the terms of the treaty; and

3.   The authority shall be in possession of full information as to the know-how for the production of atomic energy."

America was not proposing to give the atomic bomb to Russia

or to Spain or to any other country or group of countries. She was proposing to give it to peace, to an effective agency for the keeping of the peace. Unless she could secure agreement to the minimum requirements for peace she would have to keep her knowledge and do the best she could to "stay ahead in the race." America's condition was, briefly, that all the nations agree to subject themselves to the supremacy of the law of peace.

"My country is ready to make its full contribution toward the end we seek, subject, of course, to our constitutional processes, and to an adequate system of control becoming fully effective as we finally work it out.

"Now as to violations: In the agreement, penalties of as serious a nature as the nations may wish and as immediate and certain in their execution as possible, should be fixed for:

1. Illegal possession or use of an atomic bomb:

2. Illegal possession or separation of atomic material suitable for use in an atomic bomb;

3. Seizure of any plan or other property belonging to or licensed by the authority;

4. Willful interference with the activities of the authority;

5. Creation or operation of dangerous projects in a manner contrary to, or in the absence of, a license granted by the international control body."

And then Mr. Baruch spoke of the problem that was to prove the most difficult stumbling block of all—the problem without whose solution no true world control is possible. It was the veto. He said, in effect, that the veto could not be used to nullify enforcement action against a nation violating the rules laid down in the agreement. The United States was not, he emphasized, proposing to disturb the veto as to other questions. But if world authority were to be substituted for the warlike will of nations in the field of atomic weapons, it would be a clear contradiction of elemental logic to permit any one of five nations to continue to assert their supremacy to the law of peace itself. If this were permitted, then those nations would become the only enforcement agents against their own illegal acts, should they commit them.

Mr. Baruch was right. The position he took is still right.

The American representative did not stop there. He went on to show that solution of the atomic bomb problem will be, once achieved, the means of dealing with the perils of bacteriological weapons and the key to lasting peace itself.

"But before a country is ready to relinquish any winning weapons it must have more than words to reassure it. It must háve a guaranty of safety not only against the offenders in the atomic area but against the illegal users of other weapons—bacteriological, biological, gas, perhaps, why not? against war itself.

"In the elimination of war lies our solution, for only then will nations cease to compete with one another in the production and use of dread secret weapons which are evaluated solely by their capacity to kill. This devilish program takes us back not merely to the Dark Ages but from cosmos to chaos. If we succeed in finding a suitable way to control atomic weapons, it is reasonable to hope that we may also preclude the use of other weapons adaptable to mass destruction. When a man learns to say 'a' he can, if he chooses, learn the rest of the alphabet, too."

This was America's plan, her proposal, her vision. It was hoped, of course, that it would be at once accepted by all the nations. Ten of the twelve nations represented on the Atomic Energy Commission did in fact accept it at once. Only Russia and Poland refused. Nor should this have caused too deep wonderment. For America's proposal involved, inevitably, the lifting of the iron curtain from around the only other power of first magnitude in the world, which power happened also to be the strongest dictatorship of modern times.

Neither Mr. Baruch, nor President Truman, nor the whole executive department of government, nor the Congress could put into effect in the world what was now the official policy of the United States. That, some of us knew, would be a long, hard process. It would probably be a process fraught with disappointment. It would require the united, devoted, and informed support of the American people. But there could be no turning back.

One of the first essentials was the backing of the Congress. I inserted the entire text of Mr. Baruch's address to the United Nations commission in the *Congressional Record*. I collected editorial comment and inserted it as well. A number of members of Congress spoke in strong support of our country's plan. But the main thing Congress had to do was to pass legislation for domestic policy and practice regarding atomic energy which would implement our proposal to the other nations.

Such legislation had already passed the Senate. The McMahon bill was all that could be asked as demonstration that America meant business and that we were going to put our own house in such order as to fit it for participation in the world peace plan which we ourselves had advanced.

It was mid-July, however, before the bill reached the floor of the House. The debate on the bill was, especially in the early stages, profoundly discouraging. Members spoke of atomic energy and the atomic bomb as if they were completely synonymous. They attacked Senator McMahon and all his work. They attacked the Senate committee. They said that "the secret" was in a "safe place" and should be kept there—but did not explain just where that "place" was. The very central purposes of the bill were attacked. It was said that the commission was to be given "too much power," that it was "unnecessary" to do so, that the "liberties" of the nation would be endangered.

The same members who wanted to keep "the secret" locked in a vault in the War Department and who forgot that whatever secret there was resided only in the minds of a handful of civilian scientists were the stanchest advocates of turning atomic energy over to uncontrolled exploitation and outright ownership by private corporations.

Mr. Short, of Missouri, in the course of his speech said: "We are going to set up an Atomic Energy Commission and give it the power of life and death over private industry in this country." He referred, of course, principally to the provisions of the bill which prevented the patenting of atomic energy as such, and gave the commission power to require the licensing of the use of patents on *applications* of atomic energy if they were of such importance as to vitally affect the public interest. I asked Mr. Short to yield to me for a question, which he kindly did.

"I would like to ask the gentleman," I said, "whether he believes that the provisions in the bill which assure to every single American business that may arise in the future an equal opportunity to the benefits of atomic energy are destructive of private enterprise?"

Mr. Short replied: "No, but——"

I said: "That is what the bill does."

To which Mr. Short rejoined: "Well, that is state socialism."

It was a far cry from state socialism so far as I could see. And it was, and is, the only way to prevent atomic energy, once safely harnessed for peacetime uses, from becoming the exclusive property of a few special interests.

Mr. Short, however, was by no means alone in his viewpoint. Indeed, at the time a majority of the House was on his side, for the patent sections of the bill were to be successfully amended by Mr. Lanham, of Texas, in such a way as to have permitted the private patenting of atomic energy itself.

Member after member got up and contended that there was no necessity for the House passing any bill at all! One speaker lauded the Baruch proposal unreservedly and then concluded by urging that the bill before the House—the one measure which could carry out domestically the principles of the Baruch proposal—should be sent back to the committee "for further study."

To which I commented: "I agree heartily with what the gentleman said about the Baruch proposal to the United Nations Commisson on Atomic Energy. I believe that proposition ought to prove to any nation the sincerity of the United States in seeking peace. But I think it important that our action correspond to that proposal. The gentleman will agree, I hope, that those people who are responsible for the preparation of the Baruch proposal are in favor of the bill as written by the Senate."

But the reply (of Mr. Harness, of Indiana) was: "That would not influence my feeling on the bill at all."

Other members praising the Baruch plan contended that the McMahon bill would "give away the secret." This despite the obvious fact that the only way under the bill whereby any knowledge of atomics could be shared with any other nation was if all other nations—every one of them—agreed in full to that very Baruch proposal. These opponents argued against the very bill which offered the only means available to the United States to guard against the widest and most irresponsible dissemination of both fissionable material and knowledge regarding it. How any secret could be guarded under such circumstances was not explained.

I asked the chairman of the committee to give me as many minutes to speak in the general debate as he could spare. He "yielded" me twelve minutes. In those few minutes I tried to present what I considered the principal arguments for the passage of the McMahon bill. Some of the things I said were these:

"Unless a bill of this general character is passed, the development of atomic energy which has proceeded under great difficulty in recent years cannot go forward. The fact is it is not now going forward. The great majority of the most eminent scientific workers have left the project.

"I believe that American development must go on until it is possible to secure a world control, such as the Baruch Report proposes. American pre-eminence in this field, coupled with the most persistent work for peace, might give us the leverage to bring about the conditions and the enforceable disarmament which could make true peace possible.

"But it is necessary that some form of civilian commission of this sort be created together with attendant changes in the circumstances under which the work will be done if we are to bring the scientists back.

"My second reason for believing the bill necessary is that if we are to hope for international control we will have to first establish in the United States an effective control over atomic energy within our own borders. We do not have it now. There is nothing in present law to prevent any Tom, Dick, or Harry from possessing fissionable material, manfacturing bombs with it, or exporting it out of the country. We are in a situation comparable to that of a bunch of children playing with TNT.

"I believe I have at least an inkling of what atomic energy is. And not only do I know it will be our destruction unless moral and, indeed, religious and spiritual forces of corresponding strength are awakened throughout the world to meet it, but I also believe, pending that time, it must be controlled if mankind is to survive and to preserve any real vestige of his civilization on this planet."

When I sat down after making that speech I felt better. And I felt better still as I found a good deal of quiet support among members who had as yet not expressed themselves on the bill. For three days the House considered amendments to the bill. Many of them were discussed at length and several of them were adopted. An amendment requiring FBI investigation of all persons employed on atomic energy projects was adopted and I voted for it. But I bitterly opposed two other amendments, both of which were adopted in the House. One of these proposed by Mr. Elston, of Ohio, struck from the bill a provision which said that, after —and only after—an effective system of world control of atomic energy had been agreed to by all the nations and put into effect, the United States would share with other nations knowledge of atomics which might be useful to medical science, the saving of human life, and to industry.

The other amendment was that of Mr. Lanham, of Texas, which drastically amended the patent sections of the bill. I argued against the Lanham amendment as vigorously as I knew how. I said:

"We are dealing with a power here before the House today which may well transform the entire economy of the United States, and I have no fear of taking my stand on these grounds: First, I think the bill as written is quite right in refusing to allow the patentability of atomic energy itself, the very energy of the sun, for the development of which the American people as a whole have paid $2,000,000,000 and which, by every principle, must always belong to all the people. Second, I think the bill is also altogether correct in charging the commission with this duty: that if in the future a patent is taken on some application of atomic energy—if it happens that such an invention is made that would, for example, deprive every company or agency of this country that now furnishes power or heat or light to the people of the very foundation of its business—then, under those circumstances, the commission should exercise its power to require compulsory licensing, at a fair royalty, of such a patent. Unless this provision is retained, there is every likelihood of more complete monopolistic power than the world has ever seen being built on the basis of patents on this basic energy.

"Would the House want some private agency to hold a patent on the air we breathe? I believe not. But who is to say the basic energy of every piece of matter in this universe is any more a fit subject for private patent than the air? No, Mr. Chairman; these amendments are wrong. I am against them. I support the patent sections of the Senate bill."

We had now reached the end of the bill. One or two further amendments were to be considered and then the time for the final votes would come.

The danger was not so much that it would be defeated on the final roll call. The people were too deeply concerned for that. But there had been a good deal of talk about "recommitting" the bill. This would have meant sending it back to the Military Affairs Committee to begin all over the whole process of hearings, amendment in committee, reporting of the bill, consideration on the floor, and all the rest. This would have meant the death of the legislation. Congress was about to adjourn and nothing could have been done about atomic energy at all if the motion to recommit carried.

One of my most valued possessions is a dog-eared copy of the New York *Times* for July 21, 1946. For in the paper is contained this brief paragraph:

> Later, when Mr. Cooley was arguing at the microphone for killing the bill, Representative Jerry Voorhis, Democrat, of California, strode up and made the Administration's most challenging and effective speech, bringing cheers from the galleries. He declared the bill would centralize atomic control, prevent unlicensed use of fissionable material, advance the cause of medicine and industry, and had been endorsed by the President, the Secretaries of the Army and Navy and should be passed if the United States position before the United Nations was not to be repudiated.

The House did not recommit the bill. It defeated the recommittal motion by a comfortable margin and then passed the bill by an overwhelming vote. A majority of the House conferees were men who had fought as hard as anyone for a good bill.

And when the conference report was brought into the House for a vote a few days later I felt a great battle had been won. For the bill in its final form followed the original Senate Mc-Mahon bill in all important respects. The patent provisions of the Senate bill were restored and the Lanham amendment discarded. The Senate language, stricken out by the Elston amendment, was also restored. It was a good bill. The Seventy-ninth Congress, bad as its record in some other respects was, rose, in my humble opinion, to real heights of statesmanship when it passed that bill.

But the battle is not over.

The Baruch plan has not yet been accepted by all the nations. Russia's agreement to the "principle of international inspection" has been so seriously qualified as to render it almost meaningless. Principle without practice can hardly save mankind in the atomic age. But some progress is indicated and if America will stand firm, above all if she will stand united, there is still substantial hope that man can become the master of atomic energy instead of the slave to fear of it.

Most Americans have missed one important reason for the Russian attitude. Most of us have believed that the whole trouble has been Russian stubbornness and reluctance to agree to even a sincerely profferred plan for peace if it involved a lifting of the Iron Curtain. And no doubt the Politburo, like all dictatorial groups known to history, has been afraid of the consequences if that curtain were raised.

But the people of the United States—every one of us—must take some of the blame. For the actions of the Russian government are not controlled by the opinions or desires of the Russian people. They are controlled by what Russian government leaders believe they can get away with.

And what have they seen in the United States? They have seen the Acheson-Lilienthal Report of the State Department received almost coldly by all too large a percentage of our people. They have even seen David Lilienthal pilloried before a Senate committee—because politics is, in some people's minds, more important than the very lives of the next generation. These

Russian leaders did not see the United States electrified when the Baruch plan was presented to the United Nations. They did not find a profound consecration developing among this free people to do everything in their power for its acceptance by the nations. Instead they saw America take her own plan for lasting peace almost in stride. They saw that only a handful of members of Congress made it their primary business to work ceaselessly for it in their official positions. They saw news of it presented in press and radio in parallel with stories about murders and train wrecks. Pretty soon the Russians found that, apparently, some Americans had become almost weary of hearing about the Baruch plan for peace enforcement. They had "had enough" of these efforts to save the world. And the Soviet government found that it could even count on some opposition to the plan in the United States. Had not Mr. Henry Wallace and others criticized it? So if Russian leaders would hold out awhile maybe they could get something more favorable to the Soviet Union.

So they did. But had American public opinion shown genuine passionate zeal for this American peace proposal—the brightest hope for true peace in man's long bloody history—the story would, I think, have been different. It can still be different. But it will only be different if we, the American people, fully realize what an easygoing attitude in times like these may someday cost our children.

Meanwhile, another danger stares us in the face. For in every conservative Congress, which term certainly includes the present one, there will be danger of repeal of the patent sections, at least, of the McMahon bill. The Eightieth Congress was not an hour old before lobbying by the most powerful of interests for this repeal was well under way. And there were members of Congress who listened gladly. Enough has been said already to indicate the perils, both to our domestic economic liberties and to international peace, which such action would bring. But unless the people are awake and vocal, all or part of the McMahon bill may be lost.

Never was it quite so true as in this atomic age that "eternal vigilance is the price of liberty" and unremitting devotion to the common good the price of peace.

Chapter 19

THE "LITTLE" BILLS

People are always trying to induce members of Congress to introduce bills. Some of them are of the most minor and specialized kind, having to do with the erection of a monument, the building of a bridge, or the awarding of a donation to a faithful House employee. Others are of the most far-reaching nature, setting forth large-scale plans for the overcoming of unemployment or the establishment of a system of old-age pensions.

But the introduction of a bill is only the first step toward a law. And it must be followed by a long process of the most difficult and varied types of work before final success can be expected. Even then most bills that are introduced fail of enactment.

In some respects the hardest task a congressman ever faces comes to him when he decides that it is his duty to introduce a certain bill in which he alone has a deep interest. In such cases he must not only be prepared to debate and to vote. He must first develop interest among the other members. He must work with—not to say *on*—the members of the committee to which the bill has been referred. He must arrange for hearings, assemble witnesses, attempt to secure a favorable committee report. Then, unless his bill is completely non-controversial and can be passed by "unanimous consent," he must help the committee, whose interest may be only a passive one, to secure a rule for its consideration by resolution of the Rules Committee. He must persuade the Speaker and majority leader to schedule the bill for action on the floor. Then and only then can he be sure there will even be a vote on it at all. And if he succeeds in getting the bill through the House he must then, without even being a member of that body, try to bring about the same series of events in the Senate.

It happened, as the year 1946 began, that there were several measures which I believed it part of my job to see enacted into law. Before the spring had come a number more had been added to that list, which I thumbtacked to the window frame beside my desk.

This was the list:

1. H.J.R. 192: to give compensation payments to disabled veterans the status of debt payments instead of "gratuities."

2. H.R. 95: to transfer government services to the domestic rabbit industry from the Interior to the Agriculture Department.

3. H.R. 3327: to make certain amendments to the Federal Credit Union Act.

4. H.J.R. 325: to forbid the use of grain for any non-essential purpose, including liquor manufacture, during the period of acute food and feed shortage.

5. H.R. 6576: to release to the state of California sufficient of the Social Security tax collections in that state to enable its program of disability insurance to be put into operation.

6. Amend public works bills like flood control, roads, and rivers and harbors bills to provide that such works shall be undertaken in accordance with sound economic principles.

7. Amend the Wagner-Ellender-Taft Housing Bill to provide a separate administration for co-operative mutual home ownership projects, to include student co-operatives, and to make people of medium as well as low incomes eligible for guaranteed loans to mutual home ownership associations.

8. Defend appropriations for the Anti-Trust Division of the Department of Justice.

9. Prevent appropriations being made for Whittier Narrows dam.

It will be evident that the first five items on my list were bills of my own introduction which I sought to have passed; that Items 6, 7, and 8 had to do with efforts to amend legislation likely to come onto the floor; and that the last item called for opposition to an appropriation requested by the Corps of Army Engineers.

My veterans' resolution was not passed. I spoke for it several times on the floor and inserted in the *Record* resolutions by veteran organizations (principally the Disabled American Veterans) in support of it. I asked the Committee on World War Veterans' Legislation to grant me a hearing on it, and while I was promised such a hearing "at the appropriate time," no such time ever seemed to come. I repeated my request from time to time but always with the same result. The purport of my resolution was very simple. Under existing law the government of the United States pays compensation to men injured in battle not because it has any legal obligation to do so but only because it voluntarily decides to do so. Such payments are regarded in common law not as something to which the disabled veteran is entitled as a right but as something he receives out of the kindness of the government's heart. A bondholder who stayed at home could sue the government to collect his interest if the government did not pay it. But a veteran who went to war is in an inferior category according to present law. He has no legal recourse in attempting to collect "interest" on the leg he lost and an adverse decision by the Veterans' Administration on his claim is final. Such a situation has seemed to me about as wrong as anything could be. I discussed it with some of the leaders of the Disabled American Veterans in California, and it was from them, notably from Captain A. A. Roe, that I received orginally the idea of my resolution. But veterans' organizations generally did not actively support the resolution; the committee of the House was just not interested; and so, although I cared more about it, I believe, than any of the others, I failed on Item 1.

With my rabbit bill I had better luck. The reason for the bill was simple. In southern California, and in the Twelfth District particularly, the raising of rabbits has in recent years become a substantial farming business. During the war the rabbit men contributed markedly to the meat supply. In 1945, 4,000,000 animals were marketed in Los Angeles County alone.

But, in the reorganization of the executive department of government, all research work and all services to the rabbit producers were moved with the Fish and Wild Life Service over into the Interior Department. The rabbit people wanted their products to be classified as "agricultural products." They believed they should be served by the Bureau of Animal Industry. And there was no possible logical argument against their contention.

The *California Rabbit Magazine* put it this way: "Why should an industry that produces food and clothing be put under the same head as snakes, turtles, skunks, and fish?"

My bill was referred to the Committee on Agriculture—my own committee, which fact greatly simplified my problem. As a matter of fact I had succeeded in getting the bill passed by the House in the Seventy-eighth Congress, only to have it die for want of action in the Senate.

The trouble was that I was literally the only member of either house of Congress who was taking any active interest in this comparatively little-known group of small farmers.

We needed some allies. And with the beginning of the Seventy-ninth Congress we found them. Other raisers of fur-bearing animals also wanted to have their work transfered to the Agriculture Department. And these branches of animal husbandry were in many states of the union. Wisconsin was interested and Senator La Follette was prepared to help. But even more encouraging was the fact that Congressman Walter K. Granger, of Utah, one of the finest men I have ever known in Congress or out of it, was preparing to introduce a bill which would shift to the Agriculture Department all government research and service to producers of all domestically produced fur-bearing animals. His bill was so framed that it included all the provisions of my H.R. 95 and everything the rabbit men wanted, plus the provisions for the other fur farmers.

Obviously the wise thing to do for the rabbit farmers was to ally our cause with that of the others. So I told Mr. Granger that we would forget about my bill and throw all our efforts behind his.

Together we succeeded in getting the Granger bill (H.R. 2115) favorably reported by our committee. Only the Interior

Department opposed it openly, though there was covert opposition from some of the big livestock interests, partly because of the fact that many of the rabbit people were organized in co-operatives. Mr. Granger and I went before the Rules Committee and secured a rule for his bill. Then we spoke to the Speaker and majority leader and on March 20, 1946, H.R. 2115 by Mr. Granger, of Utah, was "called up" on the floor of the House and passed.

It remained to get the bill through the Senate. But this time Senator La Follette arranged an early hearing before the Senate Agriculture Committee. He testified briefly and then I was called to the stand. There were a number of other witnesses present and ready to testify, but before I had spoken more than a few minutes one of the Senators moved to report the bill favorably and the motion carried. A short time thereafter the Senate passed the bill, and it was signed by the President despite the fact that it changed one of the parts of the reorganization program of the executive department.

As congressmen do in all such instances, I had kept in touch with the rabbit people at home. As each successful step was taken I would telegraph them and advise what had to be done next. And so on April thirtieth I sent telegrams to the Secretary of the Los Angeles County Farm Bureau, to the Rabbit Breeders Co-operative, to the Grange, and to a number of individual farmers, advising them that the President had signed the Granger bill. One of the items on my list had been carried through to success. The bill with my name on it was not the one that became law. But all the provisions of it had been enacted and the constructive change which the rabbit farmers needed had been accomplished. That, after all, was the important thing.

I had equal success with the Credit Union bill. It consisted of a series of amendments to the basic Federal Credit Union Act which were needed to plug some loopholes and to help the credit unions to function more efficiently. The most important change was to increase from $100 to $300 the amount a credit union could loan to one of its members without security. A lot of credit-union funds were lying idle and this change seemed important for that reason. Other provisions had to do with the manner of calling meetings, requirements for bonding the treasurers, and so on.

I was requested by the Credit Union National Association to introduce this bill. And I felt this a great honor. I had the very able help, in working for this bill, of Mr. Hubert Rhodes, the Washington representative of the credit unions. He and I discussed the bill with individual members of the Banking and Currency Committee first of all. We made sure that a report on the bill had been submitted by the Federal Deposit Insurance Corporation, the supervising agency for credit unions. Then we asked for a hearing, and Mr. Brent Spence, the beloved chairman of the Banking and Currency Committee, scheduled it. Aside from brief testimony from a representative of the Federal Deposit Insurance Corporation, Mr. Rhodes and I were the only witnesses. I was on the stand most of the session. Some of the committee members showed some hostility to the basic idea of a credit union, a point of view hard for me to understand. However not only the Democratic members but also Mr. Wolcott, the ranking Republican, were clearly for the bill. Several perfecting amendments, however, were suggested and to these I agreed. The hearing ended with a virtual assurance to me that with the amendments included in it the bill would be favorably reported by the committee.

The question then arose, in informal discussion between Mr. Spence and me, as to the best way of handling the amendments. It was agreed between us that, instead of having the amendments adopted on the floor, which might lead to controversy, it would be better that a "clean bill" be introduced. The next question was, who should introduce this clean bill? Mr. Spence at first wanted me to do so. But it was late in the session, and a bill carrying the name of the chairman of the committee would be in the most favorable position to gain quick action. So I urged Mr. Spence to reintroduce the bill in its slightly amended form. This he did and it was passed by the House without dissent.

Senator Wagner, a long-time friend of credit unions, handled the bill in the Senate and, since he was chairman of the Banking and Currency Committee, there was no problem about arranging a hearing. One additional amendment was adopted in the Senate version of the bill but it remained in every important feature the same bill I had introduced as H.R. 3327.

On July 19, 1946, Mr. Spence made a motion in the House to agree to the Senate amendment and pass the bill. The motion carried and "H.R. 6372 by Mr. Spence of Kentucky" went to the President for his signature and became a law.

House Joint Resolution 325 never was voted upon by either the Committee on Agriculture or the House. But its purpose was largely accomplished by other means. As hunger and even starvation swept the world in the aftermath of the war and as the world supplies of grain were spread with tragic thinness to try to meet this need, the Grange and the Farm Bureau in California both passed resolutions urging that so long as this terrible shortage should last no more grain be permitted to be used for any nonessential purpose. The farm organizations had an immediate interest in the matter, but it was one which affected the entire nation as well, for it was proving necessary to slaughter livestock, especially poultry, simply because feed could not be obtained.

Acting on the basis of the Grange and Farm Bureau resolutions, and also on my own deep conviction, I drew up and introduced H.J.R. 325, which, had it passed, would have forbidden the use of any grain for any purpose other than human or livestock food until the shortage was relieved. One of the "nonessential purposes" under the bill was the manufacture of liquors.

A storm of protest of course arose from the liquor industry of the country. Already the Department of Agriculture had limited the amount of grain they could use. And as public interest became more intense and conditions more serious the department bore down more and more severely. I like to think my resolution had something to do with this. And I believe it did. Mr. Flannagan, the chairman of our committee, introduced a similar measure a little later on. Thousands of communications in support of H.J.R. 325 were received in my office and, I know, in other congressional offices. The main obstacle to its passage was the argument: "Isn't the Agriculture Department doing this already?" And they were doing about sixty-six and two-thirds per cent of it. My bill would simply have clamped the lid on tight.

With the invaluable help of a Washington citizen who must be nameless but who had access to all the facts behind the scenes, I filled the *Congressional Record* with data in support of my position. I showed that the distillers had, as of May 1946, no less than three years' supply of hard liquor already in storage; showed that their stocks were increasing every month despite the restrictions. It seemed to me we could afford to suspend making any more liquor for three or four months! On April twenty-seventh I wrote an open letter to the President in which I pointed out that the amount of grain to be used by distilleries in the next sixty days would be enough to keep some 14,000,000 people alive for that same length of time.

It was argued that some of the grain was unfit for human consumption. My reply was that it would certainly be helpful, however, to devote it to saving some of our farmers' livestock and thus protecting the basic agricultural wealth of America.

A few months later, in the election campaign, I was to discover to my astonishment that my "real purposes" in all this were very sinister ones. What I was trying to do was to "destroy small business." At least that is what propaganda of the liquor interests told the people. It is interesting to bear in mind that four huge corporations control most of the distilling business of the country.

The fifth project on my 1946 list was passage of H.R. 6576, designed to provide funds for the California disability insurance program. Early in 1946 the California state legislature had passed a law providing for such a system as a part of the unemployment insurance program. As matters stood before (and as they still stand in most states), if a person was unemployed but in good health he could draw his unemployment insurance. But if the man or woman was *both* unemployed and sick or disabled not a cent of insurance could be collected. Obviously the need was greater in the second case than in the first one. So the California legislature passed the law for disability insurance.

The governor wrote to me, as I presume he did to all California members of Congress, pointing out that unless the Social Security Board would release some of California's tax collections which had been paid into the unemployment insurance trust fund, it would not be possible to put the disability insurance into effect until one year had passed from the date of enactment of the new California law. I inquired of the Social Security Board and found they could not do this unless directed to do so by an act of Congress. I asked them what sort of act would be required and secured the text of a bill that would accomplish the purpose. This I promptly introduced as H.R. 6576. The bill was referred to the Ways and Means Committee, the most formidable in the House, and I knew full well, and so advised the governor, that only the united efforts of all California representatives could bring its enactment. Even then the only likely method was by getting the substance of the bill included in an omnibus measure amendatory of the Social Security Act. It happened that the Ways and Means Committee was at that very time considering such a bill.

California sent several representatives to Washington to, I suppose, "lobby" for this bill—or at any rate for what my bill contained. One of them in particular, Mr. Merrick, proved one of the most effective workers with the Congress I have ever known. The long and short of the matter was that the House Ways and Means Committee did not include any provision to cover our California disability insurance program. And since the Ways and Means bill came onto the floor under a special "closed" rule which forbade any amendments, there was nothing that I or anyone else could do to try to insert the language of my bill on the floor.

In the Senate, however, it was a different story. The two California senators went to work on the matter and, ably assisted, I am sure, by the genial and understanding Mr. Merrick, succeeded in getting the Senate Finance Committee to include the provisions of H.R. 6576 in the Social Security bill. These provisions were agreed to by the House conferees and became the law. I believe essentially the same results would have been obtained by the senators and Mr. Merrick even if I had never introduced my bill. They could have secured the proper language from the Social Security Board and inserted it in the Senate bill, whether or not they had had my bill to work from. But it was some satisfaction to be able to put a plus sign after my Item No. 5 and to know that disability insurance could go into effect in California in accordance with legislative language which I had been the first to write.

My amendments to the public works bills failed of adoption by the House. They were defeated because the very members who talked the most about "inflation" and "economy in government" voted against them. What those amendments provided, in a word, was that public works like river and harbor improvements, flood control dams, and the like should not be started except at the right time to start them. The amendments said that unless a project was "immediately necessary to protect human life and property" it should not be undertaken until (1) the supply of materials was adequate for this *and* other more essential purposes such as housing, and (2) there was unemployment in the construction industry and need therefore to expand its volume of business and activity. All my amendments sought to do was to write into law a sound policy whereby public works not immediately necessary would be delayed until they were needed to combat a trend toward deflation and depression. One member pointed out on the floor that my amendment might mean delaying projects in many congressional districts. To this I readily agreed, but the suggestion of the other member struck home and my amendments were defeated each time I offered them.

The Wagner-Ellender-Taft Housing bill was never even considered in the House, so there was no opportunity to do anything about the amendments I had prepared.

As to the Anti-Trust Division appropriations, I did the best I could. I offered my amendment to keep the personnel of the division from being severely reduced. The House, which had talked so much about how small business was being "destroyed by New Deal bureaucrats," defeated the amendment.

But I was successful concerning the one negative item on my program. Whittier Narrows Dam is part of the over-all plan for flood control in Los Angeles County. Taken as a whole, that plan or something like it is necessary as a means of protecting heavily populated Los Angeles County against the flash floods that sometimes come down from the California mountains.

But all the other dams included in the flood control plan, except only Whittier Narrows, have been or are to be constructed in mountain or desert sections where the land is worth little— where few people have built their homes and where sound underground support is available.

The site proposed for the Whittier Narrows Dam, on the other hand, is one that "old-timers" in the area, who have drilled wells there since the first settlers came, declare to be unsafe because it is underlain with quicksand. In the second place, the area which would be flooded is one of the most fertile and productive in all of southern California. It is populated by a great many families; it is highly cultivated and includes a number of small industrial establishments. All these families, their farms and industries, will be forced to move if the dam is built. Several beautiful schools will either have to be closed completely or will suffer the loss of a large proportion of the taxable properties that support them. Building this dam would turn an area that is now a garden spot into a desolate, swampy area in the very center of one of the most densely populated sections of the whole United States.

Furthermore, a huge dam has just been built across the San Gabriel River only eight miles above the proposed site of Whittier Narrows. At the very least, it would seem wise to wait and see how that dam operates before rushing into the very expensive Whittier Narrows project. And, should further flood protection be necessary, many competent engineers are convinced that widening and improvement of the river channel would be a more desirable and more effective method.

The proposed site of the Whittier Narrows dam is in the center of the Twelfth Congressional District and it would clearly have been my province to try to stop its construction even had I not been thoroughly convinced in my own mind that it should not be built.

This was an old fight. We had won the first round in 1945 when Mr. Frank Wright, superintendent of schools at El Monte, California, and Mr. Emory C. Metcalf, member of one of the pioneer California families, had come to Washington to testify before the Appropriations Committee and help me out in what otherwise would have been a one-man effort.

Our 1945 victory had aroused a good many powerful forces —not the least of which was the Corps of Army Engineers themselves. And there is no agency in all the government to whom Congress ordinarily listens more readily than it does to the Army Engineers. Moreover, the Board of Supervisors of Los Angeles County and the Los Angeles Chamber of Commerce were on record for the dam. One reason for this was understandable. Under the basic flood control act the federal government is obliged to pay the cost of all lands and damages wherever a reservoir is built, but the localities have to pay a considerable proportion of such costs in the case of channel improvements. Again, if the channel project were to be substituted for the dam in order to save the homes and farms, there was some oil property downstream which might be affected and the oil companies didn't like that prospect. The large city of Long Beach was officially on record in support of the dam and so were other communities of lesser size. Only El Monte and the surrounding towns were actively opposed.

In consequence, none of the other congressmen from California was in a position to help me out—even if they had wanted to. No district except mine would be hurt by the dam. And all the county-wide influences were for it.

In 1946 I again got some help from home. Mr. Wright returned and with him the Rev. Dan Cleveland, pastor of the Church in the Barn, a non-denominational church which Mr. Cleveland had built up from the very ground both physically and organizationally. The people of his church were among those who would lose their homes should the Whittier Narrows Dam be built. Furthermore, he was interested in keeping the San Gabriel River as it was—an area admirably adapted to Boy Scout and similar activities.

We went before the House Committee on Appropriations and pleaded our case. But we found that the record of the committee also contained arguments in favor of the dam, presented by the agencies above referred to. Some anxious days passed during which, I am afraid, I troubled members of the committee a good deal with questions as to what their action was likely to be. At last, however, the bill was reported to the floor of the House— and no Whittier Narrows money was included in it. We had won the second round. We had won it largely, I knew, because of a strong tendency in Congress not to do anything in a member's district which that member vigorously opposes.

I was afraid some member under pressure from other parts of our country, as I knew many of them to be, would try to introduce an amendment to put the Whittier Narrows money back in the bill. I watched uneasily during consideration of the bill until that point where such an amendment would have had to be offered was passed. No one tried. And the bill passed the House as we wanted it.

Mr. Wright and the Rev. Mr. Cleveland had to go home before the Senate took up the bill. So I went before the Senate Appropriations Committee alone. I had been there before a good many times, but still it was not the same familiar ground as the House committee. The Army Engineers wanted the appropriation and said so, though they were most courteous to me throughout. I made my argument against the dam.

Then I waited till the Senate committee reported the bill— without Whittier Narrows—waited till the bill came up on the Senate floor. I went to the Senate that day. (House members have the privilege of going on the Senate floor at any time, as do Senators with respect to the House floor.) I talked with several of the senators about the dam, told them I hoped the bill would not be amended to put it in. It wasn't. For another year at least our people's homes and farms would not be disturbed. There was still a chance of getting the alternate plan of channel improvement substituted for Whittier Narrows.

And so my "batting average" for 1946 was .444. Out of nine special legislative tasks that I had undertaken, four had been successfully carried through. On the other five I had for one reason or another failed.

Chapter 20

THE CONGRESSMAN'S JOB
AS IT IS

Practically every morning of my ten years in Congress I arrived at my office on the "attic" floor of the Old House Office Building somewhere between eight-fifty and nine-ten. A member of the staff was almost always there ahead of me. The first hour was in many respects the crucial one. It was the only hour of the day—except for Saturdays—when we could be fairly certain that there would be neither a committee meeting, a state delegation meeting, nor a session of the House. Most days it was the only hour for office work. Theoretically, it was the time to answer all the mail—a worthy objective which was, however, quite beyond the realm of practical possibility.

So let us suppose it is nine o'clock on Capitol Hill. Let us follow the congressman to his office and go with him through a typical day. If he is not smart (as I usually wasn't) he comes in the main door. He has his mind made up that he is "going to get a lot done" before committee meeting at ten o'clock. But Mr. So-and-so from such-and-such an organization is there waiting for him in the outer office. He talks to Mr. So-and-so for perhaps ten minutes. There are very few people congressmen don't have *some* obligation to talk to, for this is a democracy and it is the people's government. Then he asks one of his secretaries to please come in the inner office so they can start on the mail—not only the mail he has brought from home but the big accumulation from previous days which stands there rebuking him on the corner of his desk.

The desk looks more disorderly than it is. In its center is a pile of papers representing things that must be done that very day— telephone calls, letters whose answers must meet a date line, notices of meetings. Before he starts dictating the first letter he asks his other secretary to please get the head of a certain government department on the telephone. Usually this is unsuccessful on the first attempt, so it is a good idea to start early. While he is dictating he sees the other piles on his desk. One of them consists of several bunches of notes, letters, and documents clipped together. These are the current "major projects"—material about a small company fighting for its life against a "patent pool"; about the support price for eggs; about the dam in one part of the district which ought not to be built; about a veteran's claim, to be heard by the Appeals Board within the next few days.

Behind him on a big table is the partially completed text of a speech, together with big envelopes containing material to be used in it. In a number of separate piles is the necessary information for work on several bills the congressman is trying to get passed: one amending the Federal Credit Union Act, another exempting Series E Government Bonds from attachment, another granting disabled veterans the right of appeal to the courts on their claims, and others. Back next to the wall on this table are other piles of brown envelopes—some of them dust-covered—representing big jobs that ought to be done but aren't being taken care of—at least at the moment. One of them concerns conditions in veterans' hospitals, another the patent laws, a third a new program for maintaining farm prices.

All around the room are bookcases. Some have books in them. Some contain manila folders bulging with pamphlets and reports and booklets, arranged according to subject matter, on housing, power, agriculture, education, taxation, foreign affairs, Social Security, labor relations, unemployment, the Army, the Navy, military conscription, atomic energy, co-operatives. A lot of the literature that floods the office mail every day and which ought to be read on the spot, but can't be, goes into these collections.

These things, plus the boxes of stencils for the mailing list, the addressing machine, the mimeograph, the pictures of the family, friendly congressmen, and others on the walls, the large number of wastebaskets—these things compose the office.

Only a few letters have been written when the congressman's secretary reminds him that this is the day he is supposed to write his newspaper column. Everything else has to be dropped to write the column. There is a deadline to be met; and the column is the only means the congressman has of reporting to his constituents generally on what is going on at the national capital and what he is trying to do about it.

The telephone rings. A colleague wants to talk about the bill coming up that afternoon. They do so.

A good many other things happen. People "drop in" at the office. Some he is glad to see, some not. Most of them he sees for at least a minute or two. (Once a man got angry because I wouldn't talk to him about trying to get out of jail one of his friends who had been put there for stabbing someone in a poker game in San Francisco. Usually, however, the business of our callers concerned matters altogether worthy, if not always weighty.)

Then back to the column. By the time it is finished it is ten o'clock. Only a handful of letters have been dictated. But it is time for the committee meeting. So off the congressman goes.

That afternoon his secretary will send the draft of the newspaper column to him on the floor of the House. He will correct it and send it back to the people in the office, who will then mimeograph about a hundred copies. These will go to all the newspapers in his district. Maybe a third of them, or a fourth, or occasionally half of the papers will print it. If it is within six or seven months of the next election, not more than three or four will do so—unless the congressman is a conservative, in which case his column will appear quite regularly in all the papers.

Anyway, the congressman has gone to his committee meeting. He takes along some work—maybe part of the speech he's writing —because there may be some dull periods in the meeting.

There are days in a congressman's life when he has no committee meetings. Then he can work at his desk all morning. And there are times when there is "general debate" in the House or when the sessions are short, in which case some of the afternoon can be used. But these days are comparatively rare.

During my first term in the House I was a member of three regular committees—Flood Control, Public Lands, and World War Veterans' legislation. At the beginning of the Seventy-sixth Congress I was made a member of a fourth committee as well, the Committee on Rivers and Harbors.

In my last two terms I had only one regular committee—the Committee on Agriculture. But the "special" or "select" committee work is sometimes harder and more time-consuming than that of the standing committees. And except for the Seventy-fifth Congress, I served continuously on one special committee or another and part of the time on two of them at once.

The regular time for congressional committees to meet is from ten o'clock to twelve o'clock in the morning. This is about the only time they can meet without mixing practically everything up. Nonetheless they sometimes meet during the afternoon, even though the House is in session.

Someone in our office made a list on Monday morning, April 23, 1945, of the committee meetings I was to attend during the following week. Here is what it looked like:

COMMITTEE MEETINGS

	A.M.	P.M.
Monday April 23	10:00—Agriculture 10:30—Smith Com.	
Tuesday April 24	10:00—Agriculture 10:00—Post-War Planning 10:30—Smith Com.	4:00—Calif. Delegation
Wednesday April 25	10:00—Agriculture (Wickard) 10:00—Post-War Planning	2:00—Post-War Subcommittee on Agric.
Thursday April 26	10:00—Agriculture 10:00—Post-War Planning	2:00—Post-War subcommittee on Agric.
Friday April 27	10:00—Agriculture 10:00—Post-War Planning	

In other words, at least two of my committees were meeting every single day and all except the Smith Committee met for the full two hours from ten o'clock to twelve o'clock. To round things out, there were three afternoon meetings called in the hope, which was frequently vain, that "nothing of importance" would be transpiring on the floor of the House.

But what were these meetings about? Maybe some of them weren't important. Well, the Committee on Agriculture was holding hearings on far-reaching bills affecting the farm credit system. And Wednesday was devoted to the question of American membership in the United Nations Food and Agriculture Organization. The Post-War Committee held hearings every day that week on the financial problems of reconversion, a reasonably vital subject at the time certainly. The Smith Committee was in the midst of the OPA and the War Production Board, the immediate study being on whether the regulations on clothing and textiles were workable or not. Not only was the full Post-War Committee meeting but our subcommittee on Agriculture also met for additional hearings preparatory to issuing our report. The California delegation meeting discussed the employment problems that were expected to arise in our state as a result of the defeat of Germany and the shifting of the whole war effort to the Pacific.

The point of all this is that I could not miss a single one of these meetings and fulfill my duty as a congressman. As a practical matter, what I did was to attend one meeting for an hour or so, then go to one of the others. During this particular week I was compelled to miss four of the meetings altogether. I wasn't doing my job. I couldn't.

It would have been different if there had been people to whom I could have gone for skilled assistance. But there weren't. The staff of my own office, consisting sometimes of two, sometimes of three, people had every bit of work they could possibly do simply keeping reasonably abreast of the day-to-day tasks. All of us were working overtime every day and every week as it was.

Nor was there anyone on the committee staffs to whom I could go. True, the special committees did engage the services of one or two professional assistants. But these people were kept extremely busy on tasks assigned them by the chairmen or the committees as a whole. And their number was never great enough to even begin to cover such tremendous fields as postwar planning for example. As an individual I could not expect to command more than a few minutes per week of their time.

As for the regular committees, which constitute the very heart of the work of Congress, their entire staff consisted of one or two clerks and a "messenger." These people were always appointed by the chairman and they were almost always people from his own district who had been politically active on his behalf. They were in most cases people of genuine earnestness and fine character. But they were not even supposed to be trained for the work of advising a congressional committee regarding its legislative work. The most minor bureau in the Department of Agriculture had on its staff a dozen people far more highly trained, far better informed, and considerably better paid than anyone on the staff of the Committee on Agriculture of the House or Senate.

If one stopped to think about it, the situation was nothing short of ridiculous. The same Congress that constantly worried about the "dominance of the executive department of government" went on and on from year to year appropriating money—altogether properly—to engage staffs of well-trained experts for every department, bureau, and agency of government. But it never thought of doing the same sort of thing for its own committees. There was no one on Capitol Hill who could be a match for the departments' professional people—except some of the senators and congressmen themselves. And they hadn't time to study.

The Legislative Reference Service of the Library of Congress did an efficient job of answering congressional inquiries and supplying information upon the request of a congressman or senator. But the head of the Foreign Trade Division of Legislative Reference, for example, was paid something like $2500 or $3000 a year, while people with comparable responsibility in the executive departments were receiving three times that amount. Everybody knew the situation was all out of balance. But nobody did anything about it.

If a member like myself missed a committee meeting there wasn't anything to be done except to talk to another member who had been present and ask him to repeat as much of the testimony as he could remember.

The House ordinarily meets at twelve o'clock every weekday except Saturday. It usually stays in session until sometime between five o'clock and six o'clock. The session always opens with prayers by the chaplain. Then the journal of the previous day's proceedings is read and approved. After that the Speaker almost always recognizes members who wish to get permission to "extend their remarks in the Appendix of the *Record*." This means that they can prepare an article of their own on some subject or can, with special permission, insert something someone else has said and have it printed under an appropriate heading in the back part of the *Congressional Record* of that day. In the House, with its large membership, some of the most important material that ever gets into the *Record* goes in by this process—and some of the most worthless. In the Senate extensions are somewhat less used because there is more time per member for debate on the floor. During this opening period members can also obtain recognition to "proceed for one minute." As long as the speaker does not violate the rules of the House, any subject may be discussed. And most subjects are. Many members make most of their speeches in these one-minute periods. There are two reasons for this: because it is early in the session more members are present to listen, and the afternoon papers have not yet gone to press.

When these preliminaries have been finished the chairman of some committee will make a motion for the consideration of a bill or resolution. This is always prearranged according to the "program" of the majority party leadership which includes, of course, the Speaker. Usually this motion is adopted "without objection" and the House then proceeds to "resolve itself" into the "Committee of the Whole" and to legislate. However, before the time comes to "read the bill for amendment" there is a period for debate. This may be only an hour on a comparatively unimportant measure. It may last a week on the most important and controversial ones. During the time the debate is taking place it is possible, if a member is already familiar with the arguments pro and con, and has his mind made up how he will vote, to tend to other business.

Sometime or another most members eat lunch. Most frequently I accomplished this in the "cloakroom," which is just off the floor and where one can keep track of what is going on. But lunch was also an accepted time to talk to people from the district, from one of the government departments, or to others with ideas to discuss. In such cases we would eat together in the House Restaurant downstairs. There, bells announcing roll calls can be heard and members can dash up and answer to their names.

I used to make most of my telephone calls from the cloakroom during dull speeches, because this gave me a little more time for other types of work when I could be in the office. If other members had to be seen about some problem or question, "general debate" was a good time to do it. At times I would slip into a tiny library room just off the floor and do some of my reading or writing. It was possible meanwhile to hear all that was taking place on the floor and, if it seemed that a good speech was being delivered, to turn one's attention to it.

When debate has been concluded the reading of the bill begins and from that point on any member may offer an amendment to any paragraph. At such times it really is the duty of members to be present on the floor continuously and to remain until the amendments have all been voted "up or down" and the final vote taken on the bill.

Not only while the congressman is in his office but also while he is legislating on the floor, people come to see him about bills. Members can be, and constantly are, "called off the floor" to talk to people in the corridors of the Capitol. Sometimes they are from your district, sometimes not. Sometimes it is just to "say hello" and to give the member a kind word or a message. More often it is to talk about the bill which is at that moment under consideration. Many times I have known a member to miss the chance to vote for an amendment simply because someone kept him outside the chamber so long telling him why he should vote for it. It is most questionable whether this sort of last-minute lobbying gains any votes for the lobbyist's cause. And I am sure it loses some, since members of the House and Senate don't like to be "advised" at the last minute how they ought to vote—even when they have doubts in their own minds.

Someone has said that a congressman's job is to know a very little about practically everything. It could also be said that his job is to be doing at least three things at once all the time, for it almost works out that way. It shouldn't.

I never went to my office on Sundays. That day at least I stayed at home with my family—when we were in Washington. I took my work home in the big brown brief case of which my friends in Congress used to make so much fun. But during the day I seldom tried to work unless there was the most insistent reason for it. On Sunday evenings, however, as on every other one, I did work—sometimes an hour or two, sometimes four or five.

Had it not been for Saturdays, the situation in our office would have become desperate. The House very seldom meets on Saturday and committee meetings are hardly ever held. One reason for this is that many members living within short distances of Washington go home practically every week end. How they manage to get their work done I do not understand. For it was only on Saturdays that the accumulation of unanswered mail and of the jobs people had asked us to do for them could be attacked in earnest. We worked a full day in our congressional office every Saturday and were thankful for the day each week. I cannot remember a single occasion when any member of the staff complained of this, even though, except during the war years, most everyone else in both government service and private industry had the day off.

In recent years the congressman's job has become more and more that of an ambassador, attorney, and secretary for the people of his district in the national capital. There is certainly nothing unworthy or undesirable about this relationship. The only trouble is that the congressman simply cannot perform even reasonably well all this service that is expected of him and still do the more important work of passing laws for the United States. For example, a great deal of the service-to-constituents work consists of consulting one or more of the scores of governmental departments and agencies on behalf of some person who needs information from them or has some problem which must be taken up with them. To do this effectively the congressman needs to know as much as possible about the agencies, what their work is, whom to call about specific phases of that work, how best to present his case.

While he tries to keep up with his job in Washington the congressman must not "lose touch" with his district. I am not altogether sure whether I did lose touch with mine or whether a certain thing that happened to me in the election of 1946 was more or less inevitable. But I know I tried to keep the lines between home and Washington as active and warm as I could.

I wrote my weekly newspaper column. And I recorded, extemporaneously, a radio record every week for broadcast over Los Angeles station KFVD, whose owner, Mr. J. F. Burke, was kind enough to ask me to send his station these weekly reports on Washington.

Once I prepared a questionnaire for our district, asking the people's opinions on a number of important questions which Congress was about to have to decide. I sent it to more than 30,000 people, the extent of my mailing list at that time. A little over ten per cent of them responded by filling out the questionnaire and sending it back to me. For more than a week we worked at night, tabulating and compiling the results of the people's votes, and even then had to hire extra help.

For all of the foregoing reasons, every night when I left my office at six-thirty or seven o'clock, my big brown brief case went along. I seldom tried to begin work until supper was over and the children in bed. If there was an evening meeting or engagement, or if we went to the movies, as we did about once a week, I couldn't start until that was over. But at either eight o'clock or eleven o'clock or sometime in between I would get out the folding table and spread out the work. First I would thumb through the "pending legislation" file to see if it contained anything which bore on the legislation coming up next day. Then would come the most urgent parts of the evening's work—finishing what must be done before I went to the office in the morning, such as speeches for delivery the next day, which someone would have to begin early to type if copies were to be ready for the press and for use on the floor when the House "took up" at noon. Or perhaps there would be papers concerning the problem of some individual who was coming to see me and about which I'd better know something when he came. Sometimes, of course, there was no such pressing work that had to be done. Sometimes I could spend some time reading—but never a fraction as much as I should have done—background material that would give me a basis for legislative decisions. Congressmen who keep up their work have little if any time for this sort of reading. Yet they need it badly.

After the other work was finished I would open the big brown envelope containing the day's mail. Sometimes I went to bed at midnight, sometimes at one, occasionally not until two or three o'clock. It all depended on how many letters there were to read.

If a congressman tries to do his job as that job is laid out for him today, he faces an almost impossible task. And the only reason I say "almost" is because I have been a politician and have learned to be careful about making absolutely unqualified statements. Someone might come along who could do such a job. But he hasn't appeared as yet

Chapter 21

THE CONGRESSMAN'S JOB
AS IT OUGHT TO BE

Congressmen are supposed to pass good laws for the government of the United States. Compared to that duty and obligation, all the other things congressmen do are of almost insignificant consequence.

But had I never written a single letter, or done a single worthwhile service for a constituent, or consulted a single department, or attended a single meeting, conference, or lecture during my whole congressional career, even then I could barely have done a completely effective legislative job on the number of bills in which I believed it my clear duty to take an active interest.

Other members were in the same dilemma.

We needed help.

We needed to have our job simplified as much as possible.

We needed ready sources of information which would be absolutely unbiased and on which we could rely.

And, once the legislative job was done on a certain bill and a law passed, we needed some means of finding out how that law was being administered. For it is no use passing a law unless it is carried out in accordance with the purposes and intent of the legislative body which passes it.

For my part, I wanted to feel that I was part of a truly independent national legislature equipped with adequate machinery for working out and passing a rounded legislative program, conceived in Congress and dedicated to the meeting not alone of the immediate but of the long-range problems of the people of the United States.

After my first few months of service it became evident to me that the protection of the position of Congress as an institution required some positive, dynamic action. On February 24, 1941, in a speech in the House, I said: "I want to discuss frankly with the members present the future place of our Congress in the government of the United States. In recent years we have heard a lot of talk, most of which, it seems to me, has been pretty irresponsible, about the possibility of dictatorship in the United States and the loss of the special elements of constitutional democracy. Most of these fears I have not shared, but there are some elements in the present situation which are causing me a very deep concern. I agree with those people who entertain some fears that there is danger of loss by the legislative branch of its proper place in the American scheme of government.

"I think there is some such danger, but I do not believe that danger arises from things which the Congress has done or is likely to do. On the contrary, I think danger arises from a lack of initiative on the part of Congress and from its failure to do positively certain things which are the evident duty of the legislative branch. It is a law of nature that any organ of the body which is not exercised ceases to retain its capacity to function fully."

The passage of time has strengthened, not weakened, the convictions I expressed in that speech.

The heart of the matter is: how can we prevent a decline in the prestige of our national legislature, assure its co-equal status with the Executive, and thus guard the very central feature of representative, constitutional, democratic government? We may as well face the fact that in a world like the present one with military power, economic power, the power of press and radio concentrated as never before in history, it will be nip and tuck whether democratic government can be preserved in its full vigor even in the United States. And if such government is lost, the liberties of the people are always lost with it. This is why I have fought monopoly so hard; it is why I worked and hoped so earnestly for effective long-range postwar planning to be done through our democratic congressional machinery; it is why I supported so vigorously from the very beginning the movement for the "reorganization" or, as I chose to call it, the strengthening of Congress.

No national legislature in any nation has ever destroyed liberty. The reason is simple. A legislature like the legislatures of the early American colonies, like the Italian Parliament or the German Reichstag or the Congress of the United States is elected by the people to pass laws. But in the nature of the case a Congress cannot enforce those laws. That is the job of the executive. Hence power over the people is actually wielded not by the national legislature but by the executive department of government. The saving factor is that, so long as the national congress of a country maintains its position in the scheme of government, the executive may not and dare not enforce any law except in the manner prescribed by the legislature, or exercise any powers over the people except those which have been specifically granted by the congress. A dictator is simply a man who can exercise power in a country without the necessity of deriving that power from the people or their elected representatives. No wonder every dictator, right or left, who ever gained power has, as his first act, abolished the national legislature of the country or transformed it into a one-party "puppet" pretense.

I have been angry and fearful many times at the failure of Congress to act in accordance with the obvious future needs of America. The main reason for my anger and fear has been that I know Congress can maintain its position, its co-equal status, only if it consistently and with genuine statesmanship faces and solves reasonably well the problems of the nation before they become acute. Once they are acute, the stage is set for the executive to take over.

My concern was caused not alone by the action or inaction of Congress, but by the attitude of some people in the executive department. Perhaps it was a natural reaction to the dangerously depressed conditions of the country that certain leaders of the New Deal were very impatient with any questioning of the executive's program by the Congress, or any insistence that Congress define the manner in which specific features of that program were to be administered. But I never liked that attitude. As time went on, I liked it less and less. The ends were in most cases worthy ones. But they did not justify the use of means which involved circumvention of the law. There was another means always available—and a right one. It was to change the law. But that required time and effort. And there is a school of thought—there always has been in America— which considers Congress as little better than a necessary nuisance with whose bickerings, debates, and sometimes slow action a far wiser executive department is forced to contend. I remember how strongly this opinion was held by some of the businessmen I heard talking when I was a young man. That was when Republican presidents were in the White House. And I ran into the same thing among some—by no means all—of the administrators of governmental programs in the New Deal period.

It was obvious, of course, why a good many Americans, during the thirties and early forties, based their whole political policy on the slogan "Support the President." It was because President Roosevelt, like Jefferson, Jackson, Lincoln, Theodore Roosevelt, and Woodrow Wilson, like all "strong" presidents in our history, was considerably ahead of Congress in some of his progressive views. But as I wrote in an article published in the *American Mercury* for June 1944:

> To those groups and organizations which consider themselves "liberal" let this be said with fervent emphasis: The remedy for congressional conservatism must not be the undermining of the whole institution of Congress. The cure, in that event, would be far worse than the disease. For if Congress is enfeebled and hamstrung, all hope of decent solutions of our natural problems would be obliterated along with the Congress which thus far has failed to deal adequately with such problems.

The fault was not altogether with the liberal groups. I said later in the same article:

> One thing has been lacking. It is the one thing without which Congress cannot maintain its position as a co-equal

branch of government, the one thing which the people of America inevitably associate with national leadership. I refer to a constructive program for the solution of the nation's present and future problems.

For example, in a speech entitled "The Congress—Its Place, Its Duties, and Its Opportunity," delivered May 21, 1942, I said: "If Congress is to gain and retain the position of public confidence it should have, the most important single thing it can do right now is to pass a tax bill which will actually do a large part of the job of assuring economic balance during the war and preventing a rising spiral of living costs. The danger is not, at this time, that the tax bill will be too severe, but that it will not be as effective as the needs of the country demand.

"There must be courageous action by Congress to equalize the burdens of war—to limit to $25,000 the amount of income anyone can have during this war, to close every tax loophole; to sharply increase estate and gift tax rates; to tax the individual incomes of all those who have more than they need for a standard of living of health and decency; to recapture for the people all excess profits accruing to anyone as a result of this war; and to require that all who can possibly afford to do so shall set aside for their own future protection through purchase of non-transferable War Bonds from their government a fair and reasonable percentage of their incomes. These things in the field of taxation are our clear duty now, as I see it.

"If we do that duty, we will, I imagine, receive scant credit for doing so. Many of us will probably be defeated. But the Congress, as America's one agency of government which is really close to the people, will have been justified fully and completely. Those who have launched this drive to destroy this representative body will not be deterred from their attempt. But they will inevitably fail in it if we answer them with speedy, forthright, and dynamic action."

Two years later, regretting that no such carefully conceived congressional program had been enacted, I used, again in the *American Mercury* article, this illustration:

A concrete example will show how Congress might have acted to put itself in a position of coequality with the President in national leadership but failed to do so.

Every Member of Congress knew perfectly well from the beginning that this would be a total war in which it would be necessary artificially to restrict the output of consumers' goods; and that to the extent that taxes plus savings failed to equal the difference between national income and the available supply of consumers' goods there would be inflation. From the very beginning there were those in Congress who advocated not only a courageous tax policy but also a program of compulsory savings. This would have rendered unnecessary the inflationary sale of bonds to banks for newly created money; it would have distributed the holdings of Government bonds widely and equitably through the entire population; it would have made certain that wartime savings would remain available as a backlog of consumers' buying power to prevent deflation in the postwar period.

But because neither the Treasury nor any other executive agency recommended a compulsory-savings program, Congress never went ahead with it. Here was a superb chance for Capitol Hill to assume both responsibility and leadership. But Congress did not act. It took the weak and futile position that its own legislative action had to wait upon Executive recommendation. And so it did not enact a general savings program. Neither did it come forward with a tax program sufficiently courageous to pay even half the cost of the war as we went along.

Nor is this all. The national debt has soared to astronomical figures. Some estimate it will go to $300,000,-000,000 before the war has finally been won. And the worst of it is that at least one-third of this mounting debt never should have been a debt of the American people at all.

This Congress might have said, when the war broke out: "We will finance this war so far as humanly possible by means of a courageous tax program and the real savings of the people, not by monetary inflation through the banking system. If any new money is required it shall be created in such fashion that no interest will have to be paid upon it by the generation now bearing the brunt of the fighting." That would have constituted dynamic leadership. It would have been a program better than the Treasury's, better than the President's. Above all, it would have been a program. It would have enabled the American people to know that their choice was not between Presidential proposals and no proposals at all, but between Presidential proposals on the one hand and a constructive Congressional program on the other.

But farsighted statesmanlike action is a good deal to expect from a group of thoroughly harassed men—especially if they lack the machinery required to do the job.

So certain reforms clearly were called for. The first of these was to supply Congress with its own sources of full, scientific information. Everybody, except the direct representatives of the people, was so supplied. The Senate and House committees were securing the information upon which they framed the laws of the United States from two principal sources. The first of these was the executive agencies of government. All of them were well staffed with lifelong students of the problems with which they had to deal. Their testimony before congressional committees was and always will be essential to proper consideration of bills. They are the people who must administer the laws. But theirs cannot help being more or less slanted testimony. Each executive department has its own future to think of. It naturally wants its work to be important, to expand. Officials of those departments and agencies have behind them a record to justify and protect. Their counsel to congressional committees ought, at the very least, not to be the last word.

The second source of information was testimony on behalf of organizations with a special interest in the legislation. Of course any American citizen has a right to be heard by congressional committees. But few of them can get to Washington for this purpose. The ones who do get there are, generally speaking, those who are sent by groups with peculiar economic or other interests in the bills under consideration. The right of such organizations to be heard is unquestioned. It is part and parcel of democracy. But their testimony ought not to go unchecked or unchallenged.

What Congress has needed for a long, long time is a staff of people on its own pay roll who will be constantly engaged in gathering information, in analyzing national problems and proposals for their solution, and in keeping themselves prepared to present unbiased, factual appraisals of bills and other measures either to committees or to individual members.

Every special interest in the country has had its private "brain trust" for a long time. Why shouldn't there be at least one "brain trust" devoted exclusively to serving the general interest of all the people?

Accordingly, on May 5, 1941, I introduced, in the Seventy-seventh Congress, H.J.R. 179 to provide just such a legislative staff for the Congress. Dr. George B. Galloway, one of the most careful and experienced students of congressional problems, helped me draft the bill and encouraged my introduction of it.

This, however, was only one phase of the problem. Each senator and congressman needed at least one well-paid assistant who could carry on a large part of the non-legislative work of the office, who would handle problems of constituents, take care of a considerable portion of the mail, and thus free the member for his primary duty of writing and passing the laws of the United States.

There was necessary also a simpler committee structure—with fewer committees, each of which would deal with a truly important phase of legislation. This would enable members to simplify and concentrate their work—and do it better.

Moreover, there was needed an orderly and effective way in which the Congress itself could lay out a legislative program. If Congress was to function with the full effectiveness required of it, what was (and is) called for was a steering committee which would really "steer." The best make-up of such a committee would be to include, not only the Speaker, majority leader, and others already in positions of leadership, but also the chairmen of the important committees of the House or Senate. Such a group should meet regularly to discuss the vital problems confronting the country, to decide what legislative action might be required to meet those problems, and then to determine upon the order of consideration of the pertinent bills. All individual members of the House or Senate regardless of party should have free access to meetings of the steering committee in order to present the case for legislation believed by them to be of emergent importance. The objective of such a system would be to put the work of the Congress more nearly on a plane of farsighted statesmanship and less upon the plane of simply meeting the immediate and frequently routine tasks.

This is the key to the future position of Congress in our scheme of government. For the main reason for such decline in the power of Congress relative to the executive, as has taken place, is the fact that the executive has become the agency of government taking an over-all view not only of the nation's immediate problems but also of its long-run future needs. Meanwhile Congress has to a considerable extent permitted itself to become absorbed in year-to-year, if not day-to-day, routine matters and has thus largely abdicated its most essential function, namely that of devising on its own motion long-range legislative programs geared to the necessities of the time. It is obvious that the central function of any national legislature should be the devising of a national legislative program. Yet by and large this is the one thing that Congress has not been doing.

It was obvious, too, that a better working relationship between Congress and the executive departments was badly needed. Consequently, on the opening day of the Seventy-eighth Congress, I introduced H.R. 60, aimed to give to each standing committee of the Congress the duty and function of carrying on a "continuous review" of the administration of all laws resulting from bills reported out of that committee. According to my resolution, each committee was to report at once to Congress any failure of an executive agency to carry out the intent of Congress in the administration of a law, any instance where any executive agency was for any reason unable to carry out that intent, and any evidence that an agency was exceeding the powers duly granted to it. Together with its report would be recommendations for corrective legislation.

My resolution did not pass. But only a couple of months after I had introduced it, and exactly a week after my resignation from the Dies Committee, the Speaker appointed the newly authorized Committee to Investigate the Acts of Executive Agencies Exceeding their Proper Authority. When he asked me if I would accept a place on this committee I told him that I would be glad to.

There were those among my friends who told me they thought I had "jumped out of the frying pan into the fire" and that the job on the Smith Committee would prove as difficult and trying as the Dies Committee assignment.

But such was certainly not the case. I did not agree with all the reports of the Smith Committee. Indeed, Mr. Delaney, of New York, and I filed minority reports to two of them. Nor were the chairman of my new committee and I in agreement on many public questions. He was a conservative, whereas my position had been a consistently progressive one. But the proceedings of the Smith Committee were as orderly as those of the Dies Committee had, at certain times at least, been disorderly. Members of the committee were consulted on all questions; individual members did not anticipate its findings in public statements or speeches; and not once did I have reason to feel that plans were being made "behind my back" or to fear that either committee statements or reports would be issued without ample notice and discussion of the action contemplated. In short, the committee work was conducted as the work of a congressional investigating committee should be. In two instances Mr. Smith held up his majority report until I should have time to prepare my minority report, so that both could be issued at the same time. And, finally, much as I might disagree with Representative Smith on certain economic questions, I did not disagree at all with his general point of view as to the proper place of the Congress in our scheme of government or the relationship that should exist between the Congress and the executive departments.

Exhaustive not to say exhausting hearings were held by the Smith Committee. At least half of them had to do with that most controversial of all war agencies, the Office of Price Administration. One report dealt with the War Labor Board. In all instances, except that of one OPA report, in which I believe the committee itself went beyond the scope of its authority, the reports dealt with the question of whether or not these agencies had exceeded the powers granted them by the Congress. In the introduction to its second report, the committee summarized the reason for its existence and its central purpose:

> This committee is fully conscious of the fact that its work is being done in the midst of the greatest war in the history of mankind. It recognizes that unless victory is achieved human freedom and constitutional government as we have known them are altogether likely to be blotted out for an indefinite period of time. The committee also recognizes the necessity in the war period for the exercise of extraordinary governmental action to mobilize the economic as well as the military resources of the nation, and to direct them toward the winning of the war.
>
> But there are right and wrong ways to accomplish these purposes.
>
> The right way is through the operation of the legislative, executive and judicial functions of democratic government within the confines of constitutional limitations.
>
> The wrong way is by the usurpation of those functions by executive agencies through misinterpretation and abuse of powers granted them by the Congress and the assumption of powers not granted.
>
> The assumption of legislative and judicial functions by an executive agency constitutes a fundamental danger to constitutional government.
>
> In this critical era of world struggle for democracy there devolves upon the legislative and executive branches of government the very solemn and mutual duty to make democracy work efficiently, within the framework of its charter.
>
> Congress must delegate necessary powers to the executive branch, and the executive branch must construe and execute those powers in good faith, relying upon the Congress for an extension or enlargement of those powers which prove inadequate.

In direct accordance with the foregoing statement, the major action taken by the Smith Committee went to the very heart of the problems that had caused the House to vote the committee into existence. These were the problems involving the relationship of Congress to the executive department of government. It was clear from the hearings conducted by the committee that one major reason why executive agencies sometimes were guilty of exceeding their duly granted authority was because Congress had not specifically set forth what that authority was or the limitations upon it. Congress must do a better job of legislating. In order to do so Congress needed better sources of information, better staff, and a better direction of the work of its members. Moreover, whatever the disagreements between us on other questions, there was complete accord within the committee and particularly between Mr. Smith and me that some orderly method should be established whereby Congress could regularly and continuously ascertain whether the laws it had passed were being carried out in accordance with the intent of Congress.

Accordingly we went to work drafting a bill which would strengthen the Congress in these respects and on November 20, 1944, Chairman Smith and I introduced very nearly identical bills which were called the Legislative Organization Act of 1944. The concrete proposals contained in these bills were described in the committee report, which said of the legislation:

(1) It establishes a joint legislative staff service available to all committees of both Houses of Congress for the purpose of enabling such committees to obtain expert, unbiased and independent analyses of proposals which they may consider.

(2) It establishes a joint committee on appropriations having investigatory powers for the purpose of studying the manner in which the executive branch of Government spends the funds appropriated to it by the Congress in order that efficient and economical administration may be attained.

(3) It creates a permanent standing joint committee of the Senate and House on executive agencies and procedures to investigate executive agencies for the purpose of ascertaining whether the laws of the nation are executed and administered according to the intent of the legislative body which enacted them.

(4) It establishes a joint committee of the House and Senate to study the organization and operation of the Congress for the purpose of recommending such improve-

ments as it may deem desirable in order to enable the Congress better to meet its responsibilities as the national legislative body under the Constitution. All authority of this committee terminates upon the submission of the committee's final report.

The one difference between Congressman Smith's bill and mine was that, whereas his bill provided for one standing committee of the Senate and House to review the acts of executive agencies, my bill granted this power and duty to all regular standing committees, each acting with regard to those executive agencies which administered laws emanating from that committee.

It had been evident from the start that the scope of work which our select committee was authorized to do was so broad as to require a dozen such committees to áccomplish it. Executive agencies are numbered by the score. Our committee had dealt with the work of five or six of them. Furthermore, if there was justification for the Smith Committee at all—and I believed there was—then work of this sort ought not to be delegated spasmodically to specially appointed temporary committees which would make "investigations," report to Congress once or twice, and then pass out of existence. Neither, in my opinion, could it be entrusted to any one committee. There was simply too much for one committee conceivably to do. It ought instead to be made the province of all the regular standing committees of the House and Senate, as my Resolution 60 had earlier proposed. The review—or "investigation" if that very popular word is preferred —should be aimed not at making sensational revelations or capturing headlines but at correcting promptly and without fanfare any tendencies of executive agencies to exceed their proper authority or to fail to administer laws in accordance with the will of Congress.

In every other respect Mr. Smith's bill and mine were identical.

Brief but pointed defense of this legislation was contained in our seventh committee report:

In nation after nation it has been proven that the freedom of the people and the continuance of democratic institutions depend directly on the vigor, the effectiveness, and the strong position of the national legislature. Much of the criticism which has in recent years been heaped upon the Congress of the United States has been irresponsible and undeserved. But there has been also well-considered and constructive criticism which merits attention. No effort should be spared to make congressional organization, procedure, and functioning as nearly perfect as possible.

The Committee on Rules, of which Mr. Smith was a member, granted a hearing on these bills on the same day on which it heard arguments for the passage of the Maloney-Monroney resolution to create a special joint committee of the House and Senate on reorganization of Congress. While I believed that sufficient study had been given to the legislation introduced by Mr. Smith and me to push it forward to passage, it was evident that most members of Congress were far from prepared to take such action. For this reason I testified before the Rules Committee that, whatever was decided about our Smith Committee bills, I earnestly hoped that they would act favorably on the Maloney-Monroney resolution. This they did and the Special Committee on the Organization of Congress was the result.

A short time thereafter the Congress was severely shocked by the sudden death of Senator Maloney, of Connecticut, one of the authors of the resolution.

But the special committee organized itself by electing Senator Robert M. LaFollette, of Wisconsin, as its chairman, and Representative A. S. Mike Monroney, of Oklahoma, its vice-chairman. To these two men, far more than to anyone else, goes the credit for the first successful major effort to improve the workings of the Congress in all United States history. The committee held long and exhaustive hearings. It engaged a staff headed by Dr. Galloway, which was excellently qualified for the work in hand. Day after day in cloakrooms, in members' offices, on the floor of Senate and House, Senator LaFollette and Congressman Monroney carried on their fight for a more efficient Congress. There was far more opposition to their committee and its work than ever appeared on the surface. Powerful congressional figures were secretly opposed to anything being done to change the traditions and practices of the decades. But the weight of all the evidence was on the side of Mr. LaFollette and Mr. Monroney, and as the weeks passed public opinion came more and more overwhelmingly to their support.

Perhaps because of my early introduction of the bill to provide a legislative staff for the Congress, I was the first member of Congress from whom the committee took testimony. I appeared before it on March 15, 1945, and was on the stand most of the morning. I told why action to improve the functioning and strengthen the hand of Congress was, in my opinion, so vitally important. I pointed out how much more complex the problems of government are today than they were when the American Congress was first established, and how much more directly the citizen of today is affected by the actions of his government. And I made these specific proposals for inclusion in the bill which the special committee would in the course of time draft and seek to have enacted:

(1) That each senator and representative be provided with an administrative assistant.

(2) That the number of committees be reduced, and the work thus consolidated so that each member might be assigned to only one committee.

(3) That central policy committees consisting of the chairmen of the more important standing committees be created and given the duty of laying out the broad legislative program of the Congress.

(4) That the appropriations committees have adequate staff to make their own independent and continuous investigation of how moneys appropriated by the Congress are spent and, hence, how much should be granted a given agency in the future.

(5) That the Legislative Reference Service of the Library of Congress be expanded to a point where it could readily furnish any information or any problem analyses needed by the members of Congress.

(6) That each committee be staffed with men and women at least as competent as the experts of the executive departments or special interest organizations.

(7) That each committee be given the function of surveillance and review of the administration of laws emanating from it.

None of these proposals, except possibly the seventh one, was original with me. They had been the subject of articles and books. Many other members of Congress had discussed and expressed support of them. But I am grateful to have had the first chance to speak about them under circumstances where the speaking might result in action.

There were other problems, of course, and for some of them I could suggest no immediate solution. One was that of the admitted shortcomings of the "seniority" system. No one pays much attention to it when it brings a good and able man to a committee chairmanship. But everyone becomes very excited about the matter when a weak, arbitrary, prejudiced, or ineffective chairman is produced. The trouble has been that no one could suggest anything better. To throw the choice of its chairman into an election by committee members would almost certainly lead to all sorts of logrolling activities on the part of hopeful aspirants. To let the Speaker appoint the chairman would give him too much power. A combination of these methods whereby the committee would nominate three or four candidates from among whom the Speaker would make the selection seemed too cumbersome. A rotating chairmanship would be inefficient. It seemed better, therefore, to try to get at the problem by giving a majority of every committee more power and the chairman less power, by requiring meetings at regular intervals and giving the committee membership additional rights in determing what bills were to be considered.

Then there was the problem of the lobbyists. They are of all sorts and kinds and they take up a lot of every congressman's time.

There are the inexperienced lobbyists for world peace and international control of atomic energy, upon the success of whose efforts the future of mankind may depend. And there are the experienced lobbyists, the sugar lobbyists, the inland waterways lobbyists, the wool lobbyists, the oil lobbyists, the farm organization lobbyists, the insurance lobbyists, the AF of L lobbyists, the

CIO lobbyists, and a lot more. A lobbyist is simply a man or woman who tries to get a bill passed or keep one from passing. As such they are part and parcel of our democratic system of government. It would, therefore, be a most serious mistake to attempt to "bar lobbyists from Capitol Hill," as some have suggested. It would be impossible to draw a line between "bad" lobbyists and "good" ones, between big-business lobbyists and little-business lobbyists, between lobbyists for special interests and lobbyists for the people. The first thing to happen would be that a farmer from Maryland or Virginia would be in Washington and would drop in to his congressman's office to talk about his problems. And get himself arrested for lobbying on Capitol Hill.

So there is no practical way to abolish lobbying or lobbyists. The best that can be done is to require all lobbyists, good, bad, and indifferent, to register their names with Congress, tell who pays their salaries and how the money is raised for the purpose.

Of course what the United States really needs is a Congress which will be immune to the influence of bad lobbyists but amenable to the influences of good ones. More than that, it needs a Congress that can make up its own mind—even without the aid of lobbyists—and carry through a legislative program which will meet the country's problems. In other words, we need a Congress which can and will be a national legislative body with all that name implies—and which won't be too many other things besides.

That is the kind of Congress the LaFollette-Monroney Committee was trying to bring about. For more than a year the committee worked. It heard hundreds of witnesses from every walk of life, many of whom had made extensive study of the whole congressional problem. Senators and representatives gave the committee their suggestions. Section by section a bill was drafted. Section by section it was discussed, amended, rewritten. At last the whole measure was put together and introduced—in the Senate by Senator LaFollette, in the House by Congressman Monroney.

It wasn't a perfect bill. Everyone knew that. It contained provisions which conservative older members were violently opposed to. It contained some other provisions, such as the requirement that Congress fix an over-all limitation on the amount of appropriations, which some liberals were against. It omitted some worthwhile reforms entirely.

But it was a good bill. It would represent a long forward step. The question was whether or not it could be passed. Weeks passed and no progress had been made toward getting the bill onto the floor of the House. Interested members met to discuss "strategy." We made speeches, tried to interest some of those whom we believed to be against us. Most of them just didn't say anything. Few of them, we knew, would vote against the bill once it came onto the floor. But there were plenty of ways to keep that from taking place—especially since the bill was an "omnibus" sort of measure which might have been referred to any number of committees. At one time we were threatened with having some parts of the bill referred to one committee, other parts to another committee, still other parts to a third committee. Had this happened, the parliamentary difficulties would have been almost insurmountable.

But, if we were discouraged, it was only because we were underestimating the influence in the Senate of "Bob" LaFollette. For one fine spring day word came over from "the other end of the Capitol" that the "Reorganization bill" was on the floor of the Senate and would probably be passed that day. Senator LaFollette had to make one or two concessions by removing certain comparatively minor sections of the bill. But he succeeded in securing passage of almost everything that his committee had recommended.

This put a very different complexion on things in the House. It was now possible simply to bring up the bill as it had passed the Senate. In order to obtain agreement for this to be done, it was necessary for Mr. Monroney to make further concessions, to take several more provisions out of the bill. Some of these, unlike the Senate changes, removed important sections in which some of us were vitally interested. But it was the price that had to be paid if we were to pass a bill at all.

At last on July 23, 1946, scarcely a week before the Congress adjourned *sine die* (which means without naming a day for reassembling). Mr. Monroney was recognized to call up the Senate bill in the House. All day it was debated and amendments considered and voted upon. It was finally passed that same evening without a roll-call vote. The conference was quickly held and agreement reached between the Senate and the House. The conference reports were passed under the very shadow of adjournment. And with the President's signature, the bill became a law.

As enacted into law, the bill provided for an increase in the salaries of members of the House and Senate. It included a retirement system by which members paying certain percentages of their salaries can at age sixty-two receive retirement benefits based upon but not wholly covered by the amounts of their contributions. These provisions were the most widely publicized and the least important parts of the bill, although there is little doubt they facilitated its passage.

But the bill also brought about a streamlining of the whole committee system. It abolished a considerable number of committees in both the House and Senate and limited House members to one committee each and senators to two or three. Every one of the new committees has a broad, challenging field of jurisdiction. There are no longer any "minor" or inactive congressional committees.

The provision which I had advanced in my Resolution 60 and which had been included in the Smith Committee bills was enacted into law. It will be interesting to observe the extent to which the regular committees of Congress, now equipped to follow up and correct deficiencies in the administration of laws, carry out vigorously this new function. If they do so, we should see marked improvement in the workings of our government. If they don't, the blame for maladministration will rest squarely on the congressional doorstep.

The Congressional Reorganization Act has provided Congress for the first time in history with a staff and technical assistance somewhere nearly comparable to the importance of its work. Each committee is provided with a staff of clerical assistants and, what is more important, a staff of "professional" assistants to aid it in its work. The Legislative Reference Service in the Library of Congress is in a position to afford for the first time a salary scale adequate to attract competent specialists in various fields of legislation and national problems.

All lobbyists, big and little, "good" and "bad," must, under the terms of the bill, register their names with the Congress and tell the sources of the funds which support their activities. Passage of the LaFollette-Monroney bill was important because of its specific provisions aiming to simplify and make more effective the work of the beleaguered congressman. It was even more important in that it marked the first occasion in some hundred and fifty years when the Congress of the United States was willing critically to examine itself and then do something about the weaknesses discovered.

It is a sad commentary on the caprice of American political trends that despite their courageous leadership in this historic fight Senator LaFollette was actually defeated in the 1946 election and Congressman Monroney almost so.

It would be a most serious mistake, however, to conclude that the LaFollette-Monroney bill is sufficient to guarantee either the effective functioning or the co-equal position of the Congress of the United States. A great deal remains to be done.

In the House version of the bill no provision was made for the "executive assistants" so badly needed by the busier and abler congressmen.

We have made no progress toward a better method than pure seniority of selecting committee chairmen. Bills of importance can still be pigeonholed by committee chairmen. Provisions of the original Reorganization bill would have afforded regular opportunity for members to present before committees the main arguments for bills of their authorship and would have prevented this pigeonholing. But these provisions were dropped in the final version.

It remains possible for the Rules Committee to thwart for considerable periods of time the clear will of a majority of the House to act upon a piece of important legislation.

And most serious of all, in my opinion, no provision has yet been made for effective and responsible steering or policy committees in the House and Senate. In their absence the only charting of a legislative course for Congress will continue to be done at the White House or in purely partisan caucuses. The prestige of the Congress will continue to decline in consequence.

It may be that in the course of time the joint committee of House and Senate members created by the Full Employment Act of the Seventy-ninth Congress will assume some of the functions which in my opinion should be assumed by over-all policy committees of both Houses. Obviously the consideration of measures to promote full employment must inevitably include almost every phase of our domestic national life. This joint committee receives the reports on the economy of the nation from the Council of Economic Advisors of the President. But it need not, and certainly ought not, limit its work to analyzing those reports. It should secure all the additional information possible and then recommend a legislative program to Congress which would, so far as is possible through governmental action, assure a high level of national income, production, and employment. If the joint committee should in statesmanlike fashion seize this opportunity, in time it could accomplish much toward strengthening the Congress of the United States.

Progress has been made toward making the job of a congressman what that job really ought to be. But there is as yet little indication that either the joint committee on full employment, or any other agency of the Congress intends to grapple with the most important single problem of them all: the problem of developing within the Congress a method of working out a consistent, well-rounded program of legislation for the solution of the long-run problems of the United States. Until this is done Congress will continue to be in danger of losing its co-equal status with the executive and of sacrificing the position of trust and confidence which it should occupy in the minds and hearts of the American people.

Chapter 22

THE ROOTS
OF DEMOCRACY

On August 2, 1946, the Seventy-ninth Congress adjourned *sine die.* For the first time since the war broke out our family drove home to California together. Once again the greatness of America unfolded before us—the dairy farms of western Maryland, the coal-blackened cities of Pennyslvania, the Ohio River filled with barges, the magnificent lands of the Mississippi Valley whose rich, deep, black soil is still the greatest single source of food in the whole world. I quietly thanked God for the flatness of those lands, because it meant that it would be centuries, maybe millenniums, before any serious erosion of their fertile topsoil need be feared. I thought, too, that even atomic bombs could hardly destroy this empire of homes and farms. Because of its very vastness, this, the heart of America, would survive. Yet all this was only a part of our nation's breadth. We crossed the Great Plains that lead gradually up to the mountains, the Rockies, the deserts of Utah and Nevada with their beautiful green irrigated oases, then the Mojave and at last Cajon Pass and the orange groves of southern California.

I had been away from the district for nearly a year without a single opportunity to be at home for even a few days. Twice I had planned to return, but both times had been compelled to cancel my plans. Once it had been an important appropriation bill, the other time decisive meetings of the Committee on Agriculture which had stood in the way. So it seemed good to be back again—even though I knew from experience something of what the next three months held in store.

Now at last I could renew close acquaintance with the people from whom I had been so long separated. My best chance to do so would come through meetings such as the one held at Peter and Harriet Embrey's house shortly after we arrived home. It was not essentially different from a very large number of other meetings which we had had in the Twelfth District during the previous eleven years.

The ordinary political meeting leaves a good deal to be desired. In congressional campaigns particularly, only certain people will make the effort to attend such meetings. Many others who might like to come are unable to do so. The attendants at such meetings are largely those who are already best informed on the issues of the campaign. Moreover, there is an "audience." The meeting is divided between those who speak and those who simply listen. This is not good; there should be a two-way exchange of ideas. Half of the job of a political candidate is, of course, to speak to the people, tell them his ideas, and give some leadership to their thinking. But at least the other half of the job is to listen to the people—especially if there is any real chance of his winning the election.

Therefore it seemed a good idea to have another kind of meeting. We called them "house meetings," but "neighborhood meetings" might have been a better name. I would ask a lady who was friendly to my political work whether she would be willing to invite a group of friends and neighbors—as many or as few as she might decide—to come to her house on a certain evening or late afternoon, and whether I might come to meet with them. Usually there would be between twenty and thirty people, though sometimes there were four times that number. We had no set method of carrying on the meeting. Sometimes the entire time would be taken up in informal conversation, group by group, in greeting people and telling them good-by. But generally I would start out with a very brief talk on one or two of the most pressing questions of the time, urging that I be interrupted at any desired point. Almost always I would be interrupted, and from that point on the time would be spent in general discussion of whatever matters seemed uppermost to us.

The meeting at the Embreys' was on a Saturday night and was the only engagement I had to meet on that evening. As she almost always did, Mrs. Voorhis went with me. A few of the people had already gathered when we got there—the rest drifted in gradually. I do not remember what I talked about to start things off. But I do remember most of the discussion which followed.

One of the printers at the local newspaper began it: "What I never have understood is this business about 'overproduction' and 'surpluses.' This country would give just about anything right now if we could have some of those surpluses that were supposed to be such a problem a few years ago. But I never did believe in those things. I never believed we had overproduction or any real surpluses. The trouble was that nobody could afford to buy the stuff."

"That's right," said Mr. Smith, who had a small poultry farm. "At least, it's right in general. Part of the time we worry about the wrong things. It can just as well be too little money as too much goods. Just now I guess it's the other way, though—not enough goods. And some folks, though I hate to say it, have darn near got more money than is good for them."

"Won't last long," put in Peter Embrey dryly.

"But now," went on Mr. Smith, "I've seen the time when we did seem to have too much of certain things—eggs, for instance. Gosh! Jerry remembers when we had them running out of our ears a few years ago. The government bought a heck of a lot of eggs and I guess they didn't know what to do with some of them. But a lot of them were used to give to schools, weren't they? How does that work?"

I explained about the working of the School Lunch program, and said I believed it was at least one partial answer to the problems we had been discussing. I told them a little about the passing of the Flannagan School Lunch bill during the last session. There was not a single dissent in that meeting from the hearty expression of support for the School Lunch program which one of the women voiced.

"About all I can worry about right now is a place to live," said a young veteran's wife. "It's really terrible. My husband isn't so very well but I know if we could find a house or even a small apartment he'd pick up. We've got a priority to build and we even have our loan. But the lumberyard tells us the priority isn't any good because they aren't getting enough lumber. And do we have to pay interest on the loan even though we haven't spent any of the money? It's pretty tough. I can't see why anybody is talking about surpluses."

I told her I was afraid the big builders were getting most of the lumber that was coming in and that several people had told me great quantities of it were piled all around the mills in the Northwest. Several of the people agreed that they had heard the same thing.

"When are they going to turn loose of it?" she asked.

"I don't know, of course," I told her, "but I would bet that there will be no shortage after election. I have no doubt they're holding it till OPA ceilings are taken off."

"Why not take them off then?" she persisted.

"Because then the price might go so high that the people who need the houses most just couldn't afford it," I replied.

"Well, I don't know. It seems to me it might be better to let them have their bigger profits if we could just have a home. And what about our loan?"

I had to tell her that they did have to start paying interest from the day they signed the loan contract, even though they couldn't use the money. It was hard to do.

"If these people in the rent control office would be a little reasonable there would be a lot of houses for rent that aren't being rented now." The man who said this was Mr. Berry, the town druggist. I said I believed rent control was still necessary because otherwise, with the shortage so acute, rents might go to very high figures.

There followed the discussion of OPA which took place in all our meetings that year. First Mr. Berry's point was developed, with which many agreed. Then the almost general concern was expressed that rent control was still necessary. Third came the charges that some of the shortages were being caused by unwise and arbitrary OPA decisions. And finally there was the recital of instances of discourteous if not positively shabby treatment of people who had had dealings with the OPA offices in Los Angeles. Of the last complaint I had heard much and could not doubt that it was true. And yet I hadn't been able to conscientiously vote for the abolition of the agency, at least not until the critical supply shortages were on the way to being overcome. The grievances against OPA worried me more than almost anything else, but I will always believe that any unsatisfactory conditions were in part due to those who deliberately sought to discredit the whole program of price ceilings. I was positive people at the head of OPA didn't intend such abuses.

"OPA won't last much longer, I guess, though for my part I think it's been a good thing," said Mrs. Robinson. "But what worries me almost sick is that it looks like we'll always have that terrible open ditch running in front of our houses. Another little boy fell in it today. Mr. Frazier got him out before it was too late but the little fellow floated halfway down the block before anyone discovered him. Suppose it had happened at night?"

Then I asked what turned out to be a very naïve question: "Why don't they cover it?"

Mrs. Embrey answered me with feeling. "When we bought our place they promised us it would be covered that very year. We've been here for fourteen years now and the ditch isn't covered yet. And I don't think it ever will be. The people who control this town will never make the water company do it. Jim Fletcher has too much power. Everybody seems to be afraid of him."

"Sure. That gang doesn't care what happens to the kids. I used to be on the school board. I ought to know." This came from the man who was probably the most prominent and well-to-do citizen in the meeting. He owned considerable property and had lived in the town almost all his life. He went on: "Back in 1934 and 1935 we were really getting things done. I was chairman of the school board. I've always been a Democrat. Our superintendent was a Democrat. Our principal was a good Republican. All of us cared about the youngsters. We had a plan for two new schools located so the youngsters would not have to cross the boulevard——"

"Oh! That boulevard!" broke in one of the women. "A car just missed Louise when she was crossing it today."

The man went on. "We were going to build those new schools and get a couple of new teachers. About that time they found out the superintendent and I were Democrats. They fired him and kicked me out as board chairman. We haven't got the new schools yet."

"The worst of it was they stopped my classes for the Mexican mothers," added one of the teachers. She spoke with genuine sadness.

"Well, why can't we get the county to put in a traffic light or at least a stop sign at the boulevard crossing?" protested Mrs. Fisk. "Two children have been killed there already since we've been living here."

"Trucking companies don't want it. It's the state, not the county, that would have to do it." This from Peter Embrey, who I knew had been trying for years to get that stop sign installed. I had tried to help him as much as I could, though it was hardly a congressional problem. I told them I doubted it would do much good but that I would be glad to write the State Highway Department about the matter again.

And so our meeting went along, going over the problems of the everyday lives of that California community. Sometimes we were back in Washington in the middle of price control or the long-run problems of our whole country; occasionally we were in Europe with the foreign ministers, wrestling with world peace; more often we were right in the home community of our meeting place, talking about the struggles, the difficulties, the sadnesses, the hopes, the aspirations of that American neighborhood.

Up until the very last of the meeting, Joe, the ice cream salesman, was silent. Then we returned to the subject we had started with—the great central problem of bringing together the needs of people and the potential supply of goods. Joe listened for a while. Then he said quietly: "If you feed the lowest peon in Mexico there isn't going to be any depression. There's something wrong when people start queueing up for bread. When people get hungry they start fighting."

Somehow everybody seemed to feel that Joe had summed it up. All the struggles of the ages, the causes of wars and conflicts, all the hopes for a better world were there. Nothing much was left to be said. We bade one another good night. Mrs. Voorhis and I waited till the last to thank the Embreys for their kindness and hospitality, to tell them what a good meeting we thought they had had.

As we drove home that night my wife observed that it is among folks like those with whom we had just met that democracy has its roots. She was eternally right. It is the neighborhoods that make the nation and hold it together. The government is a great thing of course, the Congress, the Supreme Court, the presidency, the cabinet departments. We have been a long time building them, and on the whole our work has been pretty well done.

But our government is not democracy nor is it the nation. The nation is the people, and democracy is a relationship between the people. It is a relationship of mutual respect, of common concern over common problems, of willingness to work together till they're solved—even if it takes "all summer."

If a politician or a candidate or a congressman is really seeking wisdom he will do best to look for it in groups of the people such as the ones with which we were privileged to meet that night.

There are a few things a congressman may in the course of years be able to do for the people. But there is a great deal more which the people can do for him. For among them and twining close about their lives for better nourishment grow the roots of democracy, the roots of America.

Chapter 23

THE FALL OF 1946

During the week of October 13–20, 1946, I spoke at a Sunday morning church service, a rabbit breeders' co-operative meeting, three "house" meetings, a Junior Chamber of Commerce, two carpenters' local unions, one luncheon club, a young peoples' evening church meeting, an American Legion post, two general political meetings in schoolhouse auditoriums, a Democratic party dinner, a Saturday afternoon open forum in a city park, and the annual convention of the California State Grange. That week was nothing unusual. The others were a good deal like it.

It wasn't the first time. Year after year since 1936 our family had expected it, though we never quite reconciled ourselves to it and didn't like the arrangement from a family point of view. It was just part of the game.

There was no great difference between campaign years and the other years, so far as the pressure of the meetings was concerned. We had almost as many of our house meetings during the weeks that I was at home in the odd-numbered years as in the campaign years. (Members of Congress soon learn to prefer odd numbers, for the odd-numbered years are the ones when members of the House are just congressmen. In every even-numbered year they as candidates as well.)

The Twelfth District campaign of 1946 got started along in the fall of 1945, more than a year before the election. There was, of course, opposition to me in the district. There always had been. Nor was there any valid reason for me to think I lived a charmed political life. But there were special factors in the campaign of 1946, factors bigger and more powerful than either my opponent or myself. And they were on his side.

In October 1945 the representative of a large New York financial house made a trip to California. All the reasons for his trip I, of course, do not know. But I do know that he called on a number of influential people in southern California. And I know he "bawled them out." For what? For permitting Jerry Voorhis, whom he described as "one of the most dangerous men in Washington," to continue to represent a part of the state of California in the House of Representatives. This gentleman's reasons for thinking me so "dangerous" obviously had to do with my views and work against monopoly and for changes in the monetary system.

It appears that his California friends listened to him and were impressed. Just how much this Eastern gentleman and others like him had to do with the actual running of the campaign I do not know. But many of the advertisements which ran in the district newspapers advocating my defeat came to the papers from a large advertising agency in Los Angeles, rather than from any source within the Twelfth District. And payment was made by check from that same agency.

The Republican organization in the Twelfth District started very early to select a candidate to carry their banner. Without much argument they selected Richard M. Nixon, assistant city attorney of Whittier, California, and a lieutenant commander in the Navy during the war. Just when Mr. Nixon's "active" campaign started is a little hard to say. Certainly it was well under way in the earliest months of 1946. Meanwhile I was, of course, in Washington, attempting as best I could to do the congressional job and receiving the usual amount of mail from friends about my probable opponent's activities.

As the time for the primaries approached, a good many of the California congressmen went home to campaign, especially those who had been able to win both the Democratic and Republican nominations in past elections. (The California election laws permit a candidate to enter his name on any primary ballot he chooses to place it on. He need only pay the hundred-dollar filing fee in each case. The candidate in any primary who receives the highest number of votes becomes the nominee of that party—even if he belongs to another party entirely. In California this is known as "cross-filing." If the same man wins both the Democratic and Republican nominations in the primaries, he is virtually elected and need make no campaign for the final election.) I had never won both nominations. Certainly I did not expect to do so in 1946.

Anyway, I could not bring myself to leave Washington at that time. Amendment of the Social Security Act, the Case Labor bill, the British loan, terminal leave pay for soldiers, and several appropriation bills were on the House agenda. So was the most important problem our country had faced in all its history—the problem of what to do about atomic energy. I felt sure that the people of the district would rather have me stay on the job than come home to campaign.

So the primaries came and went with me still in Washington. The results were interpreted by many people as indication that I was sure to win in November. I won the Democratic nomination by about four to one and in the Republican primary received approximately half as many votes as Mr. Nixon. True, I received more total votes than did my opponent, but it was to be observed that the Democratic vote was considerably lighter than the Republican. A lot of Democrats hadn't voted at all. A lesser number of Republicans hadn't voted either. What would these people do in November when the total vote was certain to be much heavier?

There were other factors, too, that didn't appear on the surface. The most important of these was that, while my opponent had done a good deal of speaking, the real campaign of my opposition hadn't even started yet. Their Twelfth District operations had, wisely from their point of view, been comparatively restrained. No great effort had as yet been made to dissuade Republicans from voting for me, as a considerable number had done in past elections. And, technically at least, Mr. Nixon did not become the Republican nominee until the primaries had been held.

It was not until August, shortly before my family, my two secretaries, Harold Herin and Duane de Schaine, and I arrived at home, that the campaign began in earnest. I can't say I was exactly "ready for the fray." But the "fray" was certainly ready for me and from that time on there was fought out in the Twelfth District the bitterest campaign I have ever experienced.

The opposition was already well organized. Their advertising and publicity were obviously in expert hands; hardly an issue of any newspaper in the district failed to carry some item about my opponent, usually on the front page.

In most of the towns of the district their organization was already functioning, and it was apparent from the beginning that there was no lack of funds to carry on their work. But neither in these early stages nor at any other time prior to the election did the official Republican organization make any predictions that they would win. In talking to my supporters their leaders carefully expressed doubt as to the outcome and even forecast my re-election. This was only one example of the very "smart" politics which characterized their campaign from beginning to end. For it left our people overconfident to the very last.

We did the best we could. Mr. de Schaine opened an office in Alhambra, largest city of the district, and Mr. Herin and I set up the machinery for carrying on the regular work in the back room of our home. I was still the congressman and that work had to go on, campaign or no campaign. Meetings with small representative groups of my old supporters were held to plan strategy. Our meetings and speaking engagements were scheduled, though with considerably more difficulty, I noticed, than ever before. Fewer people believed they could "get up a good meeting."

In some of the larger cities our organizations had been kept together and functioning all through the intervening time since the last election. But elsewhere it was necessary to begin from the ground up and to ask good friends to form organizations especially for this campaign. In most instances they responded in as good a way as anyone could have asked. But in many cases it was evident that the job was harder than heretofore, that fewer people were genuinely concerned about the outcome.

The opposition, despite its oft-repeated statements of lack of confidence, was several jumps ahead of us in organization, campaign funds, and, above all, propaganda. And their propaganda was running with the tide, whereas ours—what there was of it—had to be forced against it.

The most important single factor in the campaign of 1946 was the difference in general attitude between the "outs" and "ins." Anyone seeking to unseat an incumbent needed only to point out all the things that had gone wrong and all the troubles of the war period and its aftermath. Many of these things were intimate experiences in the everyday lives of the people.

Most of them were inevitable accompaniments of the war. But a few of them undoubtedly could have been avoided. And it was easy to leave the impression that most of them could have been. Against this "campaign line" incumbent Democrats like myself had to "defend the record." We had to show, for example, that we had tried to straighten things out, and more important, we had to point out that the broad lines of policy—the efforts to strengthen the United Nations, the increasing firmness in our dealings with Russia, the moves made to cushion the shock of postwar depression—had been and were correct.

Consequently too many Republicans talked with confidence on every street corner, while too many Democrats listened and, forgetting the long-range issues, apologized as best they could.

The Twelfth District was plastered with posters telling the people to "vote for Nixon for a change," asking them if they had "had enough." From every newspaper the voters received the appeal to get rid of government controls by electing Republican candidates. My opponent regularly began his speeches by reminding the audience of their lack of automobiles, houses, meat, refrigerators. And behind all this there was in the minds of many people who had previously voted for me the general idea that it is good practice in a democracy to change the party in power from time to time. With that idea, of course, no one could quarrel as a basic proposition. The only question I could raise was what we were going to be changing to. I pointed out with vigor that we had "changed" in 1920 with consequences that hardly advanced either the peace of the world or in the long run the welfare or prosperity of the United States.

There was one other line of attack which had run through my opponent's speeches from the start, and which was a major emphasis of the Republican campaign nationally. I was labeled the "CIO Political Action Committee candidate." As a matter of fact I wasn't. I had not received the CIO endorsement and I knew why. In California and in Los Angeles County certain CIO unions, notably the Oil Workers, the Steel Workers, the Auto Workers, and the Rubber Workers, had been fighting against penetration by communists into the CIO. But while they had cleared the situation in their own unions, they had not yet won their fight against communist influence in the state or county CIO organizations. My position for the Hobbs Anti-racketeering bill, against peacetime subsidies, and a number of other issues was contrary to what the CIO wanted. But the main point was that I had a long and very clear record of consistent opposition to the communists and their whole philosophy. I had served on the Dies Committee and I had on numerous occasions, in House speeches, articles, and elsewhere, warned of the danger of any degree of communist control in American labor organizations. So I was not endorsed by the CIO Political Action Committee. This was a matter of public record. But it made no difference to my opposition. They just went on calling me the "CIO candidate."

Mr. Raymond Haight, Republican state leader, for example, gave out a public statement on August twenty-third in which he said, "as for Rogers, Outland, and Voorhis, all of them are seeking to return to Congress on their leftist records with the support of the C.I.O. P.A.C." This debonnaire attitude toward the truth made me angry.

I decided, therefore, to set the record straight and paid for an advertisement in all the newspapers of the district in early September.

The ad was in the form of a signed statement by me. It stated that I was proud to have the endorsement of the American Federation of Labor and the Railroad Brotherhoods. It referred to the gallant fight of the CIO unions mentioned above against the communists. It included the following two paragraphs.

> These labor men in the AF of L, the Brotherhoods and the CIO are fighting the front line battle against Communist forces in America. I am proud indeed to have their support.
>
> On the other hand, under present top leadership of the CIO in California, there is at least grave question whether the Communist party does not exercise inordinate if not decisive influence over state and county organizations. Under this leadership, I was not endorsed by the C.I.O. P.A.C.

The ad concluded like this:

> For the one effective enemy of the Communist or Fascist is not the reactionary or conservative, but the earnest progressive. If he can prove by his work that the problems of the people can be solved by democratic constitutional means, he can make totalitarian propaganda and causes both hopeless and foolish.
>
> This is and has been the central aim and purpose of my work in Congress.
>
> American labor, American progress, American forward-looking political movements cannot be mixed with Communist influences. I will stand with any labor man who opposes these influences. I cannot accept the support of anyone who does not oppose them as I do.

An astute political observer told me after reading my ad that he thought it "undoubtedly the dumbest political move he had ever heard of." "Why tell people you don't want their support?" he asked. But I felt better for having laid the cards on the table. The Communist *People's World* had recently published an editorial saying that "Voorhis is against unity with Communists on any issue under any circumstances." I had quoted this in my ad. Furthermore, I believed that my public record of opposition to all forms of totalitarianism or any kind of united front was long enough and plain enough so that I would be judged on that record rather than on any action that might or might not be taken by some group over which in the nature of the case I could have no control.

In the first of the five debates held during the campaign, however, my opponent was asked why so much had been made of an alleged CIO PAC endorsement of me when such did not exist. My opponent simply shifted his ground. He made no mention of the CIO PAC but now said that I was supported by the *National Citizens* Political Action Committee and read from a mimeographed report of a committee of the Los Angeles chapter of that organization which recommended my endorsement. He referred to it as a "communist-dominated" organization. Certainly I had desired no such endorsement, least of all had I asked for it. I knew there were some fine people affiliated with the organization. But I also knew it had taken no definite action to bar communists from participation and I had said a good many times that I believed failure to take such action was a fatal mistake.

Again, however, the important question was where a man himself stood on the vital issues of the hour. Paramount among all these was American foreign policy, particularly in its relations to Soviet Russia. On that issue my position was exactly the opposite of that of the National Citizens Political Action Committee. For that organization sponsored the meeting where Mr. Henry Wallace made his speech critical of American foreign policy and calling for a "realistic" attitude toward the "existence" of spheres of influence including a Soviet sphere. I immediately made a radio address and a statement to the press backing up Secretary Byrnes in the policy he was pursuing and pointing out that peace could never be achieved if America surrendered to the Russian desire for division of the world into the very sort of spheres of influence of which Mr. Wallace had spoken. At the same time I sent a telegram to the National Citizens Political Action Committee which was published in several of the district newspapers and read as follows:

Since Citizens Political Action Committee appears to be a factor in Secretary Wallace's speeches against present foreign policy, and since I profoundly believe Secretary Byrnes is generally right in course he has been pursuing and that attacks at home cannot but have disastrous effect on his efforts to deal with critical problems, I hereby request that whatever qualified endorsement the Citizens P.A.C. may have given me be withdrawn.

The simple fact is that when endorsements by the National Citizens Political Action Committee were published my name was no more on that list than it had been on the CIO PAC list. I received neither of these endorsements.

My opponent, so far as I know, did not mention the CIO again after that first debate. But he did not need to. On October eighth, a month after my ad had been run in their own papers, two of the largest newspapers in the district, which happen to be owned by outside interests, ran an editorial containing the following paragraph:

> *Jerry is not a Communist* but not many members of the House have voted against more measures the Communists vigorously opposed than he. It takes a smart politician to get the support of the C.I.O. Political Action Committee in Washington and appeal to the voters at home as a conservative.

This editorial was based on an alleged analysis of my voting record, fifteen measures having been selected for this purpose. Not only was the statement false about CIO PAC support, as the papers themselves well knew, but my voting record was also falsified on no less than three of the selected votes as to which the papers told their readers that I had voted exactly opposite to the way I actually did vote.

In accordance with Republican National Committee strategy, the PAC issue was raised in still a third form. Speeches and ads of the opposition began to say that whether or not I had the support of any such organization was of little consequence. The important thing was that out of forty-six votes I had voted only three times contrary to the position of the PAC. What particular PAC was referred to was not, for obvious reasons, made clear.

Nor was any indication given to the people as to what these forty-six votes were all about.

When, however, in the course of a debate I pointed out that the people had a right to know the issues on which these mysterious forty-six votes had been cast, my opponent gave the sources where they could be found, but still made no mention of what the actual bills were.

The sources were a list compiled by the CIO and three lists taken from supplements to the *New Republic*. One of these latter, incidentally, turned out to be a Union for Democratic Action list and not a PAC list at all. But what was a minor detail like that in a political campaign?

It was then possible to tell the people just what these forty-six votes were all about. I found two of the publications in my file and obtained the other two at a library. We worked until nearly four o'clock one morning preparing a little pamphlet to set forth the facts about these votes. Probably five per cent of the people who heard or read the charge against me saw my answer. There was simply no way to get it to them. But we tried our best.

For here are what these "bad" votes of mine turned out to be:

My vote for the School Lunch program

My vote for the Soldiers' Vote bill

A vote for soil conservation appropriations

The vote for the Fullbright Peace Resolution

A vote for an appropriation for the Rural Electrification Administration

Several votes on OPA issues

Several votes on foreign relief issues

My vote against higher prices for oil

My vote against eliminating the $67,200 limitation (before taxes) on wartime salaries

Four votes in favor of reciprocal trade agreements

My vote to sustain the veto of the Smith-Connally Act and my vote against the Case bill

My vote against continuing the Dies Committee in the year in which I resigned from it (No mention was made of the two votes I cast for continuance of the committee.)

Two votes for bills to abolish the poll tax

My vote for the loan to Great Britain (which communists bitterly opposed)

Two votes on the Veterans' Housing bill (which would, I believed, have prevented the runaway inflation in the cost of housing to veterans)

My vote against freezing Social Security taxes

My vote against exempting insurance companies from antitrust laws

Other votes on the list were the Hobbs Anti-racketeering bill and the amendment to gradually end OPA subsidies, on which questions they admitted I had voted contrary to the PAC position.

The main point, obviously, is that these were the big vital bills that had passed during the latter part of my service in Congress. They were not PAC issues, much less "communist" issues. There was, of course, sharp difference of opinion about many of them. But they were broad questions before the whole United States and in a majority of cases I had voted in undoubted accordance with the will of a majority of the American people. Yet, as my little pamphlet stated: "Mr. Nixon infers that in every case Mr. Voorhis should have found out what the P.A.C. would say and then voted the opposite way regardless of the merits of the issue."

The one thing most precious to a congressman is his "record." It is the only thing of real value that he has to hand down to his children and grandchildren. In my own case I had no apologies to make for what I knew was an independent record of votes cast in accordance with the very best light I could get on each issue. I would be less than honest if I did not say that the attempts to make of my voting record something it was not cut me pretty deeply.

It was some satisfaction to feel that there was at least in existence a document that effectively refuted the charges made. But neither the financial nor the mechanical problem of getting that document into the hands of any considerable number of the voters could we solve.

The opposition wasn't through. In ample advertisements and published statements it asked the people: "Do you know that your present Congressman introduced 132 public bills in the last four years? That only one of them was passed? That the one bill adopted transferred activities concerning rabbits from one federal department to another?" My only answer again was the factual record. The statement that but one of the bills introduced by me had become law was, to say the least, grossly misleading.

But the trouble was that in most cases the bills had either borne the name of another member at the time of passage or had been incorporated as amendments in other legislation.

One of these two things had happened in the case of the Credit Union bill, the School Lunch bill, some of the more important provisions of the Congressional Reorganization bill, the California Disability Insurance program, and the Rabbit Transfer bill.

It appeared to me that the important fact was that the legislation had actually passed and become a law, and that the question of whose name was attached to the bill at the time of passage was unimportant.

So we prepared another piece of literature to explain all this. Some of my friends ran it as paid advertising in their local newspapers. But here again my defense was necessarily a carefully detailed explanation, not nearly so effective in rough-and-tumble political battling as my opponent's "1 out of 132."

The main problem, as in all political campaigns, was getting our story to the people. We were quite unable to afford hired precinct workers. And even if we had been able to pay a few such workers it would have been palpably unfair to the faithful people who were volunteering their services for such work. But they could cover only a tiny fraction of the district. The newspapers of the district were not only, with few exceptions, openly favorable to my opponent, but in most cases they actually belonged, lock, stock, and barrel, to leaders in the Republican organization. Out of some thirty district papers only one was openly for my re-election and only three others could be said to be even neutral. All the rest were part and parcel of my opponent's campaign.

I hoped, however, that the joint debates arranged in various cities in the district would bring out large crowds and thus give me a chance to tell my side of the story to a considerable number of the voters. The crowds came all right. At every one of the debates my opponent and I spoke to packed houses. But they were "packed" in more ways than one. For the crowds mainly consisted of convinced supporters of one or the other of us—people who came with their minds already made up and to cheer for the candidate they had already decided to vote for. The debates were lively enough for this reason. But I doubt that they changed any appreciable number of votes one way or the other.

Not all the campaign was fought in the open. "Stories" were circulated. One of the prize ones made current among citrus growers was to the effect that I had "voted to increase the ceiling price on Florida oranges but not on California oranges." The facts that no member of Congress ever in history voted on any such proposition and that for a Californian to have done what I was accused of doing would have been evidence of insanity were "overlooked."

Merchants were warned that if they dared to sign newspaper statements in my support, as they had done in previous campaigns, their line of credit would be cut off at the bank. One large banking institution sent the word "down the line" that its employees were not to vote for Jerry Voorhis. Community Chest solicitors in some of the cities carried my opponent's literature with them and left it in every home. The one newspaper editor who wrote a friendly editorial on my behalf (and who, incidentally, gave equal space on his front page to my opponent and me to set our "platforms" before the voters) was informed the next morning by his landlord that he had read the editorial and the editor would have to "get out." He had no lease. The quarters were temporary while he was trying to find a house. So he had to move.

Small merchants in the district received letters from the League for Good Government bearing a caption, "Prohibition Is Not Coming Back," and stating that "Jerry Voorhis, who seeks legislation to curtail or stop the production of beer and liquors, is on record attacking the saloon and the cocktail lounges. His bill would help put us out of business." What this had reference to was H.J.R. 325, which I certainly did intend should, in the time of critical food and feed shortage, prevent any more grain being used to add further to a three-year stock of liquors. People in the liquor business know their politics and work at it.

And so when Election Day came it was my best judgment that,

considering all that had taken place (much of which has had to be omitted from this chapter), my opponent would be elected. But I must confess that right up until the returns began to come in I harbored certain hopes. I hoped that, as they had done five times before, the people would endorse the kind of clean campaign which ours had been.

I hoped that a good many people who disagreed with me on some issues would vote for me because I had tried through a good many years to do an honest job. I even hoped that the very evident efficiency and expense of my opponent's campaign might turn some people to our side.

But most of all I hoped that what I had said in the closing two minutes of the last debate with my opponent in San Gabriel had found a response among the people. What I said that night was something like this: "If you have 'had enough' of the hard, trying task of building world peace and establishing a supreme peace-enforcing authority that can prevent any nation from preparing or precipitating the atomic war—if you have 'had enough' of that effort, don't vote for Jerry Voorhis. If you really feel that our lack of refrigerators and automobiles and, until recently, meat is the most important thing, then don't vote for Jerry Voorhis. If you want to repeat the course our country followed after World War I—if you want another 'get-rich-quick' period followed by another crash like 1929, then don't vote for Jerry Voorhis. If you have 'had enough' of my efforts to chart a monetary and fiscal policy for our country that can prevent depressions and mass unemployment, then please don't vote for me. But if you want to go on facing the world and the monumental problems of the future as they really are, meeting them as best we can before they become acute, if you are ready to say you have not 'had enough' of effort until the brotherhood of man has been created on this earth, then I want your support very much indeed."

At last it was election night. About eight o'clock my wife and I started out to make the rounds of all the larger towns in the district. In each one of them there would be groups of our friends gathered together listening to the returns. We had the car radio turned on. The first returns from the Twelfth District didn't come in until we had made our visits at the first two cities on our route. I don't remember the exact figures but my opponent had some 500 votes to my 400. On the next report his margin was even greater. "Well," I said to Mrs. Voorhis, "I guess this is it at last." And it was.

We stopped in El Monte, the community that had stood by me best through all the years and where in 1944 I had a 2½ to 1 majority. Earliest returns showed 1346 votes for me and 843 for my opponent. It wasn't enough margin, not for El Monte. When all the votes were in El Monte did give me a 2 to 1 majority, which was all I had any right to expect. But that night I didn't know this.

Our last stop was at our headquarters in San Gabriel, a building donated for that purpose for the period of the campaign by a real estate and income tax man, one of my best friends. There was a group of forty or fifty people there, including many of those who had worked hardest and cared most about the outcome. Two people were there who had given at least half of all the modest funds that had been spent in all my six campaigns. They were my dad and mother. The ladies were making coffee. Two radios were fairly shouting the returns. Groups of us stood around and talked and tried to keep up our spirits. We did pretty well.

It was coming in thick and fast now—both over the radio and by telephone. And there was no longer the slightest doubt about the outcome.

My opponent would carry Pomona by a comfortable margin. I had never lost Pomona before, not a single time.

Whittier, my opponent's home town, almost 2 to 1 for him.

San Gabriel, the community which in some respects I had loved the best, on partial returns gave me only 774 to 1386 for my opponent.

And then—my home town, which I had been so proud to carry by good substantial margins after losing it in my first election, went against me, 491 to 401.

Well, there it was. Fortunately I remembered a line of poetry: "If you can . . . watch the things you gave your life to, broken, And stoop and build 'em up with worn-out tools. . . ·." And I was profoundly thankful to Rudyard Kipling. For he suggested the next job.

About one o'clock Mrs. Voorhis and I told everyone at the headquarters good night. We both managed smiles and hearty thank you's and then in the foggy night walked across the street to our car and drove the weary miles home. Hardly a word was spoken in those twenty miles. Our little boy was having trouble with his asthma and was coughing badly. We didn't tell him anything about the outcome and fortunately he didn't ask. I wondered how he'd take it. He'd have to go back to school in Covina, where some of the worst of all the attacks on his daddy had been published.

Harold and Duane just wouldn't believe it was true. Both of them had come up through the Voorhis School. We had lived and studied and worked together for a good many years. Both of them had been in the Army and both of them overseas. They had just come back to their old jobs. But now the "old jobs" just weren't there. All night long they stayed at the telephone. Every few minutes they would call the office of the registrar of voters in Los Angeles. The late returns, they kept insisting, would change the result. Once before this had actually happened. But not this time. It got worse and worse.

Along about three o'clock I went to bed. But the boys kept their vigil. When I came downstairs next morning I think they still didn't believe the figures. It was worse for them, after all the hard, confident work they had done, than it was for me.

Our little boy helped out more than he knew. For when his mother told him that Daddy had been defeated, his face brightened up and he threw his arms around my neck and said, "You mean you don't have to be a congressman any more, that you can stay home at nights with us?" And when I told him yes, it was pretty hard to keep my eyes dry. There are some things more important than being a congressman.

The newspapers wanted a statement, of course. So I wrote one out, worked over it a long time, and telephoned it around to them. What I said was this:

> Mr. Nixon has clearly been elected as Congressman from the Twelfth District. I wish him well as he undertakes his new duties.
> From the bottom of my heart I want to thank my many

friends who have so loyally supported me through this strenuous campaign.

I have given the best years of my life to serving this District in Congress. By the will of the people that work is ended. I have no regrets about the record I have written.

I know the principles I have stood for and the measures I have fought for are right. I know, too, that, in broad outline at least, they are vital to the future safety and welfare of our country. I know the day will come when a lot more people will recognize this than was the case on November fifth.

Officially that ended it. But there was a lot more work to be done if I was to "go out" the way I wanted to. There were all the people who had worked so hard in the campaign to be thanked some way. I had already planned for this. I had bought up five hundred copies of one of my books, *Beyond Victory,* from the publishing house for this purpose. I autographed them all to the people in the various towns who had done most in the campaign. It was impossible, of course, to cover everyone. I had to do the best I could. Then in the few days that remained before we would have to leave for Washington to pack up I delivered as many of the books as I possibly could around the district. It was hard but it was more than worth the time and effort. It gave me a chance to say thank you and good-by. Meanwhile we packed our things, thought about what the next move was going to be, and started work in earnest on this book.

A friend gave me a copy of a major oil company's magazine so I could read their jubilant article which told how their "enemies" in Congress had been routed and put my name at the head of the list. Another man just returned from New York told me the organized liquor interests there were claiming credit for my defeat. It was some satisfaction to have had the right people against me. This was a time when every word of encouragement meant a good deal to me. And, I confess, I will keep always some of the letters I received from friends both in and outside our district in the few weeks that followed the election. They were good enough to say I had done at least a better job than the last few months' propaganda against my work would have indicated.

I got a lift also from clippings sent to me from Eastern papers which had published on November second the story of a poll taken among House press gallery reporters in which I was rated the "best Pacific Coast Congressman." This story had been available over the press wire services to all the papers of California as well. It simply had not been used, except, as I later learned, by one or two weekly papers far removed from the Twelfth District.

We drove back to Washington to write up the last chapter. It consisted of going through the accumulation of material on almost every important subject, the mountains of filed letters, the other things that had gone to make the work of our congressional office possible. They were packed in boxes—dozens of them—some shipped to California, some to the basement of our little home in Alexandria. Meanwhile the last letters of a congressman were written, most of them thank-you letters to supporters or kind people who had written to tell me not to feel bad, that there would be "another day." There were some problems that had been laid in my lap that were still to be worked out. Harold and Duane had stayed in California and Miss Lucy Lonergan, who had carried on in the Washington office, stood by to the last day to help wind things up. I could not help wondering what I would have done without co-workers like these.

There was one thing that I hadn't yet done and which I wanted somehow to do before my term expired on January third. I tried again and again but the right words never seemed to come. Then at last on December seventh I wrote the letter. Here it is:

Hon. Richard Nixon
Representative in Congress-elect
Whittier, California
DEAR CONGRESSMAN:
During the past few days I have been busy going through the files and the materials on various important national problems and all the rest of the things that I have accumulated during the time that I have represented the Twelfth District. The thoughts that have come to me during this experience have prompted this letter to you, which I cannot refrain from writing.

I remember most poignantly the time in late December of 1936 when I first came to Washington as a new Congressman. Little did I realize then all that the job entailed, the long hours of very hard and frequently thankless work, the many periods of frustration when one was unable to get the things done which he believed most necessary for the country, as well as those times of encouragement when something worth while seemed to have been accomplished.

During the ten years .of my service I came to have a profound respect for the Congress of the United States and to realize the critical importance of its work, not only for the future of our country, but for the future of the whole world. For those of us who believe in democratic government, under a Constitution which protects the individual citizen's rights and liberties, it becomes more and more evident that the one essential bulwark of the people's liberties in such a nation is the vigor and effectiveness of the national legislature.

If that national legislature occupies its proper place as a co-equal branch of government, and especially if it puts forth and enacts into law a program calculated to meet the nation's present and future problems, the future of freedom will be safe. What will happen under opposite circumstances we all know.

The long and short of this letter is simply to say, as I said in my newspaper release after the election at home, that I sincerely wish you well as you undertake the tremendous responsibilities which will soon be yours.

I have refrained, for reasons which I am sure you will understand, from making any references in this letter to the circumstances of the campaign recently conducted in our District. It would only have spoiled the letter.

The fact remains that you are the new Congressman and that while I have no doubt your Republican colleagues are giving you all necessary assistance in getting started at the tasks that lie ahead, I want you to know that I will be glad to be of any help that you believe I can render. I will be in Washington for at least another month and perhaps longer.

Sincerely yours,
Jerry Voorhis

A couple of weeks passed and I began to wonder whether Mr. Nixon had received my letter. Then one day when I came back from lunch he was standing there in the outer office. He smiled and so did I. We shook hands and went into the inner office, which by that time was pretty bleak and bare. We talked for more than an hour and parted, I hope and believe, as personal friends. Mr. Nixon will be a Republican congressman. He will, I imagine, be a conservative one. But I believe he will be a conscientious one. And I know I appreciated his coming to see me very sincerely indeed.

Chapter 24

A BETTER WAY

The greater portion of this book has been about the government of the United States. Parts of it have been written in defense of certain action taken by our government in recent years in an attempt to mitigate or cure certain ills. None of the measures I have defended or advocated are, I believe, a threat to freedom. On the contrary, I believe the minimum wage law, the School Lunch program, the Social Security Act, laws to curb monopoly or improve the monetary system will broaden the true freedom of the average citizen.

There are certain functions protective of the people's rights, hopes, and opportunities which any good government should perform. It should maintain civil peace and provide defense against foreign aggression. It should protect the nation's future against wasteful exploitation of its resources. It should keep open the avenues of commerce. It should guard the helpless from destitution and restrain the power of the very strong. It should see that children, the citizens of tomorrow, have opportunity to grow in health and understanding. It should guard the integrity of the measure of value and medium of exchange of the nation.

As times and conditions change, so does the role of the government in human life. But beyond the functions just enumerated each extension of governmental activity should be embarked upon only on the most convincing evidence of its necessity. For there is a danger in governmental action, a danger that must forever be guarded against. It is that the people will learn to depend on government, that qualities of character such as self-reliance, mutual voluntary aid, the readiness to attack difficulties without complaint will be lost.

But action there must be or recurring and ever more devastating economic collapses will destroy our nation's health and, what is more serious, our people's faith. And they will drag down into despair the hopes of other nations for·the achievement of a new day of peace and freedom.

Indeed, we know that the most important contributing circumstance to the destruction of democracy and the birth of dictatorship has been the failure of nations to solve constructively the economic problems that have brought unemployment, fear, hunger, and bitterness to their people. Therefore we must develop methods of solving these problems—methods which do not involve the loss of liberty or dependence on government, methods which can be used by the people themselves—before it is too late.

On May 30, 1941, I made a speech in New York City. It was made to a gathering of earnest, hopeful Americans. They were people engaged in a certain type of business in which all of them very profoundly believed, the success of which depended, more than upon any other factor, upon the loyalty and teamwork of the group. It was the annual dinner meeting of the Eastern Cooperative Wholesale.

In the course of my speech I made this statement:

"If I were to say what I believed was the most important single need of the world today I would say it was this: for one people somewhere in the world to give to all mankind a living proof and demonstration that they can, without loss of liberty and without resort to governmental compulsion, solve the economic problems of this power age, end poverty in the midst of plenty, and make the machine the servant of man and not his master.

"There must be born a dynamic faith in America—the sort of faith that has sent out missionaries to work and perish in far-off lands. It must be a faith practical and realistic but with its sights fixed on a new world that we are beginning now to build."

Then I asked the question: "Can there be such a faith? Can the answer to unemployment, and monopoly, and the distress of people on the land, and dangerous dependence upon government be found?"

And I answered my own question: "I believe so. I believe the co-operative movement can give America that faith. And I believe it can supply these answers. I believe it is democracy in practice, the antithesis of dictatorship, monopoly power, and the rule of force. I believe—and I say it reverently—that it is the translation into everyday economic terms of the basic principles of the Christain faith."

This was neither the first nor the last time I had spoken at a co-operative meeting. It was one of the occasions I will remember longest, however, for my speech that night led to the publication of a little book called, *The Morale of Democracy,* which included this and two others of my speeches, an introduction by Wallace J. Campbell, and a conclusion by Dr. James P. Warbasse, in many senses the father of the consumers' co-operative movement in America. Dr. Warbasse's book, *Coöperative Democracy,* I had read many years before. *The Morale of Democracy* was my first book, and it was written without my knowing I was doing it, which has some advantages perhaps to both author and reader.

There are, of course, co-operatives and "co-operatives." During the depths of the depression some 130,000 unemployed people once belonged to the self-help co-operatives of Los Angeles County. These came into existence during the Hoover administration and were, as we later learned, rather directly dependent upon the presence of unsalable farm "surpluses" for such success as they achieved. Someone—and it is a pity we cannot record his name—had a sudden and astonishing idea. Here were the farmers of southern California going bankrupt by the scores and hundreds because not enough people could afford to buy their carrots, potatoes, cabbages, or eggs. They could not even afford to hire people to harvest their crops because it cost more to pay for the harvest alone than the produce would bring. More than one peach and apricot grower, for example, received not a check but a bill from the cannery because the total price to be paid by the cannery for the fruit was less than the charges for processing it.

Yet while the farmers were in this plight, across the road from them were the families of the unemployed, in desperate need of food and lacking it only because they were denied the opportunity to go to work. So the idea was this: why should not the unemployed agree with the farmers to harvest their crops and receive their pay not in the cash money of which the farmers had none, but in the real-wealth coin of food? It was done. On hundreds of truck farms and in hundreds of orchards it was done. Even fish was obtained in exchange for labor. A whole system of co-operatives grew up and exchanged produce with one another. One group would trade their labor for a mountain of carrots, another for several tons of peaches, another for hundreds of heads of cabbage, and so on. By interchanging what they had, by crediting each co-operative with what it contributed to the common pool and debiting it with what it took out, a scheme of distribution was developed. People ate again—not very well, but a lot better than before.

For several years the self-help co-operative performed a remarkably fine function in Los Angeles and neighboring counties. They met many of the basic needs of thousands of families. They restored hope and self-respect. They were doomed, however, to melt away. One reason for this was the disappearance of farm "surpluses" with the coming of the New Deal. Another was the fact that the ablest people among the self-help groups were always the first to be offered employment, if indeed there was any to be had. And the third reason was politics. There were certain things which the self-help people could not get in exchange for their labor. The most important of these was gasoline. And they had almost no money at all. So political aspirants, realizing the importance of some 100,000 or more votes, began to offer assistance. The County Board of Supervisors commenced providing gasoline and some other things for the co-operatives.

That was the beginning of the end. Not that these people were not entitled to the gasoline. But once the process of depending for success upon the largesse of the community had started, their independence was gone. Regulations followed the grants. The state and the federal government began to vie with one another and with the county in "assisting" the co-operatives. Gradually the fire went out of these once vital organizations. While people can, and sometimes must, be helped by governmental action, it is a contradiction of terms to speak of a "government-sponsored co-operative." The breath of life of a co-operative is self-dependence—the voluntary working together of a group of free people.

Despite the passing of the self-help co-operatives, and despite the almost universal failure of the "production-for-use" co-operatives that were started on the proverbial shoestrings after the defeat of Upton Sinclair, I continued to study and to believe in the principle and practice of co-operation. I knew that elsewhere their fate had been a very different and much better one. I had seen something of the success of the British co-operatives on my trip to Europe many years before. "Rochdale" lived and flourished in the British Isles. I had read Marquis Childs's book, *Sweden, the Middle Way.* California farmers by the thousands were solving many of their problems by means of co-operatives.

And so I was not altogether unprepared for John Carson. Mr. Carson enjoys the very dubious distinction of having eaten more lunches with me than any other three people were compelled to do during my time in Congress. Mr. Carson is one of those people who make our national capital, year in and year out, what it is. He served for years as a reporter in the House and Senate press galleries—for the Baltimore *Sun,* among other papers. He was for several years secretary to Senator James Couzens, of Michigan. He was consumers' counsel of the Bituminous Coal Commission —until he found out that the consumers' counsel was supposed to do no counseling—least of all on behalf of consumers. By the time I got to Washington he was on the staff of *Labor,* national newspaper of the Railroad Brotherhoods. But a few months thereafter he took the job which I believe he had always most wanted—as the Washington representative of the Cooperative League of the United States.

Through the years we worked together, attempting to do what we could through our respective positions to make the Congress and the nation aware that the co-operative movement was an important and most hopeful and constructive factor in American life. We tried to defend it against the attacks which have naturally accompanied the growth of the movement during the past several years.

I had not been long in Washington before I received my first invitation to speak before a co-operative meeting. And thereafter such invitations came rather frequently. I never was sure how much they were due to the effectiveness of my speeches, how much to Mr. John Carson's suggestions that I be invited. But whenever I could do so, without sacrificing my primary congressional duties, I accepted.

Congressmen are invited to make speeches to all manner of groups and organizations. The most obscure branches of the most obscure societies in the District of Columbia and its environs invite them. So do the national conventions of the largest and most important organizations of a religious, economic, cultural, or political nature.

Some of the invitations are genuine expressions of a desire to hear from the particular man to whom they are issued. Others are prompted only by a desire to "put on a big meeting" and with the hope that a representative, or senator's name will help attract the crowd.

Some senators and representatives have obtained very considerable additions to their incomes from going out to make speeches. Many of them go for bare expenses—or less.

I have spoken at communion breakfasts of the men of the Episcopal Church, at Columbus Day dinners of the Knights of Columbus, at meetings in churches of other denominations in nearby Virginia or Maryland. I've talked to Grange meetings in Pennsylvania, to dairymen's meetings in New England, to county Farm Bureaus, and to one or two state ones. Neither the local Parent-Teachers' Association nor the National Convention of the National Education Association has been completely spared the task of listening to one of my speeches. I have addressed local labor unions and an occasional national convention. But the most appealing speaking invitations are the ones that come to a member whose work in a certain field or for a certain cause has identified him therewith, and who is genuinely desired as a speaker by groups or organizations of like mind. In my own case, as time went on I felt more and more that the invitations from co-operatives were of this kind. It did not matter especially whether the co-op meeting would be large or small, I was sure it would be in earnest.

I managed to fit into my ten congressional years a number of meetings with co-operatives—local "consumer" co-operatives, regional associations, farmer co-operatives, state co-operative councils, and other co-ops, big and little. There were times when these meetings were like a much-needed tonic to me. The discouragements I met in trying vainly to promote the passage of bills I believed were greatly needed, or in seeing what I thought was harmful legislation enacted, would pass from my mind when I attended a co-operative meeting or spoke before one. For there I saw hope springing from the people's own action. Here was no governmental "program," but a way of carrying on business and meeting some of the needs of life by the application of a few time-tested and right principles. Here they are:

(1) Membership in a co-operative is open to all men and women of good will of every sort and condition, race, color, class, or creed. While others talk of equality and brotherhood, the co-ops quietly practice it and prove that it can work.

(2) Control of a co-operative is in the hands of its members. Each member has one vote and only one regardless of the number of shares he may have purchased. People—not dollars—control co-operative business. This is simply economic democracy. In political democracy a poor man's vote counts as much as a rich man's. The co-ops apply this same American principle to their business.

(3) Capital invested in a co-operative receives a fair but limited return, usually four per cent. Therefore, as co-operative business grows and spreads, our society will be less and less in danger from the problem of idle money in great financial centers seeking profitable investment but finding none. That problem lay at the root of the economic collapse of 1929. Co-ops lessen the likelihood of another such collapse.

(4) The earnings or savings of a co-operative are the property of its patrons—of the people whose trade makes those earnings possible—and are returned periodically to the patrons in direct

proportion to the volume of their purchases. This is the counter-part of the third principle. It means that a co-operative plows its savings back into the soil of consumer buying power, keeps the consumer's dollar always a consumer's dollar, and sustains as no other form of business can do the buying power of the people. It has been failure of that buying power which has caused failure of the market. Failure of the market has been the basic cause of unemployment. Therefore, by keeping dollars where they will be active instead of where they will be idle, co-operatives lessen the danger of mass unemployment's spreading its deathlike pall over our country again.

(5) Co-operatives do business for cash. There is no buying on the installment plan here, no incurring of burdens of debt that the family budget cannot carry or discharge.

(6) Co-operatives sell at the going market price. They do not attempt to "run anyone out of business" or to engage in "cut-throat competition." But the margin between real costs and sell-ing prices—that margin belongs all along, according to co-operative principles, to the people who paid the "overcharge," and is repaid to them each year.

(7) Co-operative businesses belong to the people who need and use their services. And since everyone has needs, co-operatives restore to the rank and file of men and women the opportunity to share in ownership of business and industry. They do not even have to have the five- or ten-dollar membership fee in cash. The people can become owners of a co-operative business simply by buying goods or services from it and by having their patronage refunds credited to a share in member-ownership. With owner-ship goes responsibility for good management. With ownership goes the sense of having a "stake" in the welfare of the society of which one is a part. The co-operative movement, therefore, is a "conservative" influence in the best and highest sense of that much-abused word.

(8) Since co-operatives belong to consumers of their goods or services and since the consumer interest is the one interest com-mon to all mankind, no true co-operative can benefit its own members without also benefiting the whole of society.

Fine as they are, however, it was not these principles alone that persuaded me of the value of co-operatives. I met people who had never owned a house or the tools with which they did their work but who were proud of the co-operative business which was partly theirs. I saw how co-operation enabled farmers to gain "parity" by their own unaided efforts, simply by selling together what they produced and buying together what they needed. I saw groups of city people who might otherwise have felt friendless and lonely brought into a company of friends through the business which they owned together. I saw a co-operative insurance company reduce the premium rates on school buses by almost eighty per cent, not because it had to but because it could. And I saw all other insurance companies make similiar reductions —to meet the co-op's competition. I even saw great tax-exempt organizations formed to fight the co-ops. Why? Because the competition of the co-operatives was bringing profit margins of grain dealers and other middlemen down to a reasonable figure. And I thought that any kind of business that awakened this sort of opposition must be all right. I saw credit unions teach people that they can learn to manage their own money, that by banding together and pooling their modest savings they can put the people's money to work to meet the people's needs—and pay interest to themselves in the bargain.

From a fundamental economic point of view, I saw that co-operatives make it possible for the human demand for goods or services to bring into being corresponding supply. Instead of relying upon high-pressure salesmanship, expensive advertising, and installment buying to break down "sales resistance" to a shoddy product, the co-ops start with a known demand on the part of their members and produce or purchase honest quality products to meet it. Co-op markets are assured markets—the only assured markets in our "free" economic system. Co-operation, therefore, can, and does to the extent of its operations, smooth out the peaks and valleys of the "business cycle" and help to prevent depressions before they start. Neither "overproduction" nor "underconsumption" is possible in co-operative business.

Again, every plant and productive facility in America is paid for—sometimes many times over—by the consumers of its products. The amortized cost of these facilities is included in the price consumers pay. But when a number of consumers are members of a co-operative they not only pay for plant and facilities as they buy their goods, but they can own them too. In a co-operative business the payment of those amortized costs is credited to the people who pay them. This is a basic reason why monopolists don't like co-operatives.

Members of co-operatives are not different from other people in most respects. Most of them don't realize they are different at all. But they are. For they are building something in which they believe and whose success they know means benefit to the whole community, not merely to themselves. Co-operatives have discovered an everyday activity, an everyday ordinary business in most cases, about which there is some of the same significance which a religious person finds when he goes to church on Sunday.

The co-operative members have a fundamental hope and faith in the future, because they are able, as individuals and as a group, to do something to shape that future right now, today, in the place where they are. They don't need to rush off to Washington to lobby for the passage of far-reaching legislation. They don't have to wait till a certain government department makes up its mind what it will do to help them. They aren't depending on the government or expecting anything, except reasonable justice, from it. In the long run they needn't even be afraid of powerful monopolies. Co-ops have been known to barge right into the back yard of the biggest of all monopolies—and start doing business. And the co-ops are still doing business in most of these instances, such as oil and fertilizer and insurance, because they have, in the mutual loyalty of people, a greater source of strength than dollars or cartel agreements or even patent pools can supply.

Co-operative members, especially some of the leaders in the movement who have been battered about by differences of opinion and the pulling and hauling that goes on in all human affairs, would be the first to say that in the preceding paragraphs I have idealized them too much.

Perhaps I have. Perhaps, too, I have given the impression that the present impact of the co-operative movement on American life is greater than it actually is. But what I am sure I have not exaggerated is the hope for the future, which lies potentially at least in the ideals and practices of co-operation.

Co-operation is a better way. It is a better way than monopoly, a better way than dependence on government, a better way certainly than recurring devastating depressions.

I hoped, as I looked into the future after my defeat, that I might find some place where I could be useful in working for the success of the co-operative movement in America.

Chapter 25

BLIND ALLEY
OR THE ROAD AHEAD

One of mankind's hours of great decision is close at hand. Within the next few years we shall reach the fork in the road.

One branch will lead through recurring conflict between owner and non-owner, increasing concentration of powers in private or bureaucratic hands, continuing greed and avarice, spreading totalitarianism, nationalism, prejudice, jealousy, suspicion, and fear to the terrible consequence of the atomic war. The other branch will lead through increasing use of the principles of cooperation, a consequent restoration of power to the people, beginnings of a spirit of brotherhood and unselfish devotion to the common good, strengthening of the means of keeping and enforcing peace, to a world community of free men.

Which road is it to be?

We live in a world devastated by war, a world of demolished homes, demolished factories, demolished governments, demolished lives. We live in a world where the very people who have suffered these disasters must carry their burdens beneath black clouds of fear.

Strange new winds rage over the earth and through men's minds and threaten to sweep away the moorings which have secured our lives to the values of the past. They began to blow in 1929 when an old system crumbled of its own stupidity into the Great Depression that brought Hitler in its wake. Those winds became a gale when Hitler's first shell burst on Poland to start World War II. Another such depression, another such war, and they can become a hurricane.

The wealth of the earth is hammered into vast, intricate machines whose sole purpose is the destruction of other such machines in other countries and the people who live in those countries. Science and invention are bent to the service of future destruction—until we are almost persuaded that we should be far better off on this earth if there had been neither science nor invention during the past half century.

Can liberty survive in such a world as this? Is peace already lost? Are the wounds of war so deep as to be past all healing? Is the "pursuit of happiness" no longer an "unalienable right" of humankind? Are governments instituted among men to preserve their rights doomed to pass from the stage of history?

No. The cause of man is not hopeless. The determination of mankind's fate is in his own hands. Most worthwhile human institutions—parliamentary representative government, for example—have been erected to save our race from dangers which otherwise would have overwhelmed it.

Upon the perfection and strengthening of such new institutions as the United Nations our international fate depends. Upon the application of the methods of co-operation to ever-widening areas of human problems our economic fate depends. Upon the awakening of bodies of men like the Congress of the United States to a vision and courage worthy of the times the fate of freedom depends.

The painting is not all black. There have been times like this before. And at some such times the very extremity of man's need has called forth moral and spiritual powers stronger than the forces that threatened him. Today, as always, moral and spiritual powers mightier than the blast of an atomic bomb lie latent in the hearts of the peoples of the earth.

We cannot believe that the Almighty has brought a race of men upon this earth and endowed them with the powers of mind and spirit which mankind possesses only to doom that race to de-

struction by its own hand. We know that violations of the moral
law of the universe bring inevitably their retribution. We also
know that evil contains within itself the seeds of its own destruction and has always so far in human history called into being
regenerative forces to counterbalance if not completely to overcome it.

The eternal truth is not shaken by the perils of the hour: and
God's laws are immutable today as they have always been.

It is precisely in times like these that people find courage and
strength equal to their tasks. It is in times like these, in countries
like our own, that the sort of dynamic faith that has inspired
every great civilization arises in humble minds and spreads from
man to man.

That faith will have its credo and I believe it will run something like this:

"We believe in the people—in all the people of every race,
creed, color, class, and kind.

"We believe in a society in which even the poorest among the
people have opportunity to grow in wisdom, in self-reliance, in
hope for their children's future.

"We believe that there should be 'equal opportunity for all,
special privilege to none'—and that the aim of all good government is to give effect to this principle.

"We believe in the right of the people to know all the truth and
all opinions—and in the principle of equality of educational
opportunity.

"We believe in the judgments of the people—and that in trusting those judgments lies the safety of the nation.

"We believe that freedom and security are not incompatible,
that they can both be achieved in the same society at the same
time.

"We believe that an economy of abundance is not only possible
but necessary—and that the people have a right to consume in
proportion to their production.

"We believe that modern economic problems can be solved—
that they can be solved within the framework of freedom and
mainly through the efforts of the people themselves.

"We believe in the institutions of freedom—and that governments founded on tyranny, oppression, or dictatorship are bound sooner or later to crumble and fall.

"We believe in parliamentary government—in government whose decisions are made in accordance with the will of the people expressed through their directly elected representatives.

"We believe that peace can be built among the nations however long and difficult that task—that men can learn to live as brothers because they must.

"We believe that the ultimate purpose of life is a religious purpose. We believe that the central teachings of the Christian religion are the hope of the world and will one day save it. We believe in the application of those teachings to the problems of men and nations.

"And, finally, because we believe in man as the agent of God's will on this earth, therefore, we believe the eternal values of life are indestructible in the mind and heart of each individual who clings to them. For him truth is stronger than falsehood, though falsehood seem to rule the world. For him love is stronger than hate, though nations steep themselves in hate. For him humble obedience to the will of God is life. By such men the world of tomorrow will be built."

The one creative power in all experience is self-sacrificing devotion. Out of the travail of motherhood and that way alone each child is born. No beauty in music or in art, no power in literature, no triumph of science or statesmanship, no inspiration from religious truth has ever come into this world except through the pain and sacrifice of him or her who brought it here.

Out of such self-sacrificing devotion to the common welfare of all mankind will come, from individuals and groups of individuals, the influences which will, if anything can do so, turn our course down the right fork of the road. And if such people seem temporarily to fail, what then? They will know at the very least that they have passed to their children one simple, all-sufficient principle by which they can live and, if need be, die without fear. It is: "Thou shalt love thy neighbor as thyself."

But such people will not fail. The forces of wrong against which they must strive may appear for a time to overwhelm them. As those powers go down to their own inevitable destruction they may pull much of the world down after them. But the wells of religious faith and strength will still be full. And in the long run there will come new light upon the earth and back to that light mankind will find his way.

> The tumult and the shouting dies;
> The Captains and the Kings depart:
> Still stands Thine ancient sacrifice,
> An humble and a contrite heart.
> Lord God of Hosts, be with us yet,
> Lest we forget—lest we forget!